TEXTS IN COMPUTER SCIENCE

Editors
David Gries
Fred B. Schneider

Springer
*New York
Berlin
Heidelberg
Barcelona
Hong Kong
London
Milan
Paris
Singapore
Tokyo*

TEXTS IN COMPUTER SCIENCE

Alagar and Periyasamy, Specification of Software Systems

Apt and Olderog, Verification of Sequential and Concurrent Programs, Second Edition

Back and von Wright, Refinement Calculus

Beidler, Data Structures and Algorithms

Bergin, Data Structure Programming

Brooks, C Programming: The Essentials for Engineers and Scientists

Brooks, Problem Solving with Fortran 90

Dandamudi, Introduction to Assembly Language Programming

Fitting, First-Order Logic and Automated Theorem Proving, Second Edition

Grillmeyer, Exploring Computer Science with Scheme

Homer and Selman, Computability and Complexity Theory

Immerman, Descriptive Complexity

Jalote, An Integrated Approach to Software Engineering, Second Edition

Kizza, Ethical and Social Issues in the Information Age

Kozen, Automata and Computability

Li and Vitányi, An Introduction to Kolmogorov Complexity and Its Applications, Second Edition

(continued after index)

Steven Homer   Alan L. Selman

COMPUTABILITY AND COMPLEXITY THEORY

With 17 Illustrations

Springer

Steven Homer
Department of Computer Science
Boston University
111 Cummington Street
Boston, MA 02215, USA
homer@cs.bu.edu

Alan L. Selman
Department of Computer Science and Engineering
226 Bell Hall
University at Buffalo
Buffalo, NY 14260-2000, USA
selman@cse.buffalo.edu

Series Editors

David Gries
Department of Computer Science
415 Boyd Studies Research Center
The University of Georgia
Athens, GA 30605, USA

Fred B. Schneider
Department of Computer Science
Upson Hall
Cornell University
Ithaca, NY 14853-7501, USA

Library of Congress Cataloging-in-Publication Data
Homer, S. (Steven)
   Computability and complexity theory / Steven Homer, Alan L. Selman.
      p.   cm. — (Texts in computer science)
   Includes bibliographical references and index.
   ISBN 0-387-95055-9
   1. Computer science.   2. Computable functions.   3. Computational complexity.
  I. Selman, Alan L. II. Title. III. Series.
  QA76 .H6236 2001
  004—dc21   00-053829

Printed on acid-free paper.

Production managed by MaryAnn Brickner; manufacturing supervised by Joe Quatela.
Typeset pages prepared using the authors' LaTeX 2$_\varepsilon$ files by Integre Technical Publishing Company, Inc.
Printed and bound by Hamilton Printing Co., Rensselaer, NY.
Printed in the United States of America.

9 8 7 6 5 4 3 2 1

ISBN 0-387-95055-9   SPIN 10769347

Springer-Verlag   New York Berlin Heidelberg
A member of BertelsmannSpringer Science+Business Media GmbH

We dedicate this book to our wives, Michelle and Sharon

Preface

The theory of computing provides computer science with concepts, models, and formalisms for reasoning about both the resources needed to carry out computations and the efficiency of the computations that use these resources. It provides tools to measure the difficulty of combinatorial problems both absolutely and in comparison with other problems. Courses in this subject help students gain analytic skills and enable them to recognize the limits of computation. For these reasons, a course in the theory of computing is usually required in the graduate computer science curriculum.

The harder question to address is which topics such a course should cover. We believe that students should learn the fundamental models of computation, the limitations of computation, and the distinctions between feasible and intractable. In particular, the phenomena of NP-completeness and NP-hardness have pervaded much of science and transformed computer science. One option is to survey a large number of theoretical subjects, typically focusing on automata and formal languages. However, these subjects are less important to theoretical computer science, and to computer science as a whole, now than in the past. Many students have taken such a course as part of their undergraduate education. We chose not to take that route because computability and complexity theory are the subjects that we feel deeply about and that we believe are important for students to learn. Furthermore, a graduate course should be scholarly. It is better to treat important topics thoroughly than to survey the field.

This textbook is intended for use in an introductory graduate course in theoretical computer science. It contains material that should be core knowledge in the theory of computation for all graduate students in computer science. It is self-contained and is best suited for a one-semester course. Most of the text can be covered in one semester by moving expeditiously through the core material of

Chapters 2 through 6 and then covering parts of Chapter 7. We will give more details about this below.

As a graduate course, students should have some prerequisite preparation. The ideal preparation would be the kind of course that we mentioned above: an undergraduate course that introduced topics such as automata theory, formal languages, computability theory, or complexity theory. We stress, however, that there is nothing in such a course that a student needs to know before studying this text. Our personal experience suggests that we cannot presume that all of our students have taken such an undergraduate course. For those students who have not, we advise that they need at least some prior exposure that will have developed mathematical skills. Prior courses in mathematical logic, algebra (at the level of groups, rings, or fields), or number theory, for example, would all serve this purpose.

Despite the diverse backgrounds of our students, we have found that graduate students are capable of learning sophisticated material when it is explained clearly and precisely. That has been our goal in writing this book.

This book also is suitable for advanced undergraduate students who have satisfied the prerequisites. It is an appropriate first course in complexity theory for students who will continue to study and work in this subject area.

The text begins with a preliminary chapter that gives a brief description of several topics in mathematics. We included this in order to keep the book self-contained and to ensure that all students have a common notation. Some of these sections simply enable students to understand some of the important examples that arise later. For example, we include a section on number theory and algebra that includes all that is necessary for students to understand that primality belongs to NP.

The text starts properly with classical computability theory. We build complexity theory on top of that. Doing so has the pedagogical advantage that students learn a qualitative subject before advancing to a quantitative one. Also, the concepts build from one to the other. For example, although we give a complete proof that the satisfiability problem is NP-complete, it is easy for students to understand that the bounded halting problem is NP-complete, because they already know that the classical halting problem is c.e.-complete.

We use the terms *partial computable* and *computably enumerable (c.e.)* instead of the traditional terminology, *partial recursive* and *recursively enumerable (r.e.)*, respectively. We do so simply to eliminate confusion. Students of computer science know of "recursion" as a programming paradigm. We do not prove here that Turing-computable partial functions are equivalent to partial recursive functions, so by not using that notation, we avoid the matter altogether. Although the notation we are using has been commonplace in the computability theory and mathematical logic community for several years, instructors might want to advise their students that the older terminology seems commonplace within the theoretical computer science community. Computable functions are defined on the set of words over a finite alphabet, which we identify with the set of natural numbers in a straightforward manner. We use the term *effective*, in the nontechnical, intuitive sense, to denote computational processes on other data types. For example, we will say that a set of Turing machines is "effectively enumerable" if its set of indices is computably enumerable.

Chapter 4 concludes with a short list of topics that students should know from the chapters on computability theory before proceeding to study complexity theory. We advise instructors who wish to minimize coverage of computability theory to refer to this list. Typically, we do not cover the second section on the recursion theorem (Section 3.10) in a one-semester course. Although we do not recommend it, it is possible to begin the study of complexity theory after learning the first five sections of Chapter 3 and at least part of Section 3.9 on oracle Turing machines, Turing reductions, and the arithmetical hierarchy.

In Chapter 5 we treat general properties of complexity classes and relationships between complexity classes. These include important older results such as the space and time hierarchy theorems, as well as the more recent result of Immerman and Szelepcsényi that space-bounded classes are closed under complements. Instructors might be anxious to get to NP-complete problems (Chapter 6) and NP-hard problems (Chapter 7) but students need to learn the basic results of complexity theory and it is instructive for them to understand the relationships between P, NP, and other deterministic and nondeterministic, low-level complexity classes. Students should learn that nondeterminism is not well understood in general, that P =? NP is not an isolated question, and that other classes have complete problems as well (which we take up in Chapter 7). Nevertheless, Chapter 5 is a long chapter. Many of the results in this chapter are proved by complicated Turing-machine simulations and counting arguments, which give students great insight, but can be time-consuming to cover. For this reason, instructors might be advised to survey some of this material if the alternative would mean not having sufficient time for the later chapters.

Homework exercises are an important part of this book. They are embedded in the text where they naturally arise, and students should not proceed without working on them. Many are simple exercises, whereas others are challenging. Often we leave important but easy-to-prove propositions as exercises. We provide additional problems at the end of chapters, which extend and apply the material covered there.

Once again, our intent has been to write a text that is suitable for all graduate students, that provides the right background for those who will continue to study complexity theory, and that can be taught in one semester. There are several important topics in complexity theory that cannot be treated properly in a one-semester course. Currently we are writing a second part to this text, which will be suitable for an optional second semester course, covering nonuniform complexity (Boolean circuits), parallelism, probabilistic classes, and interactive protocols.

Boston, Massachusetts
Buffalo, New York

Steven Homer
Alan L. Selman
January, 2001

Contents

Preface   **vii**

1 Preliminaries   **1**
   1.1 Words and Languages 1
   1.2 K-adic Representation 2
   1.3 Partial Functions 3
   1.4 Graphs 4
   1.5 Propositional Logic 6
       1.5.1 Boolean Functions 8
   1.6 Cardinality 8
       1.6.1 Ordered Sets 10
   1.7 Elementary Algebra 11
       1.7.1 Rings and Fields 11
       1.7.2 Groups 15
       1.7.3 Number Theory 17

2 Introduction to Computability   **22**
   2.1 Turing Machines 23
   2.2 Turing-Machine Concepts 26
   2.3 Variations of Turing Machines 28
       2.3.1 Multitape Turing Machines 29
       2.3.2 Nondeterministic Turing Machines 31
   2.4 Church's Thesis 34
   2.5 RAMs 36
       2.5.1 Turing Machines for RAMS 39

3   Undecidability   **41**
  3.1   Decision Problems   41
  3.2   Undecidable Problems   43
  3.3   Pairing Functions   46
  3.4   Computably Enumerable Sets   47
  3.5   Halting Problem, Reductions, and Complete Sets   50
      3.5.1   Complete Problems   52
  3.6   *S-m-n* Theorem   53
  3.7   Recursion Theorem   55
  3.8   Rice's Theorem   57
  3.9   Turing Reductions and Oracle Turing Machines   59
  3.10 Recursion Theorem, Continued   66
  3.11 References   69
  3.12 Additional Homework Problems   70

4   Introduction to Complexity Theory   **72**
  4.1   Complexity Classes and Complexity Measures   74
      4.1.1   Computing Functions   76
  4.2   Prerequisites   77

5   Basic Results of Complexity Theory   **78**
  5.1   Linear Compression and Speedup   80
  5.2   Constructible Functions   86
      5.2.1   Simultaneous Simulation   87
  5.3   Tape Reduction   90
  5.4   Inclusion Relationships   97
      5.4.1   Relations between the Standard Classes 105
  5.5   Separation Results 107
  5.6   Translation Techniques and Padding 111
      5.6.1   Tally Languages 113
  5.7   Relations between the Standard Classes—Continued 115
      5.7.1   Complements of Complexity Classes:
            The Immerman–Szelepcsényi Theorem 116
  5.8   Additional Homework Problems 120

6   Nondeterminism and NP-Completeness   **122**
  6.1   Characterizing NP 123
  6.2   The Class P 124
  6.3   Enumerations 126
  6.4   NP-Completeness 128
  6.5   The Cook–Levin Theorem 130
  6.6   More NP-Complete Problems 136
      6.6.1   The Diagonal Set Is NP-Complete 137
      6.6.2   Some Natural NP-Complete Problems 138

6.7   Additional Homework Problems 142

7 Relative Computability   **145**
7.1   NP-Hardness 147
7.2   Search Problems 151
7.3   The Structure of NP 153
      7.3.1   Composite Number and Graph Isomorphism 158
      7.3.2   Reflection 161
7.4   The Polynomial Hierarchy 162
7.5   Complete Problems for Other Complexity Classes 170
      7.5.1   PSPACE 170
      7.5.2   Exponential Time 174
      7.5.3   Polynomial Time and Logarithmic Space 175
      7.5.4   A Note on Provably Intractable Problems 179
7.6   Additional Homework Problems 179

References   **181**

Author Index   **187**

Subject Index   **191**

1

Preliminaries

1.1   Words and Languages   1

1.2   *K*-adic Representation   2

1.3   Partial Functions   3

1.4   Graphs   4

1.5   Propositional Logic   6

1.6   Cardinality   8

1.7   Elementary Algebra   11

We begin with a limited number of mathematical notions that a student should know before beginning with this text. This chapter is short because we assume some earlier study of data structures and discrete mathematics.

1.1   Words and Languages

In the next chapter we will become familiar with models of computing. The basic data type of our computers will be "symbols," for our computers manipulate symbols. The notion of symbol is undefined, but we define several more concepts in terms of symbols.

A finite set $\Sigma = \{a_1, \ldots, a_k\}$ of symbols is called a finite *alphabet*. A *word* is a finite sequence of symbols. The *length* of a word w, denoted $|w|$, is the number of symbols composing it. The *empty* word is the unique word of length 0 and is denoted as λ. Note that λ is *not* a symbol in the alphabet. The empty word is not a set, so do not confuse the empty word λ with the empty set $\emptyset$.

Σ^* denotes the set of all words over the alphabet Σ. A *language* is a set of words. That is, L is a language if and only if $L \subseteq \Sigma^*$.

A *prefix* of a word is a substring that begins the word.

Example 1.1   *Let $w = abcce$. The prefixes of w are*

$$\lambda, a, ab, abc, abcc, abcce.$$

Define *suffixes* similarly.

The *concatenation* of two words x and y is the word xy. For any word w, $\lambda w = w\lambda = w$. If $x = uvw$, then v is a *subword* of x. If u and w are not both λ, then v is a *proper* subword.

Some operations on languages:

union $L_1 \cup L_2$

intersection $L_1 \cap L_2$

complement $\overline{L} = \Sigma^* - L$

concatenation $L_1 L_2 = \{xy \mid x \in L_1 \text{ and } y \in L_2\}$.

The *powers* of a language L are defined as follows:

$$L^0 = \{\lambda\},$$
$$L^1 = L,$$
$$L^{n+1} = L^n L, \text{ for } n \geq 1.$$

The *Kleene closure* of a language L is the language

$$L^* = \bigcup_{i=0}^{\infty} L^i.$$

Note that $\lambda \in L^*$, for all L. Applying this definition to $L = \Sigma^*$, we get, as we said above, that Σ^* is the set of all words. Note that $\emptyset^* = \{\lambda\}$.

Define $L^+ = \bigcup_{i=1}^{\infty} L^i$. Then, $\lambda \in L^+ \Leftrightarrow \lambda \in L$.

Theorem 1.1   *For any language S, $S^{**} = S^*$.*

Homework 1.1   *Prove Theorem 1.1.*

The *lexicographic* ordering of Σ^* is defined by $w < w'$ if $|w| < |w'|$ or if $|w| = |w'|$ and w comes before w' in ordinary dictionary ordering.

1.2   *K*-adic Representation

Let N denote the set of all natural numbers, i.e., $N = \{0, 1, 2, 3, \ldots\}$. We need to represent the natural numbers as words over a finite alphabet. Normally we do this using binary or decimal notation, but k-adic notation, which we introduce here, has the advantage of providing a one-to-one and onto correspondence between Σ^* and N.

Let Σ be a finite alphabet with k symbols. Call the symbols $1, \ldots, k$. Every word over Σ will denote a unique natural number.

Let $x = \sigma_n \cdots \sigma_1 \sigma_0$ be a word in Σ^*. Define

$$N_k(\lambda) = 0,$$
$$N_k(x) = N_k(\sigma_n \cdots \sigma_1 \sigma_0)$$
$$= \sigma_n * k^n + \cdots + \sigma_1 * k^1 + \sigma_0.$$

$N_k(x)$ is the number that the word x represents.

Example 1.2 *Let $\Sigma = \{1, 2, 3\}$. The string 233 denotes the integer*

$$N_3(233) = 2 * 3^2 + 3 * 3^1 + 3 * 3^0 = 18 + 9 + 3 = 30.$$

Also,

$$N_k(\lambda) = 0,$$
$$N_k(xa) = k * N_k(x) + a$$

is a recursive definition of N_k.

To see that N_k maps Σ^* onto the natural numbers, we need to show that every natural number has a k-adic representation. Given m, we want a word $s_n \ldots s_1 s_0$ such that $m = s_n * k^n + \cdots + s_1 * k^1 + s_0$. Note that $m = [s_n * k^{n-1} + \cdots + s_1] * k + s_0$. Let $a_0 = s_n * k^{n-1} + \cdots + s_1$. Then, $a_0 k = \max\{ak \mid ak < m\}$. Use this equation to find a_0. Then, $s_0 = m - a_0 k$. Iterate the process with a_0 until all values are known.

1.3 Partial Functions

Suppose that P is a program whose input values are natural numbers. It is possible that P does not halt on all possible input values. Suppose that P is designed to compute exactly one output value, again a natural number, for each input value on which it eventually halts. Then P computes a *partial function* on the natural numbers. This is the fundamental data type that is studied in computability theory.

The partial function differs somewhat from the function of ordinary mathematics. If f is a partial function defined on N, then for some values of $x \in N$, $f(x)$ is well defined; i.e., there is a value $y \in N$ such that $y = f(x)$. For other values of $x \in N$, $f(x)$ is undefined; i.e., $f(x)$ does not exist. When $f(x)$ is defined, we say $f(x)$ *converges* and we write $f(x) \downarrow$. When $f(x)$ is undefined, we say $f(x)$ *diverges* and we write $f(x) \uparrow$.

Given a partial function f, we want to know whether, given values x, does $f(x)$ converge and if so, what is the value of $f(x)$? Can the values of f be computed (by a computer program), and if so can f be efficiently computed?

We will also be concerned with subsets of the natural numbers and with relations defined on the natural numbers.

Given a set A (i.e., $A \subseteq N$), we want to know, for values x, whether $x \in A$. Is there an algorithm that for all x, will determine whether $x \in A$? For relations, the question is essentially the same. Given a k-ary relation R and values $x_1, \ldots, x_k$, is $R(x_1, \ldots, x_k)$ true? Is there a computer program that for all input tuples will decide the question? If so, is there an efficient solution?

This discussion assumed that the underlying data type is the set of natural numbers, N. As we just learned, it is equivalent to taking the underlying data type to be Σ^*, where Σ is a finite alphabet. We will pun freely between these two points of view.

1.4   Graphs

A *graph* is a pair $G = (V, E)$ consisting of a finite, nonempty set V of vertices and a set E of *edges*. An *edge* is an unordered pair of distinct vertices. (For $v \in V$, (v, v) cannot be an edge because the vertices are not distinct.) If (u, v) is an edge, then u and v are vertices; we say that u and v are *adjacent*. A graph is *complete* if every pair of distinct vertices is connected by an edge.

A *subgraph* of $G = (V, E)$ is a graph $G' = (V', E')$ such that

1. $V' \subseteq V$, and
2. E' consists of edges (v, w) in E such that both v and w are in V'.

If E' consists of all edges (v, w) in E such that both v and w are in V', then G' is called an *induced subgraph* of G.

In most contexts (v, w) denotes an ordered pair, but when discussing graphs, we abuse notation by using (v, w) to denote edges, which are unordered pairs.

A *path* is a sequence of vertices connected by edges. The length of a path is the number of edges on the path. (A single vertex is a path of length 0.) A *simple path* is a path that does not repeat any vertex or edge, except possibly the first and last vertices. A *cycle* is a simple path of length at least 1 that starts and ends in the same vertex. Observe that the length of a cycle must be at least 3 because v and u, v, u are not cycles. A *Hamiltonian circuit* is a cycle that contains every vertex in the graph.

Example 1.3   *The sequence* $1, 2, 4, 3, 5, 1$ *is a Hamiltonian circuit of the graph in Fig. 1.1.*

A graph is *connected* if every two vertices has a path between them. The number of edges at a vertex is the *degree* of the vertex.

A *directed graph (digraph)* consists of a set of *vertices* and a set of *arcs*. An arc is an ordered pair. Fig. 1.2 gives an example.

A *path* in a digraph is a sequence of vertices $v_1, \ldots, v_n$ such that for every i, $1 \le i < n$, there is an arc from v_i to v_{i+1}. A digraph is *strongly connected* if there is a path from any vertex to any other vertex.

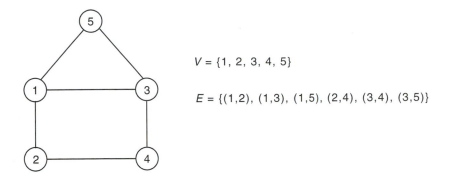

$V = \{1, 2, 3, 4, 5\}$

$E = \{(1,2), (1,3), (1,5), (2,4), (3,4), (3,5)\}$

FIGURE 1.1. A graph $G = (V, E)$.

An (undirected) *tree* is a connected graph with no cycles.

For a directed graph we define a cycle just as for an undirected graph. Note that there can be cycles of length 2 in directed graphs. For directed graphs we define a tree as follows:

1. there is exactly one vertex, called the root, that no arcs enter;
2. every other vertex is entered by exactly one arc; and
3. there is a path from the root to every vertex.

If (u, v) is an arc in a tree, then u is a *parent* of v, and v is a *child* of u. If there is a path from u to v, then u is an *ancestor* of v, and v is a *descendant* of u. A vertex with no children is called a *leaf*. A *vertex u* together with all its descendants is a *subtree*, and u is the root of that subtree.

The *depth* of a vertex u in a tree is the length of the path from the root to u. The *height* of u is the length of a longest path from u to a leaf. The *height of the tree* is the height of the root. Finally, when the children of each vertex are ordered, we call this an *ordered tree*. A *binary tree* is a tree such that each child of a vertex is either a *left* child or a *right* child, and no vertex has more than one left child or right child.

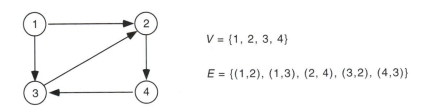

$V = \{1, 2, 3, 4\}$

$E = \{(1,2), (1,3), (2, 4), (3,2), (4,3)\}$

FIGURE 1.2. A digraph $G = (V, E)$.

1.5 Propositional Logic

Propositional logic provides a mathematical formalism that is useful for representing and manipulating statements of fact that are either true or false.

Let $U = \{u_1, u_2, u_3, \ldots\}$ be a set of Boolean variables (i.e., ranging over $\{0, 1\}$, where we identify 0 with False and 1 with True). We associate the binary Boolean connectives $\wedge$ and $\vee$, and the unary connective $\neg$, with AND, inclusive-OR, and NOT, respectively. However, their exact semantic meaning will be given shortly. For now, they are purely syntactic.

The class of *propositional formulas* is defined inductively as follows:

1. every propositional variable is a propositional formula;
2. if A and B are propositional formulas, then the expressions $(A \wedge B)$, $(A \vee B)$, and $(\neg A)$ are propositional formulas.

When convenient, we will eliminate parentheses in propositional formulas in accordance with the usual precedence rules.

Definition 1.1 *Let F be a propositional formula and let* VAR(F) *be the set of variables that occur in F. An* assignment *(or* truth-assignment*) t is a function*

$$t : \text{VAR}(F) \to \{0, 1\}.$$

An assignment induces a truth-value to the formula F by induction, as follows:

1. $t((A \wedge B)) = \begin{cases} 1 & \text{if } t(A) = t(B) = 1; \\ 0 & \text{otherwise.} \end{cases}$

2. $t((A \vee B)) = \begin{cases} 0 & \text{if } t(A) = t(B) = 0; \\ 1 & \text{otherwise.} \end{cases}$

3. $t((\neg A)) = \begin{cases} 1 & \text{if } t(A) = 0; \\ 0 & \text{otherwise.} \end{cases}$

Using these rules, given any formula F and an assignment t to VAR(F), we can evaluate $t(F)$ to determine whether the assignment makes the formula True or False. Also, these rules ascribe meaning to the connectives. It is common to present the truth-values of a formula F under all possible assignments as a finite table, called a *truth-table*.

If $u \in U$ is a Boolean variable, it is common to write $\overline{u}$ in place of $(\neg u)$. Variables u and negated variables $\overline{u}$ are called *literals*.

Example 1.4 *The propositional formula $(u_1 \vee \overline{u_2}) \wedge (\overline{u_1} \vee u_2)$ has the following truth-table:*

u_1	u_2	$(u_1 \vee \overline{u_2}) \wedge (\overline{u_1} \vee u_2)$
1	1	1
1	0	0
0	1	0
0	0	1

Definition 1.2   *An assignment t satisfies a formula F if $t(F) = 1$. A formula F is* satisfiable *if there exists an assignment to its variables that satisfies it.*

We will learn in Chapter 6 that the satisfiable formulas play an exceedingly important role in the study of complexity theory.

Definition 1.3   *A formula is* valid *(or is a* tautology*) if every assignment to its variables satisfies it.*

Proposition 1.1   *A formula F is a tautology if and only if $(\neg F)$ is not satisfiable.*

Homework 1.2   *Prove Proposition 1.1.*

Definition 1.4   *Two formulas F and G are* equivalent *if for every assignment t to $\mathrm{VAR}(F) \cup \mathrm{VAR}(G)$, $t(F) = t(G)$.*

Next we define two special syntactic "normal" forms of propositional formulas. We will show that every formula is equivalent to one in each of these forms.

A formula is a *conjunction* if it is of the form $(A_1 \wedge A_2 \wedge \cdots A_n)$, where each A_i is a formula, and we often abbreviate this using the notation $\bigwedge_{1 \leq i \leq n} A_i$. Similarly, a *disjunction* is a formula of the form $(A_1 \vee A_2 \vee \cdots A_n)$, which we can write as $\bigvee_{1 \leq i \leq n} A_i$.

A *clause* is a disjunction of literals. (For example, $u_1 \vee \overline{u_3} \vee u_8$ is a clause.) Observe that a clause is satisfied by an assignment if and only if the assignment makes at least one of its literals true.

Definition 1.5   *A propositional formula G is in* conjunctive normal form *if it is a conjunction of clauses.*

Example 1.5   *$(u_1 \vee \overline{u_2}) \wedge (\overline{u_1} \vee u_2)$ is in conjunctive normal form, the assignment $t(u_1) = t(u_2) = 1$ satisfies the formula, but it is not a tautology.*

Example 1.6   *$(u_1 \wedge \overline{u_1})$ is in conjunctive normal form and has no satisfying assignment.*

Homework 1.3   *Show that every formula is equivalent to one in conjunctive normal form. (You will need to use elementary laws of propositional logic such as DeMorgan's laws, which state that $\neg(A \wedge B)$ is equivalent to $(\neg A \vee \neg B)$ and that $\neg(A \vee B)$ is equivalent to $(\neg A \wedge \neg B)$.)*

Since a formula in conjunctive normal form is a conjunction of clauses, it is a conjunction of a disjunction of literals. Analogously, we define a formula to be in *disjunctive normal form* if it is a disjunction of a conjunction of literals.

Example 1.7   *$(u_1 \wedge \overline{u_2}) \vee (\overline{u_1} \wedge u_2)$ is in disjunctive normal form.*

Using the technique of Homework 1.3, every propositional formula is equivalent to one in disjunctive normal form.

1.5.1 Boolean Functions

A *Boolean function* is a function $f : \{0, 1\}^n \to \{0, 1\}$, where $n \geq 1$. A truth-table is just a tabular presentation of a Boolean function, so every propositional formula defines a Boolean function by its truth-table.

Conversely, let $f : \{0, 1\}^n \to \{0, 1\}$ be a Boolean function. Then, we can represent f by the following formula F_f in disjunctive normal form whose truth-table is f. For each n-tuple $(a_1, \ldots, a_n) \in \{0, 1\}^n$ such that $f(a_1, \ldots, a_n) = 1$, write the conjunction of literals $(l_1 \wedge \cdots \wedge l_n)$, where $l_i = u_i$ if $a_i = 1$ and $l_i = \overline{u_i}$ if $a_i = 0$ (where $1 \leq i \leq n$, and $u_1, \ldots, u_n$ are Boolean variables). Then, define F_f to be the disjunction of each such conjunction of literals.

1.6 Cardinality

The *cardinality* of a set is a measure of its size. Two sets A and B have the *same cardinality* if there is a bijection $h : A \to B$. In this case we write $\text{card}(A) = \text{card}(B)$. If there exists a one-to-one function h from A to B, then $\text{card}(A) \leq \text{card}(B)$. For finite sets $A = \{a_1, \ldots, a_k\}$, $k \geq 1$, $\text{card}(A) = k$. A set A is *countable* if $\text{card}(A) = \text{card}(N)$ or A is finite. A set A is *countably infinite* if $\text{card}(A) = \text{card}(N)$.

A set is *enumerable* if it is the empty set or there is a function $f : N \xrightarrow{\text{onto}} A$. In this case A can be written as a sequence: Writing a_i for $f(i)$, we have

$$A = range(f) = \{a_0, a_1, a_2, \ldots\} = \{a_i \mid i \geq 0\}.$$

To call a set enumerable is to say that its elements can be counted. Observe that an enumeration need not be one-to-one. Since $a_i = a_j$, for $i \neq j$, is possible, it is possible that some elements of A are counted more than once.

Theorem 1.2 *A set is enumerable if and only if it is countable.*

Homework 1.4 *Prove Theorem 1.2.*

The cardinality of N is denoted $\aleph_0$.

Theorem 1.3 *A set A is countable if and only if $\text{card}(A) \leq \aleph_0$.*

That is, $\aleph_0$ is the smallest nonfinite cardinality. (Of course, at the moment we have no reason to expect that there is any other nonfinite cardinality.)

Proof. Suppose $\text{card}(A) \leq \aleph_0$. Then there is a one-to-one function f from A to N. Suppose $f[A]$ has a largest element k. Then A is a finite set. Suppose $f[A]$ does not have a largest member. Let a_0 be the unique member of A such that $f(a_0)$ is the smallest member of $f[A]$. Let a_{n+1} be the unique member of A such that $f(a_{n+1})$ is the smallest member of $f[A] - \{f(a_0), \ldots, f(a_n)\}$. It follows that A is enumerable.

The reverse direction is straightforward.   □

Homework 1.5   *If* $\mathrm{card}(A) \leq \mathrm{card}(B)$ *and* $\mathrm{card}(B) \leq \mathrm{card}(C)$, *then* $\mathrm{card}(A) \leq \mathrm{card}(C)$.

Homework 1.6   *(This is a hard problem, known as the Cantor–Bernstein Theorem.) If* $\mathrm{card}(A) \leq \mathrm{card}(B)$ *and* $\mathrm{card}(B) \leq \mathrm{card}(A)$, *then* $\mathrm{card}(A) = \mathrm{card}(B)$.

Example 1.8 $\{< x, y > \mid x, y \in N\}$ *is countable. An enumeration is*

$$< 0, 0 >, < 0, 1 >, < 1, 0 >, < 0, 2 >, \ldots.$$

Example 1.9   *The set of rational numbers is countable.*

Example 1.10   *The set of programs in any programming language is countably infinite. For each language there is a finite alphabet* Σ *such that each program is in* Σ^*. *Because programs may be arbitrarily long, there are infinitely many of them. There are* $\aleph_0$ *many programs.*

The proof of the following theorem employs the technique of *diagonalization*. Diagonalization was invented by the mathematician George Cantor (1845–1918), who created the theory of sets that we now take for granted. This is an important technique in theoretical computer science, so it would be wise to master this easy application first.

Theorem 1.4   *The set of all functions from N to N is not countable.*

Proof. Let $A = \{f \mid f : N \rightarrow N\}$. Suppose A is countable. Then there is an enumeration $f_0, f_1, \ldots$ of A. (Think of all the values of each f_i laid out on an infinite matrix: The idea is to define a function that cannot be on this matrix because it differs from all of the values on the diagonal. This is illustrated in Fig. 1.3.) Define a function g by $g(x) = f_x(x) + 1$, for all $x \in N$. Then, g is a function on N, but observe that g cannot be in the enumeration of all functions.

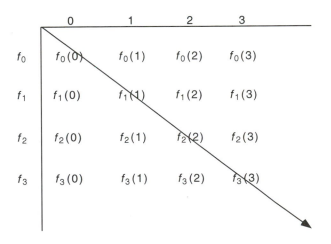

FIGURE 1.3. The diagonalization technique.

That is, if $g \in A$, then for some natural number k, $g = f_k$. But g cannot equal f_k because $g(k) \neq f_k(k)$. Thus, we have contradicted the assumption that the set of all functions can be enumerated. Thus, A is not countable.   □

Consider your favorite programming language. As there are countably many programs but there are uncountably many functions defined on N, there are functions that your favorite programming language cannot compute. All reasonable general-purpose programming systems compute the exact same set of functions, so it follows that there are functions defined on N that are not computable by any program in any programming system.

For any set A, $\mathcal{P}(A) = \{S \mid S \subseteq A\}$ denotes the *power set* of A.

Theorem 1.5 $\mathcal{P}(N)$ *has cardinality greater than* $\aleph_0$.

Proof. Let $A = \mathcal{P}(N)$. Clearly, A is infinite. Suppose A can be enumerated, and let $S_0, S_1, \ldots$ be an enumeration of A. Then, define $T = \{k \mid k \notin S_k\}$. By definition, T belongs to A. However, for every k, $T \neq S_k$ because $k \in T \Leftrightarrow k \notin S_k$. Thus, T is a set that is not in the enumeration. So we have a contradiction. Thus, A cannot be enumerated.   □

1.6.1   Ordered Sets

It is useful to consider relations on the elements of a set that reflect the intuitive notion of ordering these elements.

Definition 1.6   *A binary relation ρ on a set X is a* partial order *if it is*

1. reflexive *($a\rho a$, for all $a \in X$),*
2. antisymmetric *($a\rho b$ and $b\rho a$ implies $a = b$, for all a and b in X), and*
3. transitive *($a\rho b$ and $b\rho c$ implies $a\rho c$, for all a, b, and c in X).*

A partial order is a *linear order* on X if, in addition, for all a and b in X, $a\rho b$ or $b\rho a$. A *partially ordered set* (*linearly ordered set*) is a pair $\langle X, \rho \rangle$, where ρ is a partial order (linear order, respectively) on X. Let Z denote the set of integers.

Example 1.11
1. *$\langle Z, \leq \rangle$ and $\langle Z, > \rangle$ are linearly ordered sets, where $\leq$ and $>$ denote the customary well-known orderings on Z.*
2. *For any set A, $\langle \mathcal{P}(A), \subseteq \rangle$ is a partially ordered set.*
3. *$\langle Z, \{(a, b) \mid a, b \in Z$ and a is an integral multiple of $b\} \rangle$ is a partially ordered set.*
4. *Let $\mathcal{C}$ be any collection of sets; then*

   $\langle \{\text{card}(X) \mid X \in \mathcal{C}\}, \{(\text{card}(X), \text{card}(Y)) \mid X, Y \in \mathcal{C}$ and $\text{card}(X) \leq \text{card}(Y)\} \rangle$

   is a linear order.

1.7 Elementary Algebra

Here we present some useful algebra and number theory. In the next several pages we will barely scratch the surface of these exceedingly rich subjects. This material is not needed for the main body of the course, but is useful for understanding several examples in later chapters.

1.7.1 Rings and Fields

Definition 1.7   A ring *is a system* $\langle R, +, \cdot, 0 \rangle$ *that satisfies the following axioms, where R is a nonempty set, 0 is an element of R, and $+$ and $\cdot$ are operations on R. For arbitrary members a, b, and c of R:*

(A1) $a + b = b + a$ *(commutative law of addition);*

(A2) $(a + b) + c = a + (b + c)$ *(associative law of addition);*

(A3) $a + 0 = a$ *(zero element);*

(A4) *for every $a \in R$, there exists $x \in R$ such that $a + x = 0$ (existence of additive inverses);*

(A5) $(ab)c = a(bc)^*$ *(commutative law of multiplication);*

(A6) $a(b + c) = ab + ac$;

(A7) $(b + c)a = ba + ca$ *(distributive laws).*

A ring is commutative *if in addition it satisfies the following axiom:*

(A8) $ab = ba$ *(commutative law of multiplication).*

A ring is a ring with unity *if there is an element 1 belonging to R such that*

(A9) $1a = a1 = a$.

Definition 1.8   A field *is a commutative ring with unity $\langle R, +, \cdot, 0, 1 \rangle$ such that*

(A10) *for every $a \neq 0$, $a \in R$, there exists $x \in R$ such that $ax = 1$ (existence of multiplicative inverses).*

Note that 0 and 1 do not denote numbers—they are elements of R that obey the appropriate axioms.

Remember that Z denotes the set of integers and let Q denote the set of all rational numbers. Then, using ordinary integer addition and multiplication and integers 0 and 1, Z forms a ring but not a field. The rational numbers Q, with its ordinary operations, forms a field.

Theorem 1.6   *Each nonzero element in a field has a unique multiplicative inverse.*

---

*As is customary, we write ab instead of writing $a \cdot b$.

Proof. Suppose that s and t are two multiplicative inverses of a. Then

$$s = s1 = s(at) = (sa)t = (as)t = 1t = t. \qquad \square$$

The unique multiplicative inverse of an element a in a field is denoted a^{-1}.

Definition 1.9   *Let m be an integer greater than 1 and let a and b be integers. Then a is* congruent *to b modulo m if m divides $a - b$.*

We indicate that m divides $a - b$ by writing $m | a - b$, and we write $a \equiv b$ (mod m) to denote that a is congruent to b modulo m. Let $\mathrm{rm}(a, m)$ denote the remainder when dividing a by m (e.g., $\mathrm{rm}(5, 2) = 1$).

Theorem 1.7   *The following are elementary facts about congruence modulo m.*

1. *$a \equiv b$ (mod m) if and only if $\mathrm{rm}(a, m) = \mathrm{rm}(b, m)$.*

2. *$a \equiv b$ (mod m) $\Rightarrow$ for all integers x,*

$$a + x \equiv b + x \quad (\mathrm{mod}\ m),$$

$$ax \equiv bx \quad (\mathrm{mod}\ m),\ and$$

$$-a \equiv -b \quad (\mathrm{mod}\ m).$$

3. *Congruence modulo m is an equivalence relation.*

Homework 1.7   *Prove Theorem 1.7.*

Given $m > 1$, the equivalence class containing the integer a is the set

$$[a] = \{x \mid x \equiv a \quad (\mathrm{mod}\ m)\}.$$

We call $[a]$ an *equivalence class modulo m.* Let Z_m denote the set of equivalence classes modulo m, and let $r = \mathrm{rm}(a, m)$, so for some integer q, $a = qm + r$ and $0 \le r < m$. Then, $a - r = qm$, so $a \equiv r$ (mod m) and hence $[a] = [r]$. That is, every integer is congruent modulo m to one of the m integers $0, 1, \ldots, m - 1$. Finally, no two of these are congruent modulo m. Thus, there are exactly m equivalence classes modulo m, and they are the sets $[0], [1], \ldots, [m - 1]$. We have learned that $Z_m = \{[0], [1], \ldots, [m - 1]\}$.

Now we will show that Z_m forms a useful number system. We define operations on Z_m as follows: $[a] + [b] = [a + b]$ and $[a][b] = [ab]$. The definition is well founded, i.e., independent of choice of representative member of each equivalence class, because

$$\mathrm{rm}(a + b, m) \equiv \mathrm{rm}(a, m) + \mathrm{rm}(b, m) \quad (\mathrm{mod}\ m)$$

and

$$\mathrm{rm}(ab, m) \equiv \mathrm{rm}(a, m) \cdot \mathrm{rm}(b, m) \quad (\mathrm{mod}\ m).$$

We state the following theorem.

Theorem 1.8   *For each positive integer m, $\langle Z_m, +, \cdot, [0], [1] \rangle$ is a ring with unity.*

Homework 1.8   *Prove the theorem by verifying each of the properties A1 to A8.*

Definition 1.10   *A commutative ring with unity $\langle R, +, \cdot, 0, 1 \rangle$ is an* integral domain *if for all $a, b \in R$,*

(A11) *$ab = 0$ implies $a = 0$ or $b = 0$ (absence of nontrivial zero divisors).*

The integers with their usual operations form an integral domain.

Theorem 1.9   *Every field is an integral domain.*

Proof. Suppose that $ab = 0$. We show that if $a \neq 0$, then $b = 0$, so suppose that $a \neq 0$. Then the following holds:

$$b = 1b = (a^{-1}a)b = a^{-1}(ab) = a^{-1}0 = 0.$$

This completes the proof.   □

Our goal is to show that if p is a prime number, then Z_p is a field. First, though, let us observe that if m is not a prime number, then Z_m is not even an integral domain: Namely, there exist positive integers a and b, $0 < a < b < m$, such that $m = ab$. Hence, in Z_m, $[a][b] = 0$; yet $[a] \neq 0$ and $[b] \neq 0$.

To show that Z_p is a field when p is prime, we need to show that the equation

$$ax \equiv 1 \pmod{p}$$

is solvable* for each integer $a \in \{1, \ldots, p-1\}$. For this purpose, we introduce the following notation.

Definition 1.11   *For nonzero integers $a, b \in Z$, define*

$$(a, b) = \{ax + by \mid x, y \in Z\}$$

to be the set of all linear combinations *of a and b, and define*

$$(a) = \{ax \mid x \in Z\}.$$

Definition 1.12   *For nonzero integers $a, b \in Z$, the positive integer d is a* greatest common divisor *of a and b if*

(i) d is a divisor of a and b, and

(ii) every divisor of both a and b is a divisor of d.

We write $d = \gcd(a, b)$.

Lemma 1.1   *$(a, b) = (d)$, where $d = \gcd(a, b)$.*

---

*That is, we show for each integer $a \in \{1, \ldots, p-1\}$ that there exists an integer x such that $ax \equiv 1 \pmod{p}$.

Proof. Since a and b are nonzero integers, there is a positive integer in (a, b). Let d be the least positive integer in (a, b). Clearly, $(d) \subseteq (a, b)$.

We show $(a, b) \subseteq (d)$: Suppose $c \in (a, b)$. Then there exist integers q and r such that $c = qd + r$, with $0 \leq r < d$. Since c and d are in (a, b), it follows that $r = c - qd$ is in (a, b) also. However, since $0 \leq r < d$ and d is the least positive integer in (a, b), it must be the case that $r = 0$. Hence, $c = qd$, which belongs to (d). Thus, $(d) = (a, b)$.

All that remains is to show that $d = \gcd(a, b)$. Since a and b belong to (d), d is a common divisor of (a) and (b). If c is any other common divisor of (a) and (b), then c divides every number of the form $ax + by$. Thus, $c|d$, which proves that $d = \gcd(a, b)$. $\qquad\square$

Definition 1.13 *Two integers a and b are* relatively prime *if $\gcd(a, b) = 1$.*

Theorem 1.10 *If p is a prime number, then $\langle Z_p, +, \cdot, [0], [1] \rangle$ is a field.*

Proof. Let $[a]$ be a nonzero member of Z_p. Then, $[a] \neq [0]$, so $a \not\equiv 0 \pmod{p}$. That is, p does not divide a. Thus, since p is prime, a and p are relatively prime. Now, let us apply Lemma 1.1: There exist integers x and y such that $1 = ax + py$. We can rewrite this as $1 - ax = py$ to see that $ax \equiv 1 \pmod{p}$. Hence, $[a][x] = [1]$, which is what we wanted to prove. $\qquad\square$

Lemma 1.1 proves that the greatest common divisor of two integers always exists, but does not give a method of finding it. Next we present the *Euclidean Algorithm*, which computes $\gcd(x, y)$ for integers x and y. Later in the course we will analyze this algorithm to show that it is efficient.

If $d = \gcd(x, y)$, then d is the greatest common divisor of $-x$ and y, of x and $-y$, and of $-x$ and $-y$, as well. Thus, in the following algorithm we assume that x and y are positive integers.

> EUCLIDEAN ALGORITHM
> input positive integers x and y in binary notation;
> **repeat**
> $x := \mathrm{rm}(x, y)$;
>   exchange x and y
> **until** $y = 0$;
> output x.

Let us understand the algorithm and see that it is correct. Let $r_1 = \mathrm{rm}(x, y)$, so for some quotient q_1, $x = q_1 y + r_1$. Since $r_1 = x - q_1 y$, every number that divides x and y also divides r_1. Thus, d divides r_1, where $d = \gcd(x, y)$. Now we will show that $\gcd(x, y) = \gcd(y, r_1)$. We know already that d is a common divisor of y and r_1. If there were a common divisor $d_1 > d$ that divides y and r_1, then this value d_1 would also divide x. Thus, d would not be the greatest common divisor of x and y.

The Euclidean Algorithm reduces the problem of finding $\gcd(x, y)$ to that of finding $\gcd(y, r_1)$, where $r_1 < y$. Since the remainder is always nonnegative and keeps getting smaller, it must eventually be zero. Suppose this occurs after n iterations. Then we have the following system of equations:

$$x = q_1 y + r_1, 0 < r_1 < y,$$
$$y = q_2 r_1 + r_2, 0 < r_2 < r_1,$$
$$r_1 = q_3 r_2 + r_3, 0 < r_3 < r_2,$$
$$r_2 = q_4 r_3 + r_4, 0 < r_4 < r_3,$$
$$\vdots$$
$$r_{n-2} = q_n r_{n-1}.$$

Finally,

$$d = \gcd(x, y) = \gcd(y, r_1) = \gcd(r_1, r_2) = \cdots = \gcd(r_{n-2}, r_{n-1}) = r_{n-1},$$

and r_{n-1} is the final value of x, which completes the argument that the Euclidean Algorithm computes $d = \gcd(x, y)$.

1.7.2 Groups

Definition 1.14 *A* group *is a system* $\langle G, \cdot, 1 \rangle$ *that satisfies the following axioms, where G is a nonempty set, 1 is an element of G, and $\cdot$ is an operation on G:*

(A5) $(ab)c = a(bc)$;

(A9) $1a = a1 = 1$; *and*

(A12) *for every $a \in G$ there exists $x \in G$ such that $ax = 1$.*

A group is commutative *if in addition it satisfies axiom (A8), the commutative law of multiplication.*

The set of integers Z forms a commutative group $\langle Z, +, 0 \rangle$ known as the *additive group of the integers*; for every positive integer m, $\langle Z_m, +, 0 \rangle$ is a commutative group. It follows from Theorem 1.10 that if p is a prime number, then $\langle Z_p - \{[0]\}, \cdot, [1] \rangle$ is a commutative group. More generally, for every field $\langle F, +, \cdot, 0, 1, \rangle$, the nonzero elements of F form a commutative group $\langle F - \{0\}, \cdot, 1 \rangle$ known as the *multiplicative group of the field*.

Definition 1.15 *The* order *of a group* $\langle G, \cdot, 1 \rangle$, *written $o(G)$, is the number of elements in G if G is finite, and is infinite otherwise.*
The order *of an element a in G, $o(a)$, is the least positive m such that $a^m = 1$. If no such integer exists, then $o(a)$ is infinite.*

The order of the additive group of the integers is infinite. The order of the additive group $\langle Z_m, +, 0 \rangle$ is m, while, for p a prime, the order of the multiplicative group of the nonzero elements of Z_p is $p - 1$.

Definition 1.16   *Let H be a nonempty subset of G. H is a* subgroup *of G (or more precisely* $\langle H, \cdot, 1 \rangle$ *is a* subgroup *of* $\langle G, \cdot, 1 \rangle$*) if H contains the identity element 1 and* $\langle H, \cdot, 1 \rangle$ *is a group.*

Let $\langle G, \cdot, 1 \rangle$ be a group and $a \in G$. Then the set $H = \{a^i \mid i \in Z\}$ is a subgroup of G. We claim that H contains $o(a)$ many elements. Of course, if H is infinite, then $o(a)$ is infinite. Suppose that H is finite, and let $o(a) = m$. Let $a^k \in H$. Then for some integer q and $0 \le r < m$, $a^k = a^{qm+r} = (a^m)^q a^r = 1a^r = a^r$. Thus, $H = \{1, a, \dots, a^{m-1}\}$, so H contains at most $o(a)$ elements. If $o(H) < o(a)$, then for some i and j, $0 \le i < j < o(a)$, $a^i = a^j$. Hence, $a^{j-i} = 1$. However, $j - i < o(a)$, which is a contradiction. Thus, $o(H) = o(a)$.

Definition 1.17   *If G contains an element a such that* $G = \{a^i \mid i \in Z\}$, *then G is a* cyclic group *and a is a* generator.

For any group $\langle G, \cdot, 1 \rangle$ and $a \in G$, $H = \{a^i \mid i \in Z\}$ is a cyclic subgroup of G and a is a generator of the subgroup.

Cosets

Now we come to a remarkable point: Every subgroup H of a group G partitions G into disjoint cosets.

Definition 1.18   *Given a subgroup H of a group G and element* $a \in G$, *define* $aH = \{ah \mid h \in H\}$. *The set aH is called a* coset *of H.*

The following lemma lists the basic properties of cosets.

Lemma 1.2   *Let a and b be members of a group G and let H be a subgroup of G.*

1. $aH \cap bH \ne \emptyset$ implies $aH = bH$.

2. For finite subgroups H, aH contains $o(H)$ many elements.

Proof. Suppose that aH and bH have an element $c = ah' = bh''$ ($h', h'' \in H$) in common. Let $h \in H$. Then, $bh = bh''h''^{-1}h = a(h'h''^{-1}h)$, which belongs to aH. Thus, $aH \subseteq bH$. Similarly, bH contains every element of aH, and so $aH = bH$.

To see that aH has $o(H)$ many elements, we note that the mapping $h \mapsto ah$ (from H to aH) is one-to-one: Each element $x = ah$, $h \in H$, in the coset aH is the image of the unique element $h = a^{-1}x$.   □

The element $a = a1 \in aH$. Thus, every element of G belongs to some coset, and because distinct cosets are disjoint, every element of G belongs to a unique coset. The cosets of H partition G. Thus, the proof of the next theorem follows immediately.

Theorem 1.11   **(Lagrange)** *Let H be a subgroup of a finite group G. Then* $o(H) \mid o(G)$.

Lagrange's theorem has several important corollaries.

Corollary 1.1   *If G is a finite group and $a \in G$, then $a^{o(G)} = 1$.*

Proof. For some nonzero integer n, $o(G) = n \cdot o(a)$, so

$$a^{o(G)} = a^{n \cdot o(a)} = (a^{o(a)})^n = 1^n = 1.$$ □

Corollary 1.2   *Every group of order p, where p is prime, is a cyclic group.*

As a consequence, for each prime p, the additive group $\langle Z_p, +, 0 \rangle$ is a cyclic group.

We apply Corollary 1.1 to the multiplicative group $\langle Z_p - \{[0]\}, \cdot, 1 \rangle$ to obtain the following corollary.

Corollary 1.3   **(Fermat)** *If a is an integer, p is prime, and p does not divide a, then $a^{p-1} \equiv 1$ (mod p).*

1.7.3 Number Theory

Our goal is to show that the multiplicative group of the nonzero elements of a finite field is a cyclic group. We know from Corollary 1.3 that for each prime number p and integer a, $1 \le a \le p - 1$, $a^{p-1} \equiv 1$ (mod p). However, we do not yet know whether there is a generator g, $1 \le g \le p - 1$, such that $p - 1$ is the *least* power m such that $g^m \equiv 1$ (mod p). This is the result that will conclude this section. We begin with the following result, known as the *Chinese Remainder Theorem*.

Theorem 1.12   **(Chinese Remainder Theorem)** *Let $m_1, \ldots, m_k$ be pairwise relatively prime positive integers; that is, for all i and j, $1 \le i, j \le k$, $i \ne j$, $\gcd(m_i, m_j) = 1$. Let $a_1, \ldots, a_k$ be arbitrary integers. Then there is an integer x that satisfies the following system of simultaneous congruences:*

$$x \equiv a_1 \pmod{m_1},$$
$$x \equiv a_2 \pmod{m_2},$$
$$\vdots$$
$$x \equiv a_k \pmod{m_k}.$$

Furthermore, there is a unique solution in the sense that any two solutions are congruent to one another modulo the value $M = m_1 m_2 \cdots m_k$.

Proof. For every i, $1 \le i \le k$, define $M_i = M/m_i$. Then, clearly, $\gcd(m_i, M_i) = 1$. By Lemma 1.1, there exist c_i and d_i such that $c_i M_i + d_i m_i = 1$, so $c_i M_i \equiv 1$ (mod m_i). Take $x = \sum_i a_i c_i M_i$. For any i, consider the ith term of the sum: For each $j \ne i$, $m_i | M_j$. Thus, every term in the sum other than the ith term is divisible by m_i. Hence, $x \equiv a_i c_i M_i \equiv a_i$ (mod m_i), which is what we needed to prove.

Now we prove uniqueness modulo M. Suppose that x and y are two different solutions to the system of congruences. Then, for each i, $x - y \equiv 0 \pmod{m_i}$. It follows that $x - y \equiv 0 \pmod{M}$, and this completes the proof. $\qquad\square$

The Euler *phi function* $\phi(m)$ is defined to be the number of integers less than m that are relatively prime to m. If p is a prime, then $\phi(p) = p - 1$.

Theorem 1.13   *If m and n are relatively prime positive integers, then $\phi(mn) = \phi(m)\phi(n)$.*

Proof. We compute $\phi(mn)$. For each $1 \le i < mn$, let r_1 be the remainder of dividing i by m and let r_2 be the remainder of dividing i by n. Then $0 \le r_1 < m$, $0 \le r_2 < n$, $i \equiv r_1 \pmod{m}$, and $i \equiv r_2 \pmod{n}$. Furthermore, for each such r_1 and r_2, by the Chinese Remainder Theorem, there is exactly one value i, $1 \le i < mn$, such that $i \equiv r_1 \pmod{m}$ and $i \equiv r_2 \pmod{n}$. Consider this one-to-one correspondence between integers $1 \le i < mn$ and pairs of integers (r_1, r_2), $0 \le r_1 < m$, $0 \le r_2 < n$, such that $i \equiv r_1 \pmod{m}$ and $i \equiv r_2 \pmod{n}$: Note that i is relatively prime to mn if and only if i is relatively prime to m and i is relatively prime to n. This occurs if and only if r_1 is relatively prime to m and r_2 is relatively prime to n. The number of such i is $\phi(mn)$, while the number of such pairs (r_1, r_2) is $\phi(m)\phi(n)$. Thus, $\phi(mn) = \phi(m)\phi(n)$. $\qquad\square$

Let the prime numbers in increasing order be

$$p_1 = 2, \ p_2 = 3, \ p_3 = 5, \ldots.$$

Every positive integer a has a unique factorization as a product of powers of primes of the form

$$a = p_0^{a_o} p_1^{a_1} \cdots p_i^{a_i} \cdots$$

where $a_i = 0$ for all but at most finitely many i.

Let us compute $\phi(p^a)$ for a prime power p^a. The numbers less than p^a that are *not* relatively prime to p^a are exactly those that are divisible by p. If $n \ge p^{a-1}$, then $n \cdot p \ge p^{a-1} \cdot p = p^a$. So, the numbers less than p^a that have p as a divisor are $p, 2 \cdot p, \ldots, (p^{a-1} - 1) \cdot p$. Hence, there are $(p^{a-1} - 1)$ integers less than p^a that are not relatively prime to to p^a. It follows that there are

$$\phi(p^a) = (p^a - 1) - (p^{a-1} - 1) = (p^a - p^{a-1})$$

positive integers less than p^a that are relatively prime to p^a.

We define a function f on the positive integers by $f(n) = \sum_{d|n} \phi(d)$. We need to prove for all positive integers n, that $f(n) = n$.

Lemma 1.3 $f(p^a) = p^a$, *for any prime power p^a.*

Proof. The divisors of p^a are p^j for $0 \le j \le a$, so

$$f(p^a) = \sum_{j=0}^{a} \phi(p^j) = 1 + \sum_{j=1}^{a} (p^j - p^{j-1}) = p^a. \qquad\square$$

Lemma 1.4   *If m and n are relatively prime positive integers, then $f(mn) = f(m)f(n)$.*

Proof. Every divisor d of mn can be written uniquely as a product $d = d_1 d_2$, where d_1 is a divisor of m and d_2 is a divisor of n. Conversely, for every divisor d_1 of m and d_2 of n, $d = d_1 d_2$ is a divisor of mn. Note that d_1 and d_2 are relatively prime. Thus, by Theorem 1.13, $\phi(d) = \phi(d_1)\phi(d_2)$. It follows that

$$
\begin{aligned}
f(mn) &= \sum_{d \mid mn} \phi(d) \\
&= \sum_{d_1 \mid m} \sum_{d_2 \mid n} \phi(d_1)\phi(d_2) \\
&= \sum_{d_1 \mid m} \phi(d_1) \sum_{d_2 \mid n} \phi(d_2) \\
&= f(m)f(n).
\end{aligned}
$$
$\square$

Theorem 1.14   *For every positive integer n, $\sum_{d \mid n} \phi(d) = n$.*

Proof. The integer n is a product of relatively prime terms of the form p^a, so the proof follows immediately from Lemmas 1.3 and 1.4. $\square$

Polynomials

Let $\langle F, +, \cdot, 0, 1 \rangle$ be a field and let x be a symbol. The expression

$$
\sum_0^k a_k x^k,
$$

where the *coefficients* a_i, $i \le k$, belong to F, is a *polynomial*. The degree of a polynomial is the largest number k such that the coefficient $a_k \ne 0$; this coefficient is called the *leading* coefficient. One adds or multiplies polynomials according to the rules of high school algebra. With these operations the set of all polynomials over F forms a *polynomial ring* $F[x]$. We say that g *divides* f, where $f, g \in F[x]$, if there is a polynomial $h \in F[x]$ such that $f = gh$. An element $a \in F$ is a *root* of a polynomial $f(x) \in F[x]$ if $f(a) = 0$.

Homework 1.9   *Verify that $F[x]$ is a ring.*

Theorem 1.15   *If $f(x), g(x) \in F[x]$, $g(x)$ is a polynomial of degree n, the leading coefficient of $g(x)$ is 1, and $f(x)$ is of degree $m \ge n$, then there exist unique polynomials $q(x)$ and $r(x)$ in $F[x]$ such that $f(x) = q(x)g(x) + r(x)$, and $r(x) = 0$ or the degree of $r(x)$ is less than the degree of $g(x)$.*

The proof proceeds by applying the *division algorithm*, which we now sketch: Suppose that $f(x) = \sum_0^m a_m x^m$. We can make the leading coefficient a_m vanish by subtracting from f a multiple of g, namely, $a_m x^{m-n} g(x)$. After this subtraction, if the degree is still not less than n, then we can again remove the leading coefficient by subtracting another multiple of $g(x)$. Continuing this way, we eventually have $f(x) - q(x)g(x) = r(x)$, where the degree of $r(x)$ is of lower degree than $g(x)$ or equal to zero.

Lemma 1.5   *If a is a root of $f(x) \in F[x]$, then $f(x)$ is divisible by $x - a$.*

Proof. Applying the division algorithm, we get $f(x) = q(x)(x - a) + r$, where $r \in F$ is a constant. Substitute a for the x to see that $0 = f(a) = q(a) \cdot 0 + r = r$. Thus, $f(x) = q(x)(x - r)$. $\square$

Theorem 1.16   *If $a_1, \ldots, a_k$ are different roots of $f(x)$, then $f(x)$ is divisible by the product $(x - a_1)(x - a_2) \cdots (x - a_k)$.*

The proof is by mathematical induction in which Lemma 1.5 provides the base case $k = 1$.

Corollary 1.4   *A polynomial in $F[x]$ of degree n that is distinct from zero has at most n roots in F.*

This concludes our tutorial on polynomials. We turn now to show that the multiplicative group of the nonzero elements of a finite field is cyclic.

Let $\langle F, +, \cdot, 0, 1 \rangle$ be a finite field with q elements. Then the multiplicative subgroup of nonzero elements of F has order $q - 1$. Our goal is to show that this group has a generator g of order $q - 1$. By Lagrange's theorem, Theorem 1.11, we know that the order of every nonzero element a in F is a divisor of $q - 1$. Our first step is to show that for every positive integer $d | (q - 1)$, there are either 0 or $\phi(d)$ nonzero elements in F of order d.

Lemma 1.6   *For every $d | (q - 1)$, there are either 0 or $\phi(d)$ nonzero elements in F of order d.*

Proof. Let $d | (q - 1)$, and suppose that some element a has order d. We will show that there must be $\phi(d)$ elements of order d. By definition, each of the elements $a, a^2, \ldots, a^d = 1$ is distinct. Each of these powers of a is a root of the polynomial $x^d - 1$. Thus, by Corollary 1.4, since every element of order d is a root of this polynomial, every element of order d must be among the powers of a. Next we will show that a^j, $1 \le j < d$, has order d if and only if $\gcd(j, d) = 1$. From this, it follows immediately that there are $\phi(d)$ elements of order d.

Let $\gcd(j, d) = 1$, where $1 \le j < d$, and suppose that a^j has order $c < d$. Then $(a^c)^j = (a^j)^c = 1$ and $(a^c)^d = (a^d)^c = 1$. By Lemma 1.1, since j and d are relatively prime, there are integers u and v such that $1 = uj + vd$. Clearly, one of these integers must be positive and the other negative. Assume that $u > 0$ and $v \le 0$. Then $(a^c)^{uj} = 1$ and $(a^c)^{-vd} = 1$, so dividing on both sides, we get $a^c = (a^c)^{uj+vd} = 1$. However, since $c < d$, this contradicts the fact that $o(a) = d$. Thus, our supposition that $o(a^j) < d$ is false; a^j has order d.

Conversely, suppose that $\gcd(j, d) = d' > 1$. Then d/d' and j/d' are integers, so $(a^j)^{d/d'} = (a^d)^{j/d'} = 1$. Thus, $o(a^j) \le d/d' < d$.

This completes the proof. $\square$

Theorem 1.17 *The multiplicative group of the nonzero elements of a finite field is cyclic. If the finite field has q elements, then there exist $\phi(q-1)$ generators.*

Proof. Let $\langle F, +, \cdot, 0, 1 \rangle$ be a finite field with q elements. We need to show that the multiplicative group $\langle F - \{0\}, +, \cdot, 1 \rangle$ has a generator, an element a of order $q - 1$. Every element a has some order d such that $d \mid (q - 1)$, and by Lemma 1.6, for every such d, there are either 0 or $\phi(d)$ nonzero elements in F of order d. By Theorem 1.14, $\sum_{d \mid (q-1)} \phi(d) = q - 1$, which is the number of elements in $F - \{0\}$. Hence, in order for every element to have some order d that is a divisor of $q - 1$, it must be the case for every such d that there are $\phi(d)$ many elements of order d. In particular, there are $\phi(q - 1)$ different elements $g \in F$ of order $q - 1$. Thus, there is a generator, and the multiplicative group of nonzero elements of F is cyclic. $\square$

Corollary 1.5 *If p is a prime number, then $\langle Z_p - \{[0]\}, \cdot, [1] \rangle$ is a cyclic group.*

For example, the number 2 is a generator of Z_{19}. Namely, the powers of 2 modulo 19 are 2, 4, 8, 16, 13, 7, 14, 9, 18, 17, 15, 11, 3, 6, 12, 5, 10, 1.

Homework 1.10 *What are the other generators for Z_{19}?*

Once considered to be the purest branch of mathematics, devoid of application, number theory is the mathematical basis for the security of electronic commerce, which is fast becoming an annual trillion-dollar industry. Modern cryptography depends on techniques for finding large prime numbers p and generators for Z_p—and on the (still unproven) hypotheses of the computational hardness of factoring integers.

2.

Introduction to Computability

2.1   Turing Machines   23

2.2   Turing-Machine Concepts   26

2.3   Variations of Turing Machines   28

2.4   Church's Thesis   34

2.5   RAMs   36

This subject is primarily concerned with the limitations of computing. As one of the highlights of this study, we will learn several specific problems that computers cannot solve.

A robust theory of computability dates back to the work of Church [Chu36] and Turing [Tur36] and provides models of computation and sophisticated methods that will be useful in our study of complexity theory as well. Although much of that work predated digital computers and was without forethought of modern technology, we know that von Neumann was influenced by Turing's invention of a universal, general-purpose, stored-program computer.

The basic model of computation for our study is the Turing machine, and for complexity theory, is the multitape Turing machine. However, these subjects should not depend too much on the choice of computational model. To this end, we will discuss Church's thesis as well as an expanded version of Church's thesis. Church's thesis states that every computational device can be simulated by a Turing machine. Evidence for this thesis comes from the fact that it has withstood the test of time, and it has been proven for all known reasonable models of sequential computation, including random access machines (RAMs). One of the topics in this chapter is the simulation of RAMs by Turing machines.

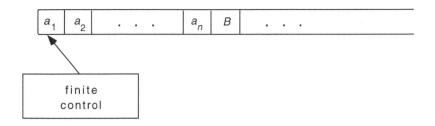

FIGURE 2.1. Diagram of a Turing machine.

We view the study of computability to be an important prelude to the study of complexity theory. First, the models and methods that we learn in these chapters will be important later as well. Second, before concerning ourselves with the question of what problems can be efficiently computed, it is good to appreciate that there is a vast world of problems that we can easily formulate as computational problems but that computers cannot solve.

2.1 Turing Machines

Even before the invention of modern computers, Alan Turing (1936) described a theoretical model of a computing machine. Although very simple in structure, the Turing machine possesses remarkable properties. In particular, a Turing machine is as powerful as any other computing device.

Computer memory is organized linearly as the cells of an infinite tape. Each cell of the tape may hold exactly one of a finite number of symbols chosen from a finite tape alphabet, Γ. Initially, an input word is placed on the otherwise empty tape as a word w in the input alphabet, Σ. This is shown in Fig. 2.1.

A *finite control* is attached to a head that scans one cell of the tape at a time. What the control does next, whether it scans a different symbol or prints a new symbol on the square, depends on its "internal state" as well as the symbol currently being scanned.

One can think of this as a machine, made of transistors or toothpicks and rubber bands. It doesn't matter. The combination of whatever the insides look like (the state) coupled with what symbol is being scanned determines what happens next.

In a move, the machine

1. prints a new symbol,
2. shifts its head one cell left or right,
3. changes state.

The number of states is finite, and at any time only a finite amount of memory is being used. A machine must have a finite description. A Turing machine has two designated special states, q_{accept} and q_{reject}. The machine halts (stops operating) when it enters either of these states. Turing machines may run forever on some inputs. This is entirely consistent with the experience of most programmers.

We let Q be the finite set of states. We permit symbols to be written on cells of the tape from a finite alphabet $\Gamma \supseteq \Sigma$.

The next move is determined by a *transition* function

$$\delta : (Q - \{q_{accept}, q_{reject}\}) \times \Gamma \to Q \times \Gamma \times \{L, R\}.$$

Hence, δ maps a (current state, current symbol scanned) pair into a triple consisting of (the next state, the new symbol to be printed, indication to move the head one cell to the left or right). There is no next move from either q_{accept} or q_{reject}.

Formally, a Turing machine is a system

$$M = \langle Q, \Sigma, \Gamma, \delta, q_0, B, q_{accept}, q_{reject} \rangle,$$

where

Q is the finite set of states,
Γ is the finite tape alphabet,
$B \in \Gamma$, the *blank*,
Σ is the input alphabet, $\Sigma \subseteq \Gamma - \{B\}$,
δ is the transition function,
$q_0 \in Q$ is the *initial state*,
q_{accept} is the accepting state, and
q_{reject} is the rejecting state.

To avoid confusion, we usually take $Q \cap \Gamma = \emptyset$.

If M tries to move left when in the leftmost square, the head stays in the same place and the computation continues. The first instance of the blank symbol B denotes the end of the input word.

Example 2.1 *A parity counter. The input is a word w in $\{0, 1\}^*$. The Turing machine M is to halt in state q_{accept} if the number of 1's on its tape is odd and to halt in state q_{reject} if the number of 1's is even.*

$\Sigma = \{0, 1\}$, $\Gamma = \{0, 1, B\}$, and $Q = \{q_0, q_1, q_{accept}, q_{reject}\}$ (q_0 for even and q_1 for odd). The transition function δ is often given as a matrix with rows of the form

$$q \quad a \mid q' \quad b \quad D$$

where q is the current state, a is the symbol currently stored in the cell being scanned, q' is the next state, b is the symbol to be written in the cell, and the *direction D is either left or right. Hence, we describe the transition function for the parity counter as follows:*

q_0	0	q_0	0	R
q_0	1	q_1	1	R
q_0	B	q_{reject}	$-$	$-$
q_1	0	q_1	0	R
q_1	1	q_0	1	R
q_1	B	q_{accept}	$-$	$-$

A Turing machine continues until it reaches the accept or reject state. If it never reaches one of these states, then the computation continues forever.

As a Turing machine computes, changes occur to the state, tape contents, and current head position. A setting of this information is called a configuration. Formally, we define an *instantaneous description* (ID) or *configuration* of a Turing machine M to be a word $\alpha_1 q \alpha_2$, where $q \in Q$ is the current state and $\alpha_1 \alpha_2$ is the contents of the tape up to the rightmost nonblank or up to the symbol to the left of the head, whichever is rightmost. The tape head is scanning the first symbol of α_2 or B, in case $\alpha_2 = \lambda$.

We define the *next move* relation, denoted by a turnstile, $\vdash_M$. Let

$$X_1 X_2 \ldots X_{i-1} q X_i \ldots X_n$$

be an ID.

1. Suppose $\delta(q, X_i) = (p, Y, L)$. If $i > 1$, then

$$X_1 X_2 \ldots X_{i-1} q X_i \ldots X_n \vdash_M X_1 X_2 \ldots X_{i-2} p X_{i-1} Y X_{i+1} \ldots X_n.$$

If $i = 1$, then

$$q X_1 \ldots X_n \vdash_M p Y X_2 \ldots X_n.$$

2. Suppose $\delta(q, X_i) = (p, Y, R)$. Then

$$X_1 X_2 \ldots X_{i-1} q X_i \ldots X_n \vdash_M X_1 \ldots X_{i-1} Y p X_{i+1} \ldots X_n$$

unless $i - 1 = n$, in which case

$$X_1 \ldots X_n q \vdash_M X_1 \ldots X_n Y p.$$

The relation $\vdash_M^*$ is the reflexive, transitive closure of $\vdash_M$. This means that $C \vdash_M^* D$, where C and D are configurations, if and only if $C = D$ or there is a sequence of configurations $C_1, \ldots, C_k$ such that

$$C = C_1 \vdash C_2 \vdash \cdots \vdash C_k = D.$$

A configuration is *accepting* if the state of the configuration is q_{accept} and is *rejecting* if the state is q_{reject}. Accepting and rejecting configurations are the only *halting* configurations. The Turing machine M *accepts* an input word w if $q_0 w \vdash_M^* I$, where I is an accepting configuration. Similarly, the Turing machine M *rejects* a word w if $q_0 w \vdash_M^* I$, where I is rejecting.

2.2   Turing-Machine Concepts

Definition 2.1   *Let M be a Turing machine. The language* accepted *by M is*

$$L(M) = \{w \in \Sigma^* \mid M \text{ accepts } w\}.$$

A language L, $L \subseteq \Sigma^*$, is Turing-machine-acceptable *if there is a Turing machine that accepts L.*

Note that M might not halt on words w that belong to $\overline{L}$.

Definition 2.2   *A language L is* Turing-machine-decidable *if L is accepted by some Turing machine that halts on every input, and a Turing machine that halts on every input and accepts L is called a* recognizer *for L.*

Usually we will write "acceptable" instead of "Turing-machine-acceptable," and write "decidable" instead of "Turing-machine-decidable." Note the distinction between these two definitions. If M accepts L, then, for all words $x \in \Sigma^*$,

$x \in L \Rightarrow M$ eventually enters state q_{accept}, and

$x \notin L \Rightarrow$ either M eventually enters state q_{reject} or M runs forever.

However, if M decides L, then

$x \in L \Rightarrow M$ eventually enters state q_{accept}, and

$x \notin L \Rightarrow M$ eventually enters state q_{reject}.

Every Turing machine M accepts some language, but a Turing machine might not be a recognizer for any language at all, simply because it does not halt on all input strings.

Proposition 2.1   *If L is decidable, then $\overline{L}$ is decidable.*

Although its proof is simple, the following theorem is an important characterization of the decidable sets and pinpoints the distinction between decidable and acceptable.

Theorem 2.1   *A language L is decidable if and only if both L and $\overline{L}$ are acceptable.*

Proof. If L is decidable, then it is acceptable, by definition. Let M be a recognizer for L. A Turing machine that is exactly like M, but with the states q_{accept} and q_{reject} reversed, is a recognizer for $\overline{L}$ (which, in passing, proves Proposition 2.1) and so $\overline{L}$ is acceptable. For the proof of the converse, let M_L and $M_{\overline{L}}$ be Turing machines that accept L and $\overline{L}$, respectively. Design N so that on an input word w, N copies the input to a second tape and then simulates M_L on some of its tapes while simultaneously simulating $M_{\overline{L}}$ on others of its tapes. N is to accept w if the simulation of M_L accepts, and is to reject w if the simulation of $M_{\overline{L}}$ accepts. Clearly, N accepts L. Since every word w belongs to either L or $\overline{L}$, either the simulation of M_L eventually accepts or the simulation of $M_{\overline{L}}$ eventually accepts. Thus, N halts on every input, which proves that L is decidable.   □

Homework 2.1   *Design Turing machines to recognize the following languages:**

1. $\{0^n 1^n 0^n \mid n \geq 1\}$;
2. $\{ww \mid w \in \{0, 1\}^*\}$;
3. $\{ww^R \mid w \in \{0, 1\}^*\}$. $(w^R$ denotes the "reversal" of w, so if $w = a_1 a_2 \cdots a_k$, then $w^R = a_k a_{k-1} \cdots a_1.)$

Primarily we will be concerned with questions about whether certain languages are either acceptable or decidable, and eventually about whether certain languages have efficient recognizers. For this reason, we formulated Turing machines as acceptors of languages. However, it is important to realize that Turing machines can also compute functions. After all, ordinary computing involves both input and output, and output is usually more complex than merely a bit indication of the machine's final state. For this reason, when computing a partial function the final state is no longer relevant. We will continue to assume that a Turing machine that computes a partial function contains the state q_{accept}, but we no longer assume that M contains the state q_{reject}. The state q_{accept} is the only halting state. We arrive at the following definition:

A Turing machine M *computes* the partial function $\phi : (\Sigma^*)^n \to \Sigma^*$ if, when the initial ID is $q_0 w_1 B w_2 B \ldots w_n$, then

1. M eventually enters an accepting configuration if and only if

$$\phi(w_1, \ldots, w_n),$$

and

2. if and when M does so, then the accepting configuration is of the form

$$\phi(w_1, \ldots, w_n) q_{\text{accept}}.$$

That is, the tape is empty except for the value of $\phi(w_1, \ldots, w_n)$, and the Turing machine halts with the head scanning the first cell to the right of this value.

When M executes on an arbitrary input word x, only two possibilities exist: Either M accepts x, in which case $x \in dom(\phi)$ and M outputs the value $\phi(x)$, or M executes forever. Observe that $L(M)$ is the domain of ϕ.

Every Turing machine M and $n \geq 1$ determines the partial function ϕ_M^n of n arguments such that M halts behind $\phi_M^n(w_1, \ldots, w_n)$ if and when M halts after being run on initial ID $q_0 w_1 B w_2 B \ldots w_n$.

---

*You should not give the formal descriptions of Turing machines that solve homework problems such as this one. Since Turing-machine programs are unreadable, as is true in general of machine-language programs, it is not desirable to give formal descriptions. Instead, describe in relative detail how the Turing machine moves its head, stores data on its tape, changes states, and so forth. In this manner describe a Turing machine that implements your algorithm for solving the problems.

A partial function ϕ is *partial computable* if there is some Turing machine that computes it. If $\phi(w_1, \ldots, w_n) \downarrow$ for all $w_1, \ldots, w_n$, then ϕ is *total computable*. Observe that a Turing machine that computes a total computable function accepts and halts on every input. Therefore, if M computes a total computable function, then $L(M) = \Sigma^*$.

It is more traditional to think of the partial computable functions as mappings on the natural numbers. Fixing 2-adic as the representation gives us a unique class of partial computable functions over the natural numbers. Many texts represent the positive integer n by the string 1^{n+1}, but, thinking ahead, from a complexity theoretician's point of view, the more succinct representation is preferable.

Homework 2.2   *Using either a 2-adic or binary representation for numbers, describe Turing machines that compute the following functions:*

1. $\lceil \log_2 n \rceil$;
2. $n!$;
3. n^2.

2.3   Variations of Turing Machines

Students of computer science should have little difficulty appreciating that Turing machines have as much power as any other computing device. That is, the Turing machine accepts or decides the exact same languages and computes the exact same partial functions as any other computing device. The Turing machine is designed to perform symbol manipulation in a simple, straightforward manner. This is one common view of computing. What might be the differences between a Turing machine and computers we use every day? Both store symbols in storage locations. The latter might store 32 or 64 symbols in one storage location, whereas the Turing machine stores only one symbol in each storage location, but that difference is not essential; rather, it makes the machines that we use more efficient. Both types of machines can change these symbols in one move and change state. The machines that we use have "random access," meaning, for example, that they can be reading the contents of memory location 100 and then, by executing one move, read memory location 1000. The Turing machine can easily simulate that, but must make 900 moves in order to move its head 900 cells to the right. Again, the difference is in efficiency rather than in fundamental computing power.

In part, the rest of this chapter is dedicated to expanding on this brief argument, to provide evidence that the Turing machine is as powerful as any other computer. This hypothesis is known as "Church's thesis." In this section we will introduce two important variations of the Turing-machine model and prove that they are equivalent to Turing machines. The next section discusses Church's thesis in more detail, and then we will examine random access machines more technically than in the previous paragraph.

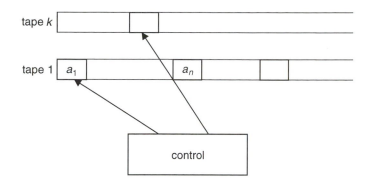

FIGURE 2.2. Diagram of a k-tape Turing machine.

2.3.1 Multitape Turing Machines

A k-tape Turing machine M, as pictured in Fig. 2.2, has k tapes, each with its own read/write head. When M is in a state q reading the scanned symbol in each tape, M writes over each of these symbols, moves left or right on each tape, and enters a new state.

Formally, the transition function is of the form

$$\delta : (Q - \{q_{\text{accept}}, q_{\text{reject}}\}) \times \Gamma^k \to Q \times \Gamma^k \times \{L, R\}^k.$$

Thus, given state q and scanned symbols $a_1, \ldots, a_k$, on tapes $1, \ldots, k$, respectively, $\delta(q, a_1, \ldots, a_k) = (p, b_1, \ldots, b_k, D_1, \ldots, D_k)$, where $b_1, \ldots, b_k$ are the new symbols to be written, $D_1, \ldots, D_k$ are the directions (left or right) in which the heads should move, and p is the next state.

Definition 2.3 *Two Turing machines are* equivalent *if they accept the same language.*

Two Turing machines might accept the same language L, and the first might be a recognizer for L, while the second does not even halt on all inputs. We will prove that every multitape Turing machine is equivalent to some ordinary (one-tape) Turing machine. Our interest in this result is twofold. First, showing that adding features does not increase a Turing machine's computational power helps us to convince ourselves that the Turing machine is a natural model of computing. Second, the multitape Turing machine is in fact the model that we will accept as our standard, and as such is the one to be used in the remainder of the course. This is a matter of efficiency. The multitape Turing machine is more efficient and easier to program than single-tape Turing machines. Also, there are efficient simulations between the multitape Turing machine and all other known models of computation.

Example 2.2 *This example illustrates the efficiency of multitape Turing machines over single-tape Turing machines. We can easily design a two-tape Turing machine to accept* *the language $L = \{ww^R \mid w \in \{0, 1\}^*\}$. Namely, given an input word that is placed on tape 1, the machine copies the input word onto the second tape. This requires one sweep of both reading heads from left to right. Next, move the reading head on tape 1 back to the left end. Then, compare the word claimed to be w^R with the word claimed to be w by moving the two heads in opposite directions, moving the head on tape 1 from left to right and on tape 2 from right to left. At each step, if the symbols on the scanned cells are identical, then continue, else halt without accepting. Finally, after the input word passes these tests, determine whether the length of the input word is even and if it is, then accept.*

Observe that this machine requires no more that a few scans of its heads from one end of the input word to the other. Hence, the number of steps is $O(n)$, where $n = |w|$. In general, we will measure the complexity of computational problems as a function of the length of the input word.

In contrast, consider your solution to Homework 2.1. First, the above solution is probably simpler. Second, your solution probably compares the first symbol of the input word with the last, placing markers to detect that they were visited. Then the machine compares the second symbol with the next-to-last symbol, and so on. The first comparison requires n steps, the second comparison requires $n - 1$ steps, and so forth, until we reach the last comparison, which requires only one step. Thus, the total number of comparisons is $O(n^2)$. Indeed, one can prove that every single-tape Turing machine that accepts L must take at least $O(n^2)$ steps.

Homework 2.3   *In the above example, why do you need to check whether the input word is even before accepting?*

Theorem 2.2   *Every multitape Turing machine has an equivalent one-tape Turing machine.*

Proof. Let M be a k-tape Turing machine. The single tape of N is viewed as consisting of k "tracks," one track for each work tape of M. This is accomplished by enlarging the tape alphabet of N so that each cell of N contains a symbol that represents k symbols of M and possibly a marker $\uparrow$ to indicate M's head position on the ith tape head. The tape alphabet of N is sufficiently large so that each tape symbol of N uniquely denotes such an array of M's tape symbols and head indicator. (For example, in the illustration given in Fig. 2.3, the second cell of N contains a symbol that uniquely denotes the array $(a_{12}, a_{22}, \ldots, \uparrow a_{k2})$.)

The one-tape Turing machine N simulates a move of M as follows: Initially N's head is at the leftmost cell containing a head marker. N sweeps right, visiting each of the cells with head markers, and stores in its control the symbol scanned by each of the k heads of M.* When N crosses a head marker, it updates the count of head markers to its right. When no more head markers are to the right, N has enough information to determine the move of M. Next, N sweeps left until it reaches the leftmost head marker. While doing so, it updates the tape symbols of

---

*By increasing the number of states, a Turing machine can always store a fixed number of symbols in its finite control. The technique is to let each new state uniquely represent a combination of stored symbols.

Track k	a_{k1}	$\uparrow a_{k2}$		a_{kd}	
Track 2	$\uparrow a_{21}$	a_{22}		a_{2d}	
Track 1	a_{11}	a_{12}		a_{1d}	

FIGURE 2.3. d cells of one-tape Turing machine N with k tracks.

M scanned by the head markers and moves the head markers one cell left or right as required. Finally, N changes M's current state, which is stored in N's control. N accepts its input word if and only the new state of M is accepting. $\square$

In this proof, if M is a recognizer for a language L, then so is N, for we need only to stipulate that N rejects if and only if the new state of M is rejecting. Also, note that N must make many moves in order to simulate one move of M. This is frequently true of simulations. Since one head of M might be moving to the left while another is moving to the right, it can take about $\Sigma_{i=1}^{n} 2i = O(n^2)$ moves of N to simulate n moves of M.

By definition, two Turing machines are equivalent if they accept the same language, and this definition will continue to be useful for us. You might think it more natural to have defined "equivalent" to mean that the two machines compute the same partial function. Clearly, this is the stronger notion, for it possible for two different partial computable functions to have the same domain. The simulation given in the proof of Theorem 2.2 holds for the stronger notion as well. Thus, we state the following corollary:

Corollary 2.1   *For every multitape Turing machine there is a one-tape Turing machine that computes the same partial computable function.*

2.3.2 Nondeterministic Turing Machines

A nondeterministic Turing machine allows for the possibility of more than one next move from a given configuration. If there is more than one next move, we do not specify which next move the machine makes, only that it chooses one such move. This is a crucial concept for our study of complexity. Unlike deterministic computing machines, we do not design nondeterministic machines to be executed. Rather, one should understand nondeterministic Turing machines to be a useful device for describing languages, and later, when we study complexity theory, for classifying computational problems.

Formally, a nondeterministic Turing machine M is the same as a multitape Turing machine, except that the transition function has the form

$$\delta : (Q - \{q_{\text{accept}}\}) \times \Gamma^k \to \mathcal{P}(Q \times \Gamma^k \times \{L, R\}^k).$$

Recall that for any set A, $\mathcal{P}(A)$ denotes the power set of A. To keep the notation manageable, let us assume for the moment that $k = 1$, so that M is a nondeterministic single-tape Turing machine. Then, given state q and scanned symbol a, $\delta(q, a) = \{(p_1, b_1, D_1), \ldots, (p_n, b_n, D_n)\}$, for some $n \geq 1$. We interpret this to mean that in state q reading the symbol a, M may make any of the possible moves indicated by one of the triples (p_i, b_i, D_i), $1 \leq i \leq n$. Thus, for some $1 \leq i \leq n$, M will write the symbol b_i in the cell that is currently scanned, move in the direction D_i, and change to state p_i.

There are two additional subtle but important distinctions between deterministic and nondeterministic Turing machines: First, it is possible that $\delta(q, a) = \emptyset$, in which case there is no next move and the machine halts without accepting. Second, we do not include the state q_{reject}, so there are no *rejecting* computations.

A nondeterministic Turing machine M and input word w specify a *computation tree* as follows: The *root* of the tree is the initial configuration of M. The *children* of a node are the configurations that follow in one move. Note that a node is a *leaf* if there is no next move. A path from the root to a leaf is an accepting computation if and only if the leaf is an accepting configuration. In general, some computation paths might be infinite, some might be accepting, and others might halt in nonaccepting states. By definition, M accepts w if and only if there is an accepting computation of M on w (in which case, the other possibilities are irrelevant). Recall that M accepts the language $L(M) = \{w \mid M \text{ accepts } w\}$. Thus, $w \in L(M)$ if and only if there is an accepting computation of M on w. This is the important point to remember. It does not matter whether certain computations run forever or whether there is a computation that halts without accepting. All that matters is that at least one computation of M on w accepts, in which case $w \in L(M)$. Conversely, w does *not* belong to $L(M)$ if and only if every computation of M on w is *not* an accepting computation. Presumably, one cannot know whether this is so without executing all possible computations of M on w.

Now we prove that nondeterministic Turing machines are not more powerful than deterministic ones after all.

Theorem 2.3   *Every nondeterministic Turing machine has an equivalent deterministic Turing machine.*

The idea of the proof is a familiar one: Given a nondeterministic Turing machine N, design a deterministic Turing machine M that on an input word w builds the computation tree of N on input w and performs a standard tree-search algorithm that halts and accepts if and only if it finds a leaf that is accepting. Implementation is not difficult, but notice one possible pitfall. Suppose that M implements a depth-first search of the computation tree. Suppose that M has an infinite computation path that is to the left of some accepting computation. Then M will descend the infinite computation path, running forever, without ever finding the accepting computation. The solution to this difficulty is to implement a breadth-first search. Then the computation tree is searched one level at a time, so, if there is a leaf that is accepting, the simulation will find it. The proof to follow gives the details.

Proof. We assume that N is a single-tape nondeterministic Turing machine. The Turing machine M will have three tapes. Tape 1 contains the input word and is never changed. Tape 2 contains a copy of N's tape on some branch of its nondeterministic computation. Tape 3 records M's location in the computation tree.

Let b be the largest number of choices given by N's transition function. Assign each node an address that is a string in $\{1, 2, \ldots, b\}$. A node has address $a_1 \ldots a_k$ if the node is at level $k + 1$, a_1 is the a_1th child of the root, and for $i = 2, \ldots, k$, $a_1 \ldots a_i$ is the a_ith child of the node with address $a_1 \ldots a_{i-1}$. The address of the root is the empty word λ. Tape 3 will contain addresses.

The computation of M proceeds as follows:

1. Initially, tape 1 contains the input word w and tapes 2 and 3 are empty.
2. M copies tape 1 to tape 2.
3. On tape 2, M simulates N on w using the string on tape 3 to determine which choices to make. If tape 3 does not contain symbols for a choice or the symbol gives an invalid choice, then M aborts this branch and goes to step 4. If this simulation reaches an accepting configuration, then M accepts, but if it reaches a halting configuration that is nonaccepting, then M aborts this branch and goes to step 4.
4. M replaces the string on tape 3 with the lexicographically next string. Then M returns to step 2.

It is self-evident that M correctly simulates N. □

Corollary 2.2 *If every computation path of a nondeterministic Turing machine N halts on every input word, then there is a deterministic Turing machine M that recognizes the language L(N).*

For the proof, notice that M must be able to determine when an input word w does not belong to $L(N)$. This occurs if and only every computation path is non-accepting. Since, by hypothesis, no computation paths are infinite, the breadth-first search will eventually search the entire computation tree and visit every leaf node, thereby gaining the information that it needs.

Example 2.3 *Given a graph G, a* clique *H is a complete subgraph of G, meaning that every two vertices in H are connected by an edge. Consider the following nondeterministic algorithm that accepts the set*

$$C = \{(G, k) \mid G \text{ is a graph, } k \text{ is a positive integer, and } G \text{ has} \\ a \text{ clique with } k \text{ vertices}\} :$$

The procedure on an input pair (G, k) nondeterministically chooses a subset of k vertices. Then the procedure tests whether there is an edge between every two vertices in the subset. If so, then the procedure accepts.

If the procedure accepts, then it has chosen a clique with k vertices, so the pair (G, k) belongs to C. Conversely, if $(G, k) \in C$, then G contains a clique H of size k. The computation path of the nondeterministic procedure that selects H is an accepting computation. Hence, the procedure has an accepting computation on input (G, k) if and only if (G, k) has a clique with k vertices.

We can easily implement this procedure on a nondeterministic Turing machine. However, in order to do so we would have to make decisions about how to represent graphs as words over a finite alphabet (because an input to a Turing machine is a word and not a graph). We postpone this discussion of representation to a later chapter. Then we would need to tend to the tedious details of Turing-machine programming. Without exercising this distraction, let us simply note that some nondeterministic Turing machine accepts a suitable representation of the set C.

A deterministic Turing machine to recognize the same language, following the idea of the proof of Theorem 2.3, systematically searches all subsets of k vertices of G and accepts if and only if one of these is a complete subgraph.

2.4   Church's Thesis

Church's thesis states that every "effective computation," or "algorithm," can be programmed to run on a Turing machine. Every "computational device" can be simulated by some Turing machine. In 1936, the same year as Turing introduced the Turing machine [Tur36], Emil Post created the Post machine [Pos65], which he hoped would prove to be the "universal algorithm machine" sought after. Also that year, Alonzo Church [Chu36] developed the *lambda calculus*. Slightly *before* Turing invented his machine, Church proposed the thesis that every function that can be computed by an algorithm can be defined using his lambda calculus. That is, he identified effective computability, a heretofore imprecise notion, with a specific mathematical formulation. Then, independently, Turing posited the thesis that every algorithm can be programmed on a Turing machine. The Church–Post–Turing formulations are provably equivalent, so these theses express the same belief. Several factors contributed to the general acceptance of Church's thesis. Turing's paper contains a convincing analysis of the basic steps of calculation and he demonstrated how this analysis led to the definition of the Turing machine. That is one important factor. Another important factor is the simplicity and naturalness of the Turing-machine model. A third factor is that the formulations of Church, Post, and Turing have been proven to be equivalent. This is no small matter, for each was independently invented from different considerations and perspectives. We should rightfully write the "Church–Turing" thesis, or even the "Church–Post–Turing" thesis, but for brevity we will continue to refer to "Church's" thesis.

Church's thesis cannot be "proven" because concepts such as "effective process" and "algorithms" are not part of any branch of mathematics. Yet evidence for the correctness of Church's thesis abounds. Two points are important to understand with regard to the notion of "algorithm" or "machine" as used here. The first is that every machine must have a "finite description." For example, even though there is no bound on the size of a Turing-machine tape, the description of the Turing machine as a tuple, including the transition function δ, has a finite length. The second is the notion of *determinacy*. For example, once a Turing machine is defined, for every input word, the transition function *determines* uniquely what sequence of IDs will occur. This never changes. Run the machine once or one hundred times, and the same sequence of IDs will occur.

In Chapter 3 we will learn about languages L that are Turing-machine-undecidable. (There exists no Turing machine that halts on every input and accepts L.) Using Church's thesis, we can understand results of this kind more broadly: There is no computational procedure (of any kind) that halts on every input and that for every input word w correctly determines whether w belongs to L.

In this course we are studying both computability theory and complexity theory. The basic model of computation for complexity theory is the multitape Turing machine. However, complexity measures should not depend too much on the choice of computational model. To this end, we introduce an *expanded version of Church's thesis*. Church's thesis states that every computational device can be simulated by a Turing machine. Our expanded Church's thesis is even stronger. It asserts that every computational device can be simulated by a multitape Turing machine with the simulation taking at most polynomial time. (That is, if M is some computational device, then there is a Turing machine T_M that simulates M such that programs run at most a polynomial number of additional steps on T_M than on M.)

This thesis is particularly fortunate because of another assertion known as Cobham's thesis (1964). Cobham's thesis asserts that computational problems can be feasibly computed on some computational device only if they can be computed in polynomial time. Truth be told, an n^{100}-time algorithm is not a useful algorithm. It is a remarkable phenomenon, though, that problems for which polynomial algorithms are found have such algorithms with small exponents and with small coefficients. Thus, combining the two theses, a problem can be feasibly computed only if it can be computed in polynomial time on some multitape Turing machine.

We are neglecting to describe the intellectual fervor that existed at the turn of the last century. What was in the air to cause brilliant scientists to converge on equivalent formulations of universal computing in 1936? This story is told extremely well in a collection of articles edited by Herken [Her94]. Alan Turing, if not the father of computer science, is frequently credited for being the father of theoretical computer science and artificial intelligence. His work in cryptography has been credited in recent years for being instrumental in enabling the Allied forces to win the Second World War. The extraordinary story of his life and work is described in the biography by Hodges [Hod83].

The next section will provide further evidence for the correctness of Church's thesis.

2.5 RAMs

A *random access machine* (RAM) is a conceptual model of a digitial computer. A RAM contains registers that serve as the computer's memory and there is random access to the registers. The basic model, as a general model of computation, is due to Shepherdson and Sturgis [SS63]. The variation that we will describe here is due to Machtey and Young [MY78]. Random access machines are important models for the analysis of concrete algorithms [CR73].

For each finite alphabet Σ, there is a RAM for that alphabet. Thus, let us fix a finite alphabet $\Sigma = \{a_1, \ldots, a_k\}$ with $k > 1$ letters. The RAM consists of a potentially infinite set of registers $R1, R2, \ldots$, each of which can store any word of Σ^*. Any given program uses only the finite set of registers that it specifically names, and any given computation that halts uses only a finite set of words of Σ^*. (Thus, any such computation needs only a finite amount of "hardware.") RAM instructions have available an infinite set of *line names* $N0, N1, \ldots$.

RAM instructions are of the following seven types:

1_j	**add**$_j$ Y,
2	X **del** Y,
3	X **clr** Y,
4	X $Y \leftarrow Z$,
5	X **jmp** X',
6_j	X Y **jmp**$_j$ X',
7	**continue**,

where X is either a line name or nothing, Y and Z are register names, X' is a line name followed by an "a" or a "b" (e.g., $N6a$), and $1 \le j \le k$.

Instructions of types 1 through 4 affect the contents of registers in obvious ways: Type 1_j adds a_j to the right end of the word in register Y. Type 2 deletes the leftmost letter of the word in Y, if there is one. Type 3 changes the word in Y to λ. Type 4 copies the word in Z into Y and leaves Z unchanged.

Types 5 and 6 are jump instructions. Normally instructions are executed in the order in which they are written. When a **jmp** Nia is executed, the next instruction to be executed is the closest instruction above bearing the line name Ni; **jmp** Nib goes to the closest instruction below bearing line name Ni. Several different instructions in a program may have the same line name. Type 6_j are conditional jumps that are performed only if the first letter of the word in Y is a_j. Type 7 are "no-ops" instructions. Table 2.1 summarizes the actions of some of these instructions.

1	**add**$_j$ $R1$	
	before	*boy*
	after	*boya*$_j$

2	**del** $R1$	
	before	*boy*
	after	*oy*

3	**clr** $R1$	
	before	*boy*
	after	λ

4	$R2 \leftarrow R1$	
	$R1$ before	*dog*
	$R2$ before	*cat*
	$R1$ after	*dog*
	$R2$ after	*dog*

Table 2.1. Summary of RAM Instructions

A RAM *program* is a finite sequence of instructions such that each jump has a place to go and such that the last line is a **continue**. A program *halts* if and when it reaches the final **continue** instruction.

A program P *computes* the partial function ϕ if when the initial contents of registers $R1, R2, \ldots, Rn$ are $w_1, w_2, \ldots, w_n$, respectively, and the initial contents of all other registers named in P are λ, then

1. P eventually halts if and only if $\phi(w_1, \ldots, w_n) \downarrow$, and
2. if and when P halts, the final contents of $R1$ are $\phi(w_1, \ldots, w_n)$.

Every RAM program P and $n \geq 1$ determines the partial function ϕ_P^n of n arguments such that P halts with $\phi_P^n(w_1, \ldots, w_n)$ as the final contents of $R1$ if and only if P halts after being run on inputs $w_1, \ldots, w_n$ initially in $R1, \ldots, Rn$, with the rest of the registers empty.

A partial function ϕ is RAM-*computable* if some RAM program computes it.

Homework 2.4 *Assume that h and g are RAM-computable. Define f as follows, where $a \in \Sigma$, $y \in \Sigma^*$, and $z \in \Sigma^*$:*

$$f(\lambda, z) = g(z);$$
$$f(ya, z) = h(y, a, f(y, z), z).$$

Then f is said to be defined by recursion *from h and g. Show that f is RAM-computable.*

We defined RAM programs with a rich instruction set in order to make programming relatively easy and to demonstrate the naturalness of this model.

Two RAM programs are *equivalent* if they compute the same partial function.

Theorem 2.4 *Every RAM program can be effectively transformed into an equivalent one that uses only instructions of types 1, 2, 6, and 7.*

Partial Proof. We will show how to replace type 4 instructions.

Replace each instruction of the form

$$X \; Y \leftarrow Y$$

by

$$X \; \textbf{continue}.$$

Replace an instruction of the form

$$X \; Rf \leftarrow Rg,$$

where f is different from g by the following code of Machtey and Young [MY78]: Let Rm be a register that is not named in the original program and let $Nh, Ni, Nj_1, \ldots, Nj_k$ be line names that are not used in the original program.

X	**clr**	Rf	
	clr	Rm	
	jmp	Nib	
Nh	**del**	Rg	
Ni	Rg **jmp$_1$**	$Nj_1 b$	[copy Rg into Rm]
	$\cdots$		
	Rg **jmp$_k$**	$Nj_k b$	
	jmp	$N1b$	
Nj_1	**add$_1$**	Rm	
	jmp	Nha	
	$\cdots$		
Nj_k	**add$_k$**	Rm	
	jmp	Nha	
Nh	**del**	Rm	
$N1$	Rm **jmp$_1$**	$Nj_1 b$	[copy Rm into Rf and Rg]
	$\cdots$		
	Rm **jmp$_k$**	$Nj_k b$	
	jmp	Nib	
Nj_1	**add$_1$**	Rf	
	add$_1$	Rg	
	jmp	Nha	
	$\cdots$		

$$N j_k \quad \textbf{add}_k \quad R f$$
$$\textbf{add}_k \quad R g$$
$$\textbf{jmp} \quad N h a$$
$$N 1 b \quad \textbf{continue} \qquad \Box$$

Homework 2.5 *Complete the proof by showing how to replace type 3 and 5 instructions.*

Homework 2.6 *Show that type 1, 2, 6, and 7 instructions form a minimal set of instructions for the RAM by showing that if we eliminate any one of these types of instructions, then we will no longer have programs for computing all of the RAM-computable functions.*

Observe carefully how many instructions are used to replace instructions of types 3, 4, and 5. That is, observe that a RAM with the minimal instruction set executes at most a polynomial number of additional instructions than the RAM with the full instruction set.

2.5.1 Turing Machines for RAMS

Here we will show that every RAM program can be simulated by a Turing machine. (It is true also that every Turing machine can be simulated by a RAM program, but as it is the generality of Turing machines that we are seeking evidence of, we will not include the proof in this direction.)

Theorem 2.5 *Every RAM-computable function is Turing-machine-computable. In particular, there is an effective procedure* that given a RAM program outputs a Turing machine that computes the same partial function.*

Proof. Let P be a RAM program that uses only the registers $R1, \ldots, Rm$. We design an m-tape Turing machine M that simulates P. Let $r1, \ldots, rm$ denote the contents of the registers $R1, \ldots, Rm$, respectively. If the input registers are $R1, \ldots, Rt$ with $R(t+1), \ldots, Rm$ empty, for some $1 \leq t \leq m$, then the input to M is $r1 B r2 B \ldots B rt$. M begins with an initialization phase that writes ri on tape i, for each $1 \leq t$, leaves tapes $t+1, \ldots, m$ empty, and then erases $r2, \ldots, rm$ on tape 1 so that only $r1$ remains.

By Theorem 2.4, we need to show how to simulate instructions 1, 2, 6, and 7. If P consists of n instructions, then M will consist of n simulating blocks of instructions. Each block begins with a unique state. M uses these unique states to connect the blocks for the same flow of control as the instructions of P. Except for jump instructions, the last instruction of each block moves M into the state that begins the next block.

---

*As all students are familiar with compilers, you are familiar with programs that take a program written in one programming language as its input and outputs an equivalent program in another programming language.

To simulate instruction 1, an instruction of the form **add**$_j$ Rq, M writes the symbol a_j to the right end of rq on tape q. M simulates instruction 2, of the form **del** Rq, by shifting the symbol in the second cell of tape q one cell to the left, then the symbol in the third cell on cell to the left, and so on, until it has shifted the last symbol of rq to the left and replaced the contents of the cell that contained rq with the blank symbol B.

To simulate a type 6 instruction, of the form Rq **jmp**$_j$, if the first symbol on tape q is a_j, then M moves to the state that begins the block to which the jump instruction refers; otherwise, it moves to the next block. Finally, M simulates the final **continue** statement by entering its accepting state and halting.

It should be clear that M is equivalent to P. Furthermore, the proof provides instructions for constructing M from P, which proves the second claim as well.

□

3

Undecidability

3.1   Decision Problems   41

3.2   Undecidable Problems   43

3.3   Pairing Functions   46

3.4   Computably Enumerable Sets   47

3.5   Halting Problem, Reductions, and Complete Sets   50

3.6   *S-m-n* Theorem   53

3.7   Recursion Theorem   55

3.8   Rice's Theorem   57

3.9   Turing Reductions and Oracle Turing Machines   59

3.10 Recursion Theorem, Continued   66

3.11 References   69

3.12 Additional Homework Problems   70

3.1   Decision Problems

A *decision problem* is a general question to be answered, usually possessing several parameters, or free variables, whose values are left unspecified. An *instance* of a problem is obtained by specifying particular values for all of the problem parameters.

Example 3.1   *The Hamiltonian Circuit problem.*

HAMILTONIAN CIRCUIT
>   **instance** *A graph G = (V, E)*
>   **question** *Does G contain a Hamiltonian circuit?*

A "problem" is not the same as a "question." For example, "Does the graph in Fig. 1.1 have a Hamiltonian circuit?" is a question. It refers to a specific instance.

A *solution* to a decision problem is an algorithm that answers the question that results from each instance. A decision problem is *decidable* if a solution exists and is *undecidable* otherwise.

We will be concerned with the question of whether certain decision problems are decidable. For those that are, in general, computer science is concerned with finding efficient solutions. Later in the course we will address the question of whether certain decidable decision problems have efficient solutions.

According to Church's thesis, every computational device can be simulated by some Turing machine that solves the problem. To show that a decision problem is undecidable, we take the point of view that it suffices to show that no Turing machine solves the problem. Conversely, to show that a Turing machine exists to solve a decision problem, it suffices to present an informal algorithm. It should take you no effort to find an algorithm that solves the Hamiltonian Circuit problem in Example 3.1, but one of the central open questions that drives research in complexity theory is the question of whether the Hamiltonian Circuit, and hundreds of similar decision problems, has an efficient solution.

Recalling that input to a Turing machine must be presented as a word over a finite alphabet, we must address our first technical issue of *encodings*. For example, in order for a Turing machine to solve a decision problem about graphs, graphs must be encoded as words over some finite alphabet. If we cared only about whether or not decision problems are decidable, then this would be enough. However, since we will be concerned also with the question of whether decision problems are feasible, meaning that they have an efficient solution, then we must insist that encodings are *reasonable*. Encodings must be reasonable in the sense that the length of the word that represents the graph must be no more than a polynomial in the length of whatever is considered to be a natural presentation of a graph.

Reasonable encodings should be concise and not "padded" with unnecessary information or symbols. For example, numbers should be represented in 2-adic, binary, or any other concise representation, but should not be represented in unary. If we restrict ourselves to encoding schemes with these properties, then the particular choice of representation will not affect whether a given decision problem has a feasible solution. For example, the natural presentation of a graph $G = (V, E)$ may be either by a vertex list, edge list, or an adjacency matrix. For our purpose either is acceptable. Once such a decision is made, it is straightforward to encode the natural presentation as a word over a finite alphabet. Now let us do this. We will show how to represent a graph as a string over the finite alphabet $\{1, 2, ,, [,], (,)\}$. Suppose that $V = \{1, \ldots, k\}$ and E consists of pairs of the form (e_1, e_2). Then:

1. denote each integer by its 2-adic representation. Let $C_2(i)$ denote the 2-adic representation of the number i;

2. for each i, $i = 1, \ldots, k$, let $[C_2(i)]$ represent the vertex i;
3. in general, if $x_1, \ldots, x_n$ represent the objects $X_1, \ldots, X_n$, let $(x_1, \ldots, x_n)$ represent the object $(X_1, \ldots, X_n)$. Thus, in particular, the string $([C_2(e_1)], [C_2(e_2)])$ represents the edge (e_1, e_2).

In this manner, every graph is representable as a string. Any other data structure can be encoded in a similar manner.

3.2 Undecidable Problems

In this chapter we will assume that all Turing machines compute partial computable functions. Thus, a Turing machine halts on an input word if and only if it accepts the input word, so we no longer need to distinguish halting from accepting. The characteristic function of a set S is the function f_S defined by $f_S(x) = 0$ if $x \in S$, and $f_S(x) = 1$ if $x \notin S$. By the following easy-to-prove proposition, restricting to Turing machines that compute partial functions does not limit our ability to recognize languages.

Proposition 3.1   *A set S is decidable if and only if its characteristic function is computable.*

Now we turn our attention to the existence of undecidable problems. We will show that a number of decision problems about Turing machines themselves are undecidable. For example, we will see that the following Program Termination problem for Turing machines is undecidable.

Example 3.2   *The Program Termination problem for Turing machines*

PROGRAM TERMINATION
>**instance** *A Turing machine M*
>**question** *Does M eventually halt on every input?*

First we must encode Turing machines as words so that Turing machines can be presented as input strings to other Turing machines. This is straightforward using the efficient encoding method that we gave in the last section. Let us note just a few of the details. Suppose we want to encode Turing machine

$$M = \langle Q, \Sigma, \Gamma, \delta, q_0, B, q_{\text{accept}} \rangle.$$

Assume that $Q = \{q_0, q_1, \ldots, q_{k-1}\}$. Represent the state q_i by $c(q_i) = [C_2(i)]$, and represent the set of states Q by the string $\{c(q_0), c(q_1), \ldots, c(q_{k-1})\}$. Similarly, represent Σ and Γ as strings. Write a move $\delta(q_i, a_j) = (q_k, a_l, D)$, where $D = 1$, for a shift left, and $D = 2$, for a shift right, as a five-tuple (q_i, a_j, q_k, a_l, D). Then, of course, we represent the five-tuple by the string

$$(c(q_i), c(a_j), c(q_k), c(a_l), D).$$

Then δ is a sequence of such five-tuples, so we can represent the sequence as a string as well. Finally, represent the entire seven-tuple that defines M as a string.

Observe that the current representation of a Turing machine M is a word w over the language $\{1, 2, ,, \{, \}, [,], (,)\}$ consisting of nine symbols. We will make one more refinement. Identify this alphabet with the symbols $\{1, \ldots, 9\}$. Then, for each word w over the alphabet $\{1, \ldots, 9\}$, let $T(w) = C_2(N_9(w))$. (Recall that $N_9(w)$ is the natural number n whose 9-adic representation is w, and that $C_2(n)$ is the 2-adic representation of n.) $T(w)$ is the result of inputing w to an algorithm that converts 9-adic notation to 2-adic notation, and $T(w)$ is a word over the two-letter alphabet $\{1, 2\}$. For a Turing machine M, where w is the representation of M as a word over the nine-letter alphabet, we call the word $T(w)$ the *encoding* of M.

For each Turing machine M, w_M will denote the word that encodes M. We will say that a problem about Turing machines is *decidable* if the set of words corresponding to Turing machines that satisfy the problem is decidable. Thus, the Program Termination decision problem, stated in Example 3.2, is decidable if and only if $\{w_M | M$ halts on every input$\}$ is a decidable set. Given M one can effectively find w_M; conversely, given a word w one can effectively determine whether $w = w_M$ for any M and if so, then effectively find M.

Since every word is a number and vice versa, we may think of a Turing-machine code as a number. The code for a Turing machine M is called the *Gödel number* of M. If e is a Gödel number, then M_e is the Turing machine whose Gödel number is e.

Let U be a Turing machine that computes on input e and x and that implements the following algorithm:

if e is a code
>   **then** simulate M_e on input x
>   **else** output 0.

(Why are you convinced that a Turing machine with this behavior exists?) U is a *universal* Turing machine. To put it differently, U is a general-purpose, stored-program computer: U accepts as input two values: a "stored program" e, and "input to e," a word x. If e is the correct code of a program M_e, then U computes the value of M_e on input x.

Early computers had their programs hard-wired into them. Several years after Turing's 1936 paper, von Neumann and co-workers built the first computer that stored instructions internally in the same manner as data. Von Neumann knew Turing's work, and it is believed that von Neumann was influenced by Turing's universal machine. Turing's machine U is the first conceptual general-purpose, stored-program computer.

For every natural number e, define

$$\phi_e = \lambda x\, U(e, x).^*$$

---

*This denotes the function of one variable that one obtains by holding the value of e fixed and letting x vary. Lambda-notation is familiar, for example, to students who have studied the programming language Lisp.

If e is a Gödel number, then ϕ_e is the partial function of one argument that is computed by M_e. If e is not the code of any Turing machine, then by the definition of U, $\phi_e(x) = 0$ for all x.

Let's use the Program Termination problem to illustrate all of this new notation: The Program Termination problem is decidable if and only if

$\{w_M \mid M \text{ halts on every input}\}$
$\quad = \{e \mid e \text{ is a Gödel number and } \phi_e \text{ halts on every input}\}$

is decidable, which holds if and only if

$\{e \mid \phi_e \text{ is total computable}\} = \{e \mid L(M_e) = \Sigma^*\}$

is decidable. Note that there is an algorithm to determine whether a natural number e is a Gödel number; in case it is not, then, by definition, ϕ_e is total.

Observe that every partial computable function of one argument is ϕ_e for some e, and conversely, every ϕ_e is a partial computable function. Thus, $\{\phi_e\}_{e \geq 0}$ is an *effective enumeration* of the set of all partial computable functions.

Now comes our first undecidability result. We will show that the Program Termination problem is undecidable.

Theorem 3.1 *The Program Termination problem (Example 3.2) is undecidable. There is no algorithm to determine whether an arbitrary partial computable function is total. Thus, there is no algorithm to determine whether a Turing machine halts on every input.*

We need to show that no such algorithm exists. We use the diagonalization technique that we introduced in Chapter 1 in order to show that every proposed algorithm must fail on some input.

Proof. Suppose there is an algorithm TEST such that, for every i,

$\text{TEST}(i) = $ "yes" if ϕ_i halts on every input value, and
$\text{TEST}(i) = $ "no" otherwise.

Define a function δ by

$\delta(k) = \phi_k(k) + 1$ if $\text{TEST}(k) = $ "yes" and
$\delta(k) = 0$ if $\text{TEST}(k) = $ "no."

By definition, δ is defined on every input and δ is computable, so δ is a total computable function. Let e be the Gödel number of a Turing machine that computes δ. Thus, $\delta = \phi_e$ and $\text{TEST}(e) = $ "yes." However, in this case, $\delta(e) = \phi_e(e) + 1$, which contradicts the assertion that $\delta = \phi_e$. Thus, the initial supposition must be false. $\qquad\square$

3.3 Pairing Functions

Before continuing with our discussion of undecidability, we digress here to introduce an encoding of ordered pairs of natural numbers and of k-tuples of natural numbers that will remain fixed and that we will use for the remainder of this book.

Definition 3.1   A pairing function *is a computable one-to-one mapping*

$$< , >: N \times N \rightarrow N.$$

whose inverses

$$\tau_1(< x, y >) = x \text{ and } \tau_2(< x, y >) = y,$$

are computable also.

Observe that for every z,

$$< \tau_1(z), \tau_2(z) >= z.$$

We claim that the function $< , >$ defined by

$$< x, y >= \frac{1}{2}(x^2 + 2xy + y^2 + 3x + y)$$

is a pairing function. Clearly, $< , >$ is computable. We claim that $< , >$ maps $N \times N$ one-to-one and onto N by the correspondence that lists ordered pairs in the order

$$< 0, 0 >, < 0, 1 >, < 1, 0 >, < 0, 2 >, < 1, 1 >, < 2, 0 >,$$
$$< 0, 3 >, < 1, 2 >, \ldots$$

as given in Fig. 3.1.

Homework 3.1   *Use the fact that $x + y = k$ is the equation of the kth line in Fig. 3.1, together with the identity*

$$1 + 2 + \cdots + k = \frac{1}{2}k(k + 1),$$

to verify that $< , >$ gives this correspondence.

It follows immediately that $< , >$ is one-to-one and onto.

Homework 3.2   *Show how to compute τ_1 and τ_2.*

We can use this pairing function to define tuples of any size: Inductively define

$$< x > = x$$
$$< x_1, \ldots, x_{n+1} > = << x_1, \ldots, x_n >, x_{n+1} > .$$

Let $\tau_k(x_1, \ldots, x_k)$ denote the computable function that outputs $< x_1, \ldots, x_k >$, and let the inverses be $\tau_{k1}, \ldots, \tau_{kk}$, so that $\tau_{ki}(< x_1, \ldots, x_k >) = x_i$ for all $i = 1 \ldots k$.

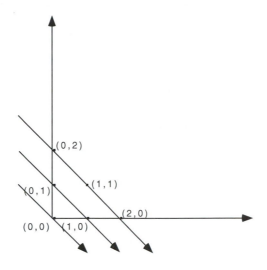

FIGURE 3.1. Enumeration of ordered pairs.

3.4   Computably Enumerable Sets

Recall that a nonempty set is S is enumerable if some function f maps N onto S, in which case we say that f enumerates S. Indeed, $S = \{f(0), f(1), \ldots, \}$.

Definition 3.2   *A set S is* computably enumerable *(c.e.) if $S = \emptyset$ or $S = range(f)$, for some total computable function f.*

A collection of Turing machines is *effectively* enumerable if the corresponding set of Gödel numbers is c.e., so, in particular, the set of all Turing machines is effectively enumerable.

Let C be any set of partial computable functions. Let $P_C = \{e \mid \phi_e \in C\}$ be the set of all programs that compute partial functions belonging to C. P_C is called an *index* set.

Example 3.3   *Let C be the set of all total computable functions. Then*

$$P_C = \{e \mid \phi_e \text{ is total computable}\}.$$

A set of partial computable functions is decidable (effectively enumerable) if its index set is decidable (c.e.). So the set of all partial computable functions $\{\phi_0, \phi_1, \ldots\}$ is effectively enumerable. A subtlety: Every partial computable function has infinitely many programs. (Think about why this is true.) Hence, if an index set is nonempty, then it must be infinite.

Homework 3.3　*(i) Use Theorem 3.1 directly to show that the following problem is undecidable: Given two Turing machines M and N, determine whether they are equivalent. That is, show that the set*

$$\{(e, j) \mid L(M_e) = L(M_j)\}$$

is not decidable.

(ii) Use the result of part (i) to show that the function that maps a program e to its smallest equivalent program is not computable.

The next theorem shows that the Program Termination problem is not computably enumerable.

Theorem 3.2　$\{e \mid \phi_e \text{ is total computable}\}$ is not *computably enumerable.*

Proof. Let $S = \{e \mid \phi_e \text{ is total computable}\}$, and suppose that S is c.e. As $S \neq \emptyset$, there is a computable function g such that $range(g) = S$. Next, we can use g in order to define a "universal function U_S for S." For all e and all x, define $U_S(e, x) = \phi_{g(e)}(x)$. U_S is a total computable function: To compute $U_S(e, x)$, first compute $g(e) = k$, and then compute $\phi_k(x) = y$. Note that both $g(e)$ and $\phi_k(x)$ must converge.

Now define $h(x) = U_S(x, x) + 1$ for all x. So h is a total computable function. Thus, there is a program $k \in S$ so that $h = \phi_k$ and for some e, $k = g(e)$. Finally,

$$\phi_k(e) = h(e)$$
$$= U_S(e, e) + 1$$
$$= \phi_{g(e)}(e) + 1$$
$$= \phi_k(e) + 1,$$

which is impossible. Thus, the original supposition that S is computably enumerable is false.　　　□

Now we will prove several useful properties and characterizations of the computably enumerable sets. After doing so, we will easily and quickly derive several more undecidable problems. (We could do so now, but developing some tools first will make things easier later.)

Lemma 3.1　*The graph of a computable function is decidable.*

The proof is easy. Let f be a computable function. Let

$$G = \{(x, y) \mid f(x) = y\}.$$

Design a Turing machine that on input (x, y), computes $f(x)$ and then if $f(x) = y$ accepts and otherwise halts without accepting.

Theorem 3.3　*A set S is computably enumerable if and only if there is a decidable relation $R(x, y)$ such that*

$$x \in S \Leftrightarrow \exists y R(x, y). \tag{3.1}$$

Proof. If $S = \emptyset$, then

$$x \in S \Leftrightarrow \exists y[x = x \wedge y \neq y]$$

and the relation $[x = x \wedge y \neq y]$ is decidable.

If $S \neq \emptyset$ is computably enumerable, then S is the range of a computable function f. Thus,

$$x \in S \Leftrightarrow \exists y[f(y) = x].$$

By Lemma 3.1, the relation $[f(y) = x]$ is decidable.

Conversely, suppose that there is a decidable relation $R(x, y)$ such that

$$x \in S \Leftrightarrow \exists y R(x, y).$$

If $S = \emptyset$, then S is c.e. by definition. So assume that S is not empty. Let a be a fixed member of S. Now we will use the pairing function that we defined in the last section. Define

$$f(x) = \begin{cases} a & \text{if } R(\tau_1(x), \tau_2(x)) \text{ is false,} \\ \tau_1(x) & \text{if } R(\tau_1(x), \tau_2(x)) \text{ is true.} \end{cases}$$

Then f is a total computable function and clearly, $range(f) \subseteq S$. If $x \in S$, consider a value y such that $R(x, y)$. Then $f(\langle x, y \rangle) = x$. So $S \subseteq range(f)$. $\square$

The next theorem demonstrates that the c.e. sets are none other than the acceptable sets. The two basic concepts, acceptable and computably enumerable, are identical!

Theorem 3.4 *A set S is computably enumerable if and only if it is Turing-machine-acceptable.*

Given a Turing machine M, recall that an accepting computation of M is a sequence of configurations $I_0, I_1, \ldots, I_n$ such that I_0 is an initial configuration, I_n is an accepting configuration, and for each $i < n$, $I_i \vdash_M I_{i+1}$. Thus, a computation is a word over the finite alphabet that defines M.

Proof. Assume that S is Turing-machine-acceptable and let M be a Turing machine that accepts S. Define the relation R_M by

$$R_M(x, y) \Leftrightarrow [x \text{ is an input word to } M \text{ and } y \text{ is an accepting computation of } M \text{ on } x]. \tag{3.2}$$

It should be clear that R_M is a decidable relation. Moreover,

$$x \in S \Leftrightarrow \exists y R_M(x, y).$$

Thus, by Theorem 3.3, S is computably enumerable.

Conversely, suppose that S is c.e. and let R be a decidable relation such that Equation 3.1 holds. A Turing machine M will accept S in the following manner: M contains a counter y and initializes y to 0. On input x, M writes the pair $(x, y) = (x, 0)$ and then determines whether $R(x, y)$ holds. If so, M accepts x. If not, then M increments the value y and repeats the test. Observe that if $x \in S$, then for some value of y, $R(x, y)$ holds. In this case M eventually accepts. (However, if $x \notin S$, then M runs forever.) Thus, M accepts S, and this completes the proof.

$\square$

Corollary 3.1 *A set S is decidable if and only if S and $\overline{S}$ are both computably enumerable.*

The corollary follows immediately from Theorem 2.1 and Theorem 3.4. In particular, every decidable set is c.e., so Theorem 3.2 is a more general result than Theorem 3.1.

Corollary 3.2 *A set S is computably enumerable if and only if S is the domain of some partial computable function.*

Proof. Surely, the domain of a partial computable function is Turing-machine-acceptable and, therefore, c.e. Conversely, if S is c.e., then S is the domain of the partial computable function f_S defined by $f_S(x) = 0$ if $x \in S$, and $f_S(x) \uparrow$ otherwise.

$\square$

Suppose that S is a c.e. set and R is a decidable relation such that Equation 3.1 holds. Define a computable function f by

$$f(x, y) = \begin{cases} 0 & \text{if } R(x, y), \\ 1 & \text{otherwise.} \end{cases}$$

Let $g(x) = \min\{y \mid f(x, y) = 0\}$. Then g is a partial computable function with domain S. This is an alternative proof of one direction of Corollary 3.2.

Define $W_e = dom(\phi_e)$. Then, $\{W_e\}_{e \in \mathbb{N}}$ provides us with a standard effective enumeration of the computably enumerable sets.

Every programmer knows that the purpose of sorting a (finite) set S is to make searching efficient. Searching is simply the problem, given a possible element w of S, to determine whether $w \in S$, that is, "searching" is the decision problem for S. The next homework problem is to demonstrate that this phenomenon holds for infinite sets as well.

Homework 3.4 *Prove that an infinite set is decidable if and only if it can be enumerated in increasing order by a one-to-one computable function.*

Homework 3.5 *Show that if A and B are c.e., then $A \cup B$ and $A \cap B$ are c.e.*

Homework 3.6 *Prove that every infinite c.e. set contains an infinite decidable subset.*

3.5 Halting Problem, Reductions, and Complete Sets

In this section we will learn that the famous Halting problem for Turing machines is undecidable. Along the way, we will build more useful tools.

Example 3.4   *The Halting problem for Turing machines*

HALTING PROBLEM
>   **instance** *A Turing machine M and input word w*
>   **question** *Does M eventually halt on input w?*

We begin by considering the "diagonal" set

$$K = \{x \mid \phi_x(x) \downarrow\} = \{x \mid U(x, x) \downarrow\}.$$

Observe that the function $\lambda x\, U(x, x)$ is partial computable. It follows from Corollary 3.2 that K is computably enumerable.

Theorem 3.5 K *is not decidable. In particular,* $\overline{K}$ *is not c.e.*

Thus, K is an example of a set that is c.e. but not decidable.

Proof. We prove that $\overline{K}$ is not c.e., for the two assertions are equivalent.
Suppose that $\overline{K}$ is c.e., then for some Gödel number e,

$$\overline{K} = W_e = dom(\phi_e).$$

In particular,

$$e \in \overline{K} \Leftrightarrow \phi_e(e) \downarrow$$
$$\Leftrightarrow e \in K.$$

This is a contradiction. Thus, the supposition that $\overline{K}$ is c.e. must be false. □

No diagonalization argument is more fundamental than the one we have just seen. Next we will introduce a tool that plays an important role in both computability theory and complexity theory. This is the notion of reductions. We have seen the idea in an informal way already. In some of your homework problems you showed that certain problems are undecidable by demonstrating that a solution would yield a solution to a problem that you already knew to be undecidable. In other words, you "reduced" one problem to another.

Definition 3.3   *A set A is* many-one reducible *to a set B, denoted by* $A \leq_m B$*, if there is a total computable function such that*

$$x \in A \Leftrightarrow f(x) \in B.$$

Lemma 3.2   *1. If* $A \leq_m B$ *and B is c.e., then A is c.e.*
    2. If $A \leq_m B$ *and B is decidable, then A is decidable.*

Proof. By hypothesis, $x \in A \Leftrightarrow f(x) \in B$ for some computable function f.
To prove the first assertion, $x \in B \Leftrightarrow \exists y R(x, y)$. So $x \in A \Leftrightarrow \exists y R(f(x), y)$. Finally, $R(f(x), y)$ is a decidable relation. Thus, A is c.e.
To prove the second assertion, the following algorithm determines whether an input word x belongs to A: If $f(x) \in B$, then "accept"; else "reject." □

Homework 3.7   *Show that $\leq_m$ is reflexive and transitive.*

Our interest will be primarily in the contrapositive of Lemma 3.2, item 2: Suppose that A is some set that we know is undecidable, for example, A might be the set K, and suppose that B is some set that we want to show is undecidable. If we can demonstrate that $A \leq_m B$, then it follows immediately that B is undecidable. This is the "reduction method" that we will employ.

Now we will use the reduction method to show that the Halting problem is undecidable. Define the set

$$L_U = \{(e, w) \mid M_e \text{ accepts } w\}.$$

Since L_U is the language accepted by the universal Turing machine U, L_U is computably enumerable. We will show that L_U is not decidable. Thus, there is no algorithm that, given an arbitrary Turing machine M and input w, determines whether M will accept w. Thus, the Halting problem for Turing machines is undecidable.

Theorem 3.6   *The Halting problem is undecidable. Specifically, the set L_U is not decidable.*

Proof. Note that

$$x \in K \Leftrightarrow (x, x) \in L_U.$$

The mapping $x \mapsto (x, x)$ is computable. So $K \leq_m L_U$, from which it follows that L_U is not decidable.   □

3.5.1 Complete Problems

Let A be any c.e. set whatsoever. For some e, $A = W_e$. Recall that

$$x \in W_e \Leftrightarrow (e, x) \in L_U.$$

Since the mapping $x \mapsto (e, x)$ is computable, $A \leq_m L_U$.

Thus, L_U is c.e., and every c.e. set many-one reduces to L_U. This observation leads to the following definition.

Definition 3.4   *A language L is* many-one complete *for the computably enumerable sets if*

1. L is computably enumerable, and

2. for every c.e. set A, $A \leq_m L$.

Thus, L_U is a many-one complete set.

Homework 3.8   *Show that K is a many-one complete set. Note that it suffices to show that $L_U \leq_m K$. This is not an easy problem. (Do not use the s-m-n theorem.)*

The question of whether there exist c.e. sets that are neither decidable nor complete was posed by Post [Pos44] in 1944. This problem has since become known as Post's problem. It was solved independently by Friedberg and Muchnik in 1956. The proof, known as a priority argument, is beyond the scope of this text.

Summary

At this point we know that the decidable sets are a proper subclass of the set of all c.e. sets. K and L_U are examples of c.e. sets that are not decidable; they are many-one complete. The sets $\overline{K}$ and $\{e \mid L(M_e) = \Sigma^*\}$ are not even c.e.

3.6 *S-m-n* Theorem

Suppose that you have program e, that is, a Turing machine M_e, to compute the product of two natural numbers x and y. Namely, $M_e(x, y) = x * y$. Obviously, you could modify this program to obtain one to compute $2 * y$. The new Turing machine will store the value 2 in its finite control. On input y, the new machine will shift y to the right, write $2By$ on its input tape, and then proceed to simulate M_e. In this manner, knowing a program e to perform multiplication, for any constant value x, you can *compute* a new program $f(e, x)$ that for each value y computes the function $\lambda\, y\, (x * y)$. In symbols, there is a computable function f so that for every x and y,

$$\phi_{f(e,x)}(y) = \phi_e(x, y).$$

In general, any program that computes a function of some $m + n$ variables can easily be modified to hold m of the variables fixed. Furthermore, the modification can be obtained effectively. This is the gist of the *s-m-n* theorem.

Theorem 3.7   *For every $m, n \geq 1$, there is a computable function $s_n^m : N^{m+1} \to N$ such that for all values $e, x_1, \ldots, x_m, x_{m+1}, \ldots, x_{m+n}$,*

$$\phi_{s_n^m(e,x_1,\ldots,x_m)}(x_{m+1}, \ldots, x_{m+n}) = \phi_e(x_1, \ldots, x_m, x_{m+1}, \ldots, x_{m+n}).$$

Taking $m = n = 1$, the theorem states that

$$\phi_{s_1^1(e,x)}(y) = \phi_e(x, y).$$

Corollary 3.3   *For every partial computable function $\lambda e, x\ \psi(e, x)$, there is a computable function f so that*

$$\phi_{f(e)}(x) = \psi(e, x).$$

Proof of the corollary.   For some Gödel number i, $\psi = \phi_i$. So

$$\psi(e, x) = \phi_i(e, x)$$
$$= \phi_{s_1^1(i,e)}(x).$$

Define $f = \lambda\, e\, s_1^1(i, e)$.   □

Proof of Theorem 3.7 for the case $m = n = 1$.   Given a natural number i, let $[i]$ denote the 2-adic representation of i. For each e and x, let $S(e, x)$ be a Turing machine that, given an input value y, performs the following actions:

1. computes the pair $< x, y >$ (i.e., writes $[< x, y >]$ on the otherwise empty tape);

2. writes $[e]B[< x, y >]B$ on the otherwise empty tape;

3. behaves like the universal machine U on the current tape (i.e., computes $\phi_e(x, y)$).

Let $s_1^1(e, x)$ be the Gödel number of $S(e, x)$. So, for each number e and x, $s_1^1(e, x)$ is the Gödel number of a program that, for each y, computes $\phi_e(x, y)$.

We need to show that the mapping

$$e, x \mapsto s_1^1(e, x)$$

is computable.

We could (and probably should) construct a Turing machine that implements the mapping. As usual, though, we will take the easier route, sketch the procedure, and yield to Church's thesis:* There is an effective procedure that, given e and x, produces the Turing machine program $S(e, x)$. Second, there is an effective procedure that, given any Turing machine, produces its Gödel number. Thus (here is where we use Church's thesis) there is a computable function that, given e and x, has value $s_1^1(e, x)$. □

Our first application of the *s-m-n* theorem formalizes the comment we just made. We demonstrate that there is a compiler that translates programs from any "acceptable" programming system into a Turing-machine program. To this end, we present the following definitions. A *programming system* is an effectively enumerable listing $\psi_0, \psi_1, \ldots$ that includes *all* of the partial computable functions of one argument. A programming system is *universal* if the partial function ψ_{univ} such that $\psi_{univ}(i, x) = \psi_i(x)$, for all i and x, is itself a partial computable function. (In this case, there is a program k that computes the partial computable function $\psi'(\langle i, x \rangle) = \psi_{univ}(i, x)$; i.e., $\psi_k(\langle i, x \rangle) = \psi_i(x)$ for all i and x.) A programming system is *acceptable* if it is universal and it satisfies the *s-m-n* theorem.

Theorem 3.8 *Let $\phi_0, \phi_1, \ldots$ and $\psi_0, \psi_1, \ldots$ be any two acceptable programming systems. There is a total computable function t that translates the system $\psi_0, \psi_1, \ldots$ into the system $\phi_0, \phi_1, \ldots$, that is, $\psi_i = \phi_{t(i)}$ for all i.*

Proof. Let ψ_{univ} be a universal partial computable function for the system $\psi_0, \psi_1, \ldots$. Let $\psi'(\langle i, x \rangle) = \psi_{univ}(i, x)$ for all i and x. Since the system $\phi_0, \phi_1, \ldots$ contains all partial computable functions of one variable, there is a program k such that $\psi' = \phi_k$. Then, by Theorem 3.7,

---

*Church's thesis, remember, is a statement of philosophical belief and so should not be cited as part of the proof of the theorem. For this reason, let us clarify our position. We are not yielding to Church's thesis as much as we are to our reader's ability as trained programmers. We take it for granted that if we understand a procedure, then we can program a Turing machine to implement the procedure.

$$\phi_{s_1^1(k,i)}(x) = \phi_k(\langle i, x \rangle)$$
$$= \psi'(\langle i, x \rangle)$$
$$= \psi_{univ}(i, x)$$
$$= \psi_i(x)$$

for all i and x. We complete the proof by defining $t(i) = s_1^1(k, i)$ for all i. □

The following is a typical application of the *s-m-n* theorem.

Theorem 3.9 *There is a computable function f such that*

$$range\ \phi_{f(e)} = dom\ \phi_e.$$

Proof. We want a partial computable function ψ of two variables such that

$$\psi(e, x) = \begin{cases} x & \text{if } x \in dom\ \phi_e, \\ \uparrow & \text{otherwise,} \end{cases}$$

for then, for each e, $range[\lambda x\ \psi(e, x)] = dom\ \phi_e$. To see that ψ exists, define a Turing machine on input e and x to simulate the universal Turing machine and to output x if it eventually halts.

By Corollary 3.3, there is a computable function f such that $\phi_{f(e)}(x) = \psi(e, x)$. Thus, $range\ \phi_{f(e)} = dom\ \phi_e$. □

Homework 3.9 *Prove that there is a computable function g such that*

$$dom\ \phi_{g(e)} = range\ \phi_e.$$

The definition of computably enumerable sets states that a nonempty set S is computably enumerable if and only if S is the range of a *total* computable function. However, we learn as a corollary to Homework 3.9 that a set is computably enumerable even if it is the range of a partial computable function.

Corollary 3.4 *A set S is computably enumerable if and only if S is the range of some partial computable function.*

Proof. If $S = \emptyset$, then S is the range of the empty function, which is computed by a Turing machine that on arbitrary input runs forever. If S is nonempty, then the definition applies directly.

We need to prove that if S is the range of some partial computable function, then S is c.e. Suppose that $S = range\ \phi_e$. Then, by Homework 3.9, $S = dom\ \phi_{g(e)}$. By Corollary 3.2, S is c.e. □

3.7 Recursion Theorem

The *recursion theorem* is a deep and powerful result with several important applications. In this section we will content ourselves with studying only one version of this result and only a limited number of applications. Other forms of the recursion theorem justify the use of recursion in programming by guaranteeing appropriate solutions to recursive procedures. These will appear in a later section.

Theorem 3.10 *For every computable function f there is a number n such that*

$$\phi_n = \phi_{f(n)}.$$

A number n with this property is called a *fixed point* of f.

Proof. We define the function $\theta(e, x) = U(U(e, e), x)$. Observe that

$$\theta(e, x) = \phi_{\phi_e(e)}(x)$$

if $\phi_e(e)$ is defined. By our standard corollary of the *s-m-n* theorem, Corollary 3.3, there is a computable function g such that

$$\phi_{g(e)}(x) = \theta(e, x).$$

Let f be any computable function. The composition $f \circ g$ is computable. Thus, there is a program k such that for all e,

$$\phi_k(e) = f(g(e)).$$

Thus, for all e,

$$\phi_{f(g(e))} = \phi_{\phi_k(e)}.$$

Set $e = k$ so that for all x,

$$\begin{aligned}
\phi_{f(g(k))}(x) &= \phi_{\phi_k(k)}(x) \\
&= \theta(k, x) \\
&= \phi_{g(k)}(x).
\end{aligned}$$

We conclude that $\phi_{f(g(k))} = \phi_{g(k)}$. Let $n = g(k)$. It follows that

$$\phi_{f(n)} = \phi_n. \qquad \square$$

With regard to this proof, observe that $\phi_e(e)$ cannot be defined for all values of e. Since $\phi_e(e)$ is a partial computable function, so is the function $\phi_e(e) + 1$. Thus, some program i computes this function, that is,

$$\phi_i(e) = \phi_e(e) + 1.$$

It follows immediately that $\phi_i(i)$ is not defined.

Corollary 3.5 *There is a number (i.e., program) n such that ϕ_n is the constant function with output n.*

Hence, n is a "self-reproducing" program—the Turing machine whose code is n does nothing on any input value other than print its own code.

Proof. Consider the computable function ψ defined by $\psi(e, x) = e$, for all e and x. By Corollary 3.3, there is a computable function f such $\phi_{f(e)}(x) = \psi(e, x)$.

By Theorem 3.10, let n be a fixed point of f. Then, for all x,

$$\phi_n(x) = \phi_{f(n)}(x)$$
$$= \psi(n, x)$$
$$= n. \qquad \square$$

Homework 3.10 *Write a program in Lisp that prints itself and nothing else.*

Corollary 3.6 *For every computable function f, there exists n such that*

$$W_n = W_{f(n)}.$$

As an application, we can see that there is a program n such that $W_n = \{n\}$. To see this, first define a partial computable function ψ such that for all e, $\psi(e, e) = e$ and $\psi(e, x)$ is undefined for all other values of x. Now, use Corollary 3.3 to obtain a computable function f such that $\phi_{f(e)}(x) = \psi(e, x)$. Then, *dom* $\phi_{f(e)} = \{e\}$ for all e. So $W_{f(e)} = \{e\}$. Thus, by Corollary 3.6, there exists n such that

$$W_n = W_{f(n)} = \{n\}.$$

We are seeing that programs can be self-referencing.

Theorem 3.11 *For every partial computable function $\psi(e, x)$, there is a value e_0 such that*

$$\psi(e_0, x) = \phi_{e_0}(x).$$

For example, there is a program e_0 such that $\phi_{e_0}(x) = e_0 * x$.

Proof. Given ψ, obtain as usual, using Corollary 3.3, a computable function f such that $\psi(e, x) = \phi_{f(e)}(x)$. Then, by Theorem 3.10, there exists e_0 such that $\phi_{f(e_0)} = \phi_{e_0}$. So, for all x,

$$\phi_{e_0}(x) = \phi_{f(e_0)}(x) = \psi(e_0, x). \qquad \square$$

Observe that there is a standard pattern to the proof of these results. First, we use the *s-m-n* theorem or its corollary to obtain a computable function f with whatever property we find useful. Then, we use the recursion theorem or its corollary to select a fixed point of f.

Homework 3.11 *Show that there is no algorithm that given as input a Turing machine M, where M defines a partial function of one variable, outputs a Turing machine M' such that M' defines a different partial function of one variable.*

Homework 3.12 *Show that there is a program e such that $W_e = \{e^2\}$.*

3.8 Rice's Theorem

Recall that the set of all Gödel numbers of some collection of partial computable functions is called an *index set*. That is, if C is any set of partial computable functions, then the set $P_C = \{e \mid \phi_e \in C\}$ is an index set. Here we will learn that *every* nontrivial index set is undecidable. This remarkable theorem, due to Rice [Ric53], tells us that undecidability is not an exception—it is the rule.

Theorem 3.12   **(Rice [Ric53])** *An index set P_C is decidable if and only if $P_C = \emptyset$ or $P_C = N$.*

Proof. If $P_C = \emptyset$ or $P_C = N$, then, of course, P_C is decidable. We need to prove the converse.

Suppose that $P_C \neq \emptyset$ and $P_C \neq N$. Let $j \in P_C$ and $k \in \overline{P_C}$. Define the function f by

$$f(x) = \begin{cases} k & \text{if } x \in P_C, \\ j & \text{if } x \notin P_C. \end{cases}$$

Suppose that P_C is decidable. Then f is a computable function. Thus, by Theorem 3.10, the recursion theorem, f has a fixed point. That is, there is a number n such that $\phi_n = \phi_{f(n)}$. Since n and $f(n)$ are programs for the same partial computable function, either they both belong to P_C or they both belong to $\overline{P_C}$. However, this is impossible because we defined f so that for all x, $x \in P_C \Leftrightarrow f(x) \notin P_C$. Thus, the supposition that P_C is decidable is false.   □

Recall that a set S is computably enumerable if $S = \emptyset$ or $S = range(f)$, for some total computable function f. Given a collection C of computably enumerable sets, the corresponding index set is the set $P_C = \{e \mid range(\phi_e) \in C\}$, and C is decidable if and only if P_C is decidable.

Corollary 3.7   *The following properties of computably enumerable sets are not decidable:*

1. *emptiness;*
2. *finiteness;*
3. *regularity;*
4. *context freedom.*

Proof. We will give details for item 1. For the other items, we will just indicate the set C, from which we can easily note that there exist sets that have the specified property and there exist sets that do not have the specified property.

1. In this case, $C = \{\emptyset\}$ and

$$P_C = \{e \mid range\ \phi_e = \emptyset\}$$
$$= \{e \mid e \text{ computes the totally undefined function}\}.$$

   So $P_C \neq \emptyset$ and $P_C \neq N$. (The same proof demonstrates that one cannot decide whether a Turing-machine program e will halt on some input.)

2. C is the set of all finite computably enumerable sets.
3. C is the set of all regular sets.
4. C is the set of all context-free languages.   □

To use Rice's theorem to show that a set A is not decidable, the set A must be an index set. Therefore, if one program e to compute ϕ_e belongs to A, then every program i such that $\phi_i = \phi_e$ must also belong to A. Thus, Rice's theorem only applies to machine-independent properties. For an example of a *machine-dependent* property, consider the following important property of Turing machines. We say that a Turing machine M *operates in polynomial time* if there is a polynomial p such that for every input word x, M on x halts within $p(|x|)$ steps. In Chapter 6 we will study this property of Turing machines in some detail, and in Section 6.3 we will prove that the set

$$S = \{i \mid M_i \text{ operates in polynomial time}\}$$

of all (encodings of) Turing machines that operate in polynomial time is not even computably enumerable. However, S is not an index set, so the result cannot be obtained using Rice's theorem.

3.9   Turing Reductions and Oracle Turing Machines

Suppose that $A \leq_m B$ for two sets A and B. Then there is a computable function f such that $x \in A \Leftrightarrow f(x) \in B$. This reduction can be used to define an algorithm for an acceptor for A that makes a subroutine call to the set B:

begin
input x;
if $f(x) \in B$ **then** accept **else** reject;
end.

Let us consider the most general possible set of programs that contain subroutine calls to B. We want to be able to write a program that is an acceptor for A and allow it to make subroutine calls of the form "$y \in B$." These calls should return *true* if the Boolean test is true and should return *false* otherwise. Such a program is called a *reduction procedure* and the set B is called an *oracle*.

Since our programming language is the Turing machine, we make these ideas precise by extending the notion of Turing machine to enable Turing machines to make subroutine calls—only they are not called subroutine calls; they are called *oracle calls*.

An *oracle* Turing machine is a Turing machine with a distinguished oracle tape and three special states, Q, YES, and NO. When the Turing machine enters state Q, the next state is YES or NO depending on whether or not the word currently written on the oracle tape belongs to the oracle set. (In this way, the machine receives an answer to a Boolean test of the form "$y \in B$" in one move.) Also, we assume that the word written on the oracle tape is immediately erased.

Consider the reduction procedure given in Fig. 3.2. First, it should be clear that this reduction procedure can be implemented by an oracle Turing machine.

```
begin
read x in {0, 1}*;
z := x;
while |z| < 2 * |x| do
        if z ∈ B then z := z1 else z := z0
if z ∈ B then ACCEPT else REJECT
end.
```

FIGURE 3.2. A reduction procedure.

Observe that for every choice of oracle set, this procedure will halt on every input. (This is not always the case; given an arbitrary oracle Turing machine M, there are three possibilities: (i) For every choice of oracle set, there exist inputs on which M does not eventually halt; (ii) there are some oracle sets A such that M with oracle A halts on every input, and there exist other oracles B such that M with oracle B does not halt on every input; (iii) for every choice of oracle, M halts on every input.) Also observe that this reduction procedure is *adaptive*. This means that queries made to the oracle at a later stage of a computation depend on what answers were given to queries made at earlier stages of the computation.

We let M^A denote an oracle Turing machine M with A as its oracle.

Definition 3.5 *A is* decidable in B *if $A = L(M^B)$, where M^B halts on every input.*

Definition 3.6 *A is* Turing-reducible to B *if and only if A is decidable in B. In notation: $A \leq_T B$.*

Homework 3.13 *Prove each of the following properties.*

1. *$\leq_T$ is transitive;*
2. *$\leq_T$ is reflexive;*
3. *for all sets A, $A \leq_T \overline{A}$;*
4. *if B is decidable and $A \leq_T B$, then A is decidable;*
5. *if A is decidable, then $A \leq_T B$ for all sets B;*
6. *$A \leq_m B \Rightarrow A \leq_T B$;*
7. *$\exists A, B[A \leq_T B$ and $A \not\leq_m B]$;*
8. *$\exists A, B[A \leq_T B$ and B is c.e. and A is not c.e. $]$.*

Definition 3.7 *A is* Turing-acceptable in B *if $A = L(M^B)$ for some M^B.*

Definition 3.8 *A partial function ψ^A is* partial computable *in A if ψ^A is computable by some oracle Turing machine with oracle A.*

Definition 3.9 *A set A is* computably enumerable in B *if $A = \emptyset$ or $A = range(f^B)$, where f^B is a total computable in B function.*

Theorem 3.13 *A is c.e. in B if and only if A is Turing-acceptable in B.*

The proof is the same as the proof for Turing machines without oracles. In particular, since an oracle Turing machine is just a certain kind of Turing machine, oracle Turing machines have Gödel numbers and there is an effective enumeration of oracle Turing machines.

As before, ϕ_i^A denotes the partial computable function in A that is computed by the oracle Turing machine M_i^A with Gödel number i and oracle A (and denotes the constant 0 function if i is not the Gödel number of any oracle Turing machine). Let $W_i^A = dom(\phi_i^A)$.

Definition 3.10 *For each set A,*

$$K^A = \{x \mid \phi_x^A(x) \text{ converges}\}$$
$$= \{x \mid x \in W_x^A\}$$
$$= \{x \mid M_x^A \text{ accepts } x\}.$$

One of the goals of computability theory is to classify undecidable sets and undecidable problems. The answer to the question "are some undecidable problems more undecidable than other undecidable sets?" is "yes." We will see that some undecidable problems are "harder" than others.

Theorem 3.14 $K^A \nleq_T A$.

The proof that follows is the same diagonalization as in the corresponding non-oracle result.

Proof. If $K^A \leq_T A$, then $\overline{K^A}$ is accepted by some oracle Turing machine M_e^A that halts on every input. Then $e \in \overline{K^A} \Leftrightarrow M_e^A$ accepts $e \Leftrightarrow e \in K^A$. □

Thus, $K^{(1)} = K = K^\emptyset$, $K^{(2)} = K^K$, ..., $K^{(n+1)} = K^{K^n}$ forms an infinite hierarchy of undecidable sets—each more undecidable than the one before it.

Proposition 3.2 *Neither $K^{(2)}$ nor $\overline{K^{(2)}}$ are computably enumerable.*

Proof. If $K^{(2)}$ is c.e., then $K^{(2)} \leq_m K$, because K is a complete c.e. set. Thus, if $K^{(2)}$ is c.e., then $K^{(2)} \leq_T K$, which contradicts Theorem 3.14. Thus, $K^{(2)}$ is not computably enumerable.

If $\overline{K^{(2)}}$ is c.e., then $\overline{K^{(2)}} \leq_m K$, which implies that $\overline{K^{(2)}} \leq_T K$, because $\overline{K^{(2)}} \leq_T K^{(2)}$. Again, this is a contradiction. Thus, $\overline{K^{(2)}}$ is not computably enumerable. □

The next theorem says that for each set A, K^A is a complete set for the collection of all sets that are c.e. in A.

Theorem 3.15
1. K^A *is c.e. in A.*
2. *If B is c.e. in A, then $B \leq_m K^A$.*

The proof of 1 is the same as the proof that shows that K is c.e. and the proof of 2 is the same as the proof of your homework problem to show that K is complete, except that now we will simplify the proof by using the corollary to the *s-m-n* theorem, Corollary 3.3.

Proof. Let B be c.e. in A. For some oracle Turing machine M^A with oracle A, $B = L(M^A)$. We want to show that $B \leq_m K^A$, and thus we want a computable function f such that $x \in B \Leftrightarrow f(x) \in K^A$.

We claim that the following function ψ^A is partial computable in A:

$$\psi^A(x, y) = \begin{cases} y & \text{if } M \text{ with oracle } A \text{ accepts } x, \\ \uparrow & \text{otherwise} \end{cases}$$

To compute $\psi^A(x, y)$, simulate M with oracle A on input x and output y if this simulation eventually accepts. If M^A does not converge, then neither will the simulation.

Notice that the computation ignores the second input string y. By Corollary 3.3 (which still holds in the relativized version), there is a computable function f such that $\phi^A_{f(x)}(y) = \psi^A(x, y)$. Moreover,

- if M^A accepts x, then for all y, $\phi^A_{f(x)}(y) = y$;

- if M^A does not accept x, then for all y, $\phi^A_{f(x)}(y)$ is undefined.

Thus,

$$x \in B \Leftrightarrow M^A \text{ accepts } x$$
$$\Leftrightarrow \text{for all } y, \phi^A_{f(x)}(y) \text{ is defined}$$
$$\Leftrightarrow \phi^A_{f(x)}(f(x)) \text{ is defined}$$
$$\Leftrightarrow f(x) \in K^A.$$

Thus, f is a many-one reduction from B to K^A. $\qquad\square$

Recall that $K \equiv_m L_U$. Thus, K has the same difficulty as the halting problem. By the previous theorem, $K^{(2)}$ is more difficult than the halting problem. We will demonstrate a natural decision problem that is equivalent to $K^{(2)}$ and therefore that is harder than the halting problem. But first it may be useful to derive still more machinery.

For any class of languages $\mathcal{C}$, define

$$co\text{-}\mathcal{C} = \{\overline{L} \mid L \in \mathcal{C}\}$$

to be the class of all complements of languages that belong to $\mathcal{C}$. Next, we define an infinite hierarchy of classes of sets called the Kleene–Mostowksi *arithmetical hierarchy.*

Definition 3.11   *The arithmetical hierarchy is the collection of all classes $\{\Sigma_k, \Pi_k\}_{k \geq 0}$, where these classes are defined inductively as follows:*

Define $\Sigma_0 = \Pi_0$ to be the class of all decidable sets.

For any class of sets C, define

$$\Sigma_1(C) = \{B \mid B \text{ is c.e. in some set belonging to } C\}.$$

Then, by induction, for each $k \geq 0$, define

$$\Sigma_{k+1} = \Sigma_1(\Sigma_k),$$

and, for each $k \geq 1$, define

$$\Pi_k = co\text{-}\Sigma_k.$$

By the definition, Σ_1 is the class of all computably enumerable sets and Π_1 is the class of complements of c.e. sets.

Note that $\Sigma_0 \subset \Sigma_1 \cup \Pi_1$, that $\Sigma_0 \neq \Sigma_1$, and that $\Sigma_1 \neq \Pi_1$. Also note that $K^{(2)}$ is not in $\Sigma_1 \cup \Pi_1$.

Now let's focus attention on the class Σ_2. By definition,

$$\Sigma_2 = \Sigma_1(\Sigma_1)$$
$$= \{B \mid B \text{ is c.e. in some c.e. set}\}.$$

That is,

$$B \in \Sigma_2 \Leftrightarrow \exists \text{ c.e. } C[B \text{ c.e. in } C]\}.$$

In particular, $K^{(2)} \in \Sigma_2$.

Recall that a set B is c.e. if and only if $B \leq_m K$ and if and only if B is expressible in the form $\exists y R(x, y)$, for some decidable relation $R(x, y)$. The next theorem gives a similar result for Σ_2.

Theorem 3.16

$$B \in \Sigma_2 \Leftrightarrow B \text{ is c.e. in } K$$
$$\Leftrightarrow B \leq_m K^{(2)}$$
$$\Leftrightarrow B \text{ is expressible in the form } \exists y \forall z R(x, y, z),$$

where R is a decidable relation.

Proof. We begin by proving the first equivalence. Suppose that B is c.e. in K. Since K is a c.e. set, $B \in \Sigma_2$ by definition. Now suppose that $B \in \Sigma_2$. Then, by definition, there is a c.e. set A such that B is c.e. in A. So, for some oracle Turing machine M^A, $B = L(M^A)$. Let f be a computable function that gives $A \leq_m K$. Here is an oracle Turing machine M_1^K that accepts B with K as the oracle: on input x simulate M except whenever M goes into its query state with a word y on its query tape, instead, M_1 should write $f(y)$ on its query tape, and then M_1 should enter its query state. Obviously, a query of y to A is equivalent to a query of $f(y)$ to K. So, B is c.e. in K. Thus, the first equivalence holds.

Now we prove the second equivalence. If B is c.e. in K, then $B \leq_m K^{(2)}$ by the previous theorem. Suppose $B \leq_m K^{(2)}$, and let f be a computable function that gives this reduction. By the previous theorem $K^{(2)}$ is c.e. in K. So there is an oracle Turing machine M^K such that $K^{(2)} = L(M^K)$. We have $x \in B \Leftrightarrow f(x) \in K^{(2)} \Leftrightarrow M^K$ accepts $f(x)$. Let M_1 be an oracle Turing machine that on input x computes $f(x)$ and then simulates M^K on $f(x)$. Obviously, $x \in B \Leftrightarrow M_1^K$ accepts x. Thus, B is c.e. in K. We proved the second equivalence.

To prove the third equivalence, suppose there is a decidable relation R such that

$$x \in B \Leftrightarrow \exists y \forall z R(x, y, z).$$

Consider the set $S = \{\langle x, y \rangle \mid \forall z R(x, y, z)\}$. S is the complement of a c.e. set. Thus, S is is decidable in a c.e. set (namely, in its own complement). So B is c.e. in a c.e. set. Thus, $B \in \Sigma_2$.

In order to prove the third equivalence in the other direction, we make some general observations first. Let z be an arbitrary computation on an arbitrary oracle Turing machine. By this we mean that z is a sequence of configurations. A *query configuration* is a configuration in which the current state is Q, the query state. If C_i is a query configuration, then the next configuration C_{i+1} has state either YES or NO. Let $y_1, \ldots, y_k$ denote the words on the query tape of each query configuration of z for which the next state is YES. Let $n_1, \ldots, n_l$ denote the words on the query tape of each query configuration of z for which the next state is NO. Observe that the list of words $y_1, \ldots, y_k, n_1, \ldots, n_l$ is effectively found from z.

Now suppose that B is c.e. in K and let M be an oracle Turing machine such that $B = L(M^K)$.

$$x \in B \Leftrightarrow \exists z[(z \text{ is an accepting computation of } x \text{ on } M)$$
$$\wedge y_1 \in K \wedge y_2 \in K \wedge \cdots \wedge y_k \in K$$
$$\wedge n_1 \notin K \wedge n_2 \notin K \wedge \cdots \wedge n_l \notin K].$$

Observe that the expression (z is an accepting computation of x on M) defines a decidable relation. Call this relation $S(x, z)$. Of course, K is c.e. and so is expressible in the form $\exists u R(x, u)$ for some decidable relation $R(x, u)$. Thus, we may rewrite the above equivalence as

$$x \in B \Leftrightarrow \exists z[S(x, z)$$
$$\wedge \exists u_1 R(y_1, u_1) \wedge \exists u_2 R(y_2, u_2) \wedge \cdots \wedge \exists u_k R(y_k, u_k)$$
$$\wedge \forall v_1 \overline{R}(n_1, v_1) \wedge \forall v_2 \overline{R}(n_2, v_2) \wedge \cdots \wedge \forall v_l \overline{R}(n_l, v_l)].$$

Then, by placing this expression in prenex normal form, we get

$$x \in B \Leftrightarrow \exists z \exists u_1 \ldots u_k \forall v_1 \ldots v_l[S(x, z)$$
$$\wedge R(y_1, u_1) \wedge R(y_2, u_2) \wedge \cdots \wedge R(y_k, u_k)$$
$$\wedge \overline{R}(n_1, v_1) \wedge \overline{R}(n_2, v_2) \wedge \cdots \wedge \overline{R}(n_l, v_l)].$$

We are almost there: What is inside the brackets is a decidable relation and the quantifiers are in the right order; there are just too many of them. For brevity, call the bracketed expression $R(x, z, u_1, \ldots, u_k, v_1, \ldots, v_l)$. Then, we have

$$x \in B \Leftrightarrow \exists z \exists u_1 \ldots u_k \forall v_1 \ldots v_l R(x, z, u_1, \ldots, u_k, v_1, \ldots, v_l).$$

Now pairing functions come in handy:

$$x \in B \Leftrightarrow \exists y \forall z R(x, \tau_{k+1,1}(y), \tau_{k+1,2}(y), \ldots, \tau_{k+1,k+1}(y),$$
$$\tau_{l1}(z_1), \ldots, \tau_{ll}(z_l)).$$

We're done. $\qquad\square$

Homework 3.14   *Prove that*

$$\Sigma_2 \cap \Pi_2 = \{A \mid A \text{ is decidable in some language belonging to } \Sigma_1\}.$$

Although we will not do so, Theorem 3.16 and this homework exercise generalize. That is, we could, by induction, prove the following properties of the arithmetical hierarchy.

1. For all $n \geq 1$, $K^{(n)} \in \Sigma_n$, $K^{(n)} \notin \Sigma_{n-1}$, and $K^{(n)}$ is $\leq_m$-complete for Σ_n.
2. For all $n \geq 1$, A belongs to Σ_n if and only if A is expressible in Σ_n-quantifier form, where this means that there is a decidable relation $R(x, y_1, \ldots, y_n)$ such that

$$x \in A \Leftrightarrow \exists y_1 \forall y_2 \ldots Q_n y_n R(x, y_1, \ldots, y_n),$$

where the quantifiers alternate ($Q_n = \forall$ if n is even, and $Q_n = \exists$ if n is odd). Dually, A belongs to Π_n if and only if A is expressible in Π_n-quantifier form, which means that

$$x \in A \Leftrightarrow \forall y_1 \exists y_2 \ldots Q'_n y_n R(x, y_1, \ldots, y_n).$$

3. For all $n \geq 1$,

$$\Sigma_{n+1} \cap \Pi_{n+1} = \{A \mid A \text{ is decidable in some language belonging to } \Sigma_n\}.$$

Consider the problem of determining, for an arbitrary Turing machine M, whether $L(M) = \Sigma^*$. We will show that this problem is Turing-equivalent to $K^{(2)}$. The way to get insight about what level of the arithmetical hierarchy a problem belongs is to express it in quantifier form: $L(M) = \Sigma^*$ if and only if *for every* input x *there exists* an accepting computation y of M on x. Clearly, this is expressible in Π_2 form. So we should expect the following to be true.

Theorem 3.17   *The problem for an arbitrary Turing machine M, whether $L(M) = \Sigma^*$, is Turing-equivalent to $K^{(2)}$. In particular,*

$$\overline{\{e \mid L(M_e) = \Sigma^*\}} \equiv_m K^{(2)}.$$

Proof. Let $B = \overline{\{e \mid L(M_e) = \Sigma^*\}}$. Then $x \in B \Leftrightarrow \exists w \langle x, w \rangle \notin L_U$. So B is c.e. in L_U. (Observe how we obtained this from the form of the expression that relates B to L_U.) Since $L_U \equiv_m K$, B is c.e. in K. Thus, $B \leq_m K^{(2)}$.

Conversely, we show that $K^{(2)} \leq_m B$. We need a computable function f such that

$$\phi_x^K(x) \downarrow \quad \Leftrightarrow \quad \exists w \phi_{f(x)}(w) \uparrow \, .$$

$f(x)$ is to be the Gödel number of the following partial computable function ψ. Given x, try for w steps to find a valid converging computation of $\phi_x^K(x)$, but do not use the oracle and do not check for correct oracle usage. If unsuccessful, set $\psi(w) = w$. If successful, then for each query q that is claimed to be in K, use w steps to try to check. If unsuccessful, set $\psi(w) = w$. If all steps are successful, consider queries for which it is claimed that $q \notin K$. Begin an enumeration of K and if and when it is shown that such a q in fact belongs to K, set $\psi(w) = w$. Otherwise, $\psi(w)$ diverges.

It should be clear that this f does the job. □

3.10   Recursion Theorem, Continued

Now we continue our study of the recursion theorem. We must explain first that the recursion theorem is not just one theorem, but rather a collection of slightly varying results. All forms of the recursion theorem are due to Kleene.

We begin our discussion with the following example:

Example 3.5   *Consider the computation rule defined by*

if $x = 1$ **then** $\psi(x) = 2$
    else if *even(x)* **then** $\psi(x) = 2\phi(x \div 2)$.

This rule define a function ψ in terms of a known function ϕ and value for x. Think of the rule as a definition of a *type 2* function F that maps a function ϕ and number x to the integral value $\psi(x)$ of another function ψ.

In general, a computation rule F that takes as parameters a partial computable function ϕ and integer values $x_1, \ldots, x_n$ of the form

$$F(\phi; x_1, \ldots, x_n) = \psi(x_1, \ldots, x_n)$$

is called a *functional*. We say that a functional F is partial computable if given a program s for computing ϕ, we can compute the value of ψ. That is, F is a *partial computable functional* if there is a partial computable function η such that

$$\eta(s, x_1, \ldots, x_n) = F(\phi; x_1, \ldots, x_n),$$

where s is any Gödel number of ϕ. Observe that a computation of η, i.e., a computation of F on inputs ϕ_s and $x_1, \ldots, x_n$, might involve using s in order to compute some values of ϕ_s, but there can exist at most some finitely many numbers $n_1, \ldots, n_k$ for which $\phi(n_1), \ldots, \phi(n_k)$ are required.

The forms of the recursion theorem that we study next, which explains why the result is so named, addresses the question of whether, for every partial computable functional F, the *recursive definition*

$$F(\xi; x_1, \ldots, x_n) = \xi(x_1, \ldots, x_n) \tag{3.3}$$

is guaranteed a solution.

Example 3.6 *Does the rule*

> **if** $x = 1$ **then** $\phi(x) = 2$
> **else if** *even(x)* **then** $\phi(x) = 2\phi(x \div 2)$

define a partial computable function ϕ?

Given two partial functions ϕ and ψ, we say that ψ is an *extension* of ϕ, in symbols $\phi \subseteq \psi$, if $graph(\phi) \subseteq graph(\psi)$. If ψ extends ϕ, F is a partial computable functional, and $F(\phi; x)$ converges, then $F(\psi; x)$ converges and $F(\psi; x) = F(\phi; x)$.

Theorem 3.18 *Let $F(\xi; x_1, \ldots, x_n)$ be a partial computable functional, in which ξ is a function variable that ranges over partial functions of n variables. Then there is a solution ϕ of Equation 3.3 such that*

1. *$F(\phi; x_1, \ldots, x_n) = \phi(x_1, \ldots, x_n)$,*
2. *ϕ is partial computable, and*
3. *if $F(\psi; x_1, \ldots, x_n) = \psi(x_1, \ldots, x_n)$ is any other solution of Equation 3.3, then $\phi \subseteq \psi$.*

Given any recursive definition, the theorem guarantees the existence of a partial computable solution. The function that is implicitly computed, whose existence is guaranteed, is called the *least fixed point* of F.

Proof. (For ease of notation, we assume that $n = 1$.) Let ϕ_0 be the completely undefined function. Then inductively define

$$\phi_{i+1}(x) = F(\phi_0; x)$$

for $i \geq 0$.

Lemma 3.3 *For all $i \geq 0$, ϕ_{i+1} extends ϕ_i. That is, $\phi_i(x) = y$ implies $\phi_{i+1}(x) = y$.*

Given Lemma 3.3, we define ϕ to be the "limit" function. That is, for each x, $\phi(x)$ converges if and only if for some i, $\phi_i(x)$ converges, in which case, $\phi(x)$ is the common value of $\phi_i(x)$ for all i greater than or equal to the least such i.

Proof of Lemma 3.3. The proof is by induction on i. Since ϕ_0 is completely undefined, clearly ϕ_1 extends ϕ_0. Let $i \geq 1$ and assume as induction hypothesis that ϕ_{j+1} extends ϕ_j for $j < i$.

Suppose that $\phi_i(x) = y$. Then $\phi_i(x) = F(\phi_{i-1}; x) = y$. By induction hypothesis, ϕ_i extends ϕ_{i-1}. Since the computation of F on ϕ_{i-1} and x converges with output y, so must F on ϕ_i and x. That is, since ϕ_{i-1} is already sufficiently defined to determine a value for $F(\phi_{i-1}; x)$, extending ϕ_{i-1} to ϕ_i cannot change F's computation. Thus, $F(\phi_i; x) = y$ also. That is, $\phi_{i+1}(x) = y$. □

Now we prove that assertion 1 holds.

Lemma 3.4 *For all x, $\phi(x) = F(\phi; x)$.*

Proof. Suppose $\phi(x) \downarrow$. Then, for some i, $\phi(x) = F(\phi_i; x)$. Since ϕ extends ϕ_i, $F(\phi; x) = F(\phi_i; x) = \phi(x)$.

Conversely, suppose that $F(\phi; x)$ is defined. The computation of F on ϕ and x is of finite length; i.e., there are some finitely many values $n_1, \ldots, n_k$ such that $\phi(n_1), \ldots, \phi(n_k)$ are required. There exist $i_1, \ldots, i_k$ such that $\phi(n_1) = \phi_{i_1}(n_1)$, $\ldots, \phi(n_k) = \phi_{i_k}(n_k)$. Let $i = \max\{i_1, \ldots, i_k\}$. Then $\phi(n_1) = \phi_i(n_1), \ldots,$ $\phi(n_k) = \phi_i(n_k)$. So, $F(\phi; x) = F(\phi_i; x)$, and the value of $F(\phi_i; x)$, by definition, is $\phi(x)$. □

Lemma 3.5 *ϕ is partial computable.*

Proof. We indicate a proof by using Church's thesis. To compute $\phi(x)$, one needs to compute $F(\phi; x)$. To compute $F(\phi; x)$, at most some finitely many values $\phi(n_1), \ldots, \phi(n_k)$ are required. If no such values are required, then $\phi(x) = \phi_1(x) = F(\phi_0; x)$. Otherwise, assume as induction hypothesis that for some i, $\phi(n_1) = \phi_i(n_1), \ldots, \phi(n_k) = \phi_i(n_k)$ and that each of these can be obtained. Then compute $F(\phi; x)$ using these values. □

Lemma 3.6 *If $F(\psi; x) = \psi(x)$, then ψ extends ϕ.*

Proof. We show by induction on i that ψ extends each ϕ_i. Clearly, ψ extends ϕ_0. By induction hypothesis, assume that ψ extends ϕ_i. Let $\phi_{i+1}(x) = y$. Then

$$\begin{aligned} y &= \phi_{i+1}(x) \\ &= F(\phi_i; x) \\ &= F(\psi; x), \quad \text{because } \psi \text{ is an extension of } \phi_i, \\ &= \psi(x). \end{aligned}$$

So ψ is an extension of ϕ_{i+1}. □

This completes the proof of Theorem 3.18. □

Theorem 3.18 gives a partial computable solution ϕ to Equation 3.3 so that for any $x_1, \ldots, x_n$, the value of $\phi(x_1, \ldots, x_n)$ can be computed in terms of ϕ and $x_1, \ldots, x_n$. A program e to compute ϕ is not explicitly given.

The following consequence of Theorem 3.11 is closely related to Theorem 3.18; in some ways it is stronger, in other ways weaker.

Theorem 3.19 *Let $F(\xi; z, x_1, \ldots, x_n)$ be a partial computable functional in which ξ is a function variable that ranges over partial functions of n variables. Then there is a number* *e such that*

$$\phi_e(x_1, \ldots, x_n) = F(\phi_e; e, x_1, \ldots, x_n).$$

Proof. There is a partial computable function η such that

$$\eta(s, z, x_1, \ldots, x_n) = F(\phi; z, x_1, \ldots, x_n)$$

for any Gödel number s of ϕ. That is,

$$\eta(s, z, x_1, \ldots, x_n) = F(\phi_s; z, x_1, \ldots, x_n).$$

Now let us consider the function ψ defined by

$$\psi(s, x_1, \ldots, x_n) = \eta(s, s, x_1, \ldots, x_n).$$

By Theorem 3.11, there is a number e such that

$$\begin{aligned}
\phi_e(x_1, \ldots, x_n) &= \psi(e, x_1, \ldots, x_n) \\
&= \eta(e, e, x_1, \ldots, x_n) \\
&= F(\phi_e; e, x_1, \ldots, x_n).
\end{aligned}$$
$\square$

Theorem 3.19 is stronger than Theorem 3.18 in that F is permitted to depend not only on ϕ but also on the Gödel number of a Turing machine for computing ϕ, but it is also weaker in that there is no reason to suppose that the solution ϕ_e is a least fixed point. That is, there is no reason to suppose that all other solutions are extensions of the one that Theorem 3.19 obtains.

Does Theorem 3.18 essentially reduce to Theorem 3.11 in the case that we do not include a Gödel number in the recursion? In that case, there is a partial computable function η such that

$$\eta(s, x_1, \ldots, x_n) = F(\phi_s; x_1, \ldots, x_n).$$

So, by Theorem 3.11, there is a number e such that

$$\begin{aligned}
\phi_e(x_1, \ldots, x_n) &= \eta(e, x_1, \ldots, x_n) \\
&= F(\phi_e; e, x_1, \ldots, x_n).
\end{aligned}$$

Again, we do not know whether ϕ_e is the least fixed point.

3.11 References

Chapters 2 and 3 of this text contain material on computability and undecidability that was developed prior to 1960. For students wishing to pursue a deeper study of computability theory, we cite the classic text by Rogers [Rog67] and the seminal paper of Post [Pos44]. Davis' source book [Dav65] contains many of the original papers on undecidability. For developments in computability theory since 1960, consult the text by Soare [Soa80].

3.12   Additional Homework Problems

Homework 3.15   *Show that every infinite decidable set has an undecidable c.e. subset.*

Homework 3.16   *Let A be an undecidable c.e. set and let B be an infinite decidable subset of A. Show that A − B is an undecidable c.e. set.*

Homework 3.17   *Show that if A is a decidable language, then so is the concatenation AA. Provide an example to demonstrate that the converse is false.*

Homework 3.18   *The* graph *of a partial function f is the set $\{\langle x, f(x) \rangle \mid f(x) \downarrow\}$. Show that a partial function f is partial computable if and only if its graph is c.e.*

Homework 3.19   *Prove that it is decidable to determine whether a Turing machine ever writes a nonblank symbol when started on a blank tape.*

Homework 3.20   *Prove that it is undecidable to determine whether a Turing machine halts on every input word that has an even number of symbols.*

Homework 3.21   *Give an example of a language L such that L is not many-one reducible to $\overline{L}$. That is, $L \not\leq_m \overline{L}$. (Observe, therefore, using Homework 3.13, item 3, that many-one and Turing reducibilities are different relations on $\mathcal{P}(N)$.)*

Homework 3.22   *Let A and B be disjoint c.e. sets. Show that $A \leq_T A \cup B$ and $B \leq_T A \cup B$.*

Homework 3.23   *Given disjoint sets A and B, we say that a set C separates A and B if $A \subseteq C$ and $C \cap B = \emptyset$. Show that if A and B are disjoint sets such that both $\overline{A}$ and $\overline{B}$ are c.e., then there is a decidable set that separates them.*

Homework 3.24   1. *Give an example of sets A, B, and C such that $A \subseteq B$, $B \subseteq C$, A and C are decidable, and B is undecidable.*
2. *Give an example of sets A, B, and C such that $A \subseteq B$, $B \subseteq C$, A and C are undecidable, and B is decidable.*

Homework 3.25   *Show that the set*

$$L = \{(e, w) \mid \text{ the head of } M_e \text{ shifts left at some point during the}$$
$$\text{computation of } M_e \text{ on input } w\}$$

is decidable.

Homework 3.26   *Prove that the set*

$$L = \{e \mid M_e \text{ accepts the input string } 11\}$$

is undecidable.

Homework 3.27   *Prove that the the set*

$$L = \{< i, j > \mid \text{ there is some input } x \text{ on which both } M_i(x) \text{ and } M_j(x) \text{ halt }\}$$

is undecidable.

Homework 3.28 *One of the following languages is computably enumerable and the other is not. Answer which is which, demonstrate that the language you claim to be c.e. is, and prove that the other language is not c.e.*

$$L_1 = \{e \mid M_e \text{ accepts at least 20 different inputs}\}.$$

$$L_2 = \{e \mid M_e \text{ accepts at most 20 different inputs}\}.$$

Homework 3.29 *A c.e. set is* simple *if its complement is infinite but does not have any infinite c.e. subset.*

1. *Explain whether a simple set can be decidable.*
2. *Prove that simple sets exist by constructing one. (This is a difficult problem.)*

Homework 3.30 *A c.e. set A is* creative *if there is a total computable function f such that for all m, if $W_m \subseteq \overline{A}$, then $f(m) \in \overline{A} - W_m$.*

1. *Show that K is creative.*
2. *Show that no creative set is simple.*

Homework 3.31 *Construct a computably enumerable, undecidable set B of pairs of natural numbers with the property that for each natural number x, both sets $\{y \mid (x, y) \in B\}$ and $\{y \mid (y, x) \in B\}$ are decidable.*

Homework 3.32 *Let us define the set $K^{(\omega)}$ as follows:*

$$K^{(\omega)} = \{\langle i, j \rangle \mid i \in K^{(j)}\}.$$

1. *Show for every $j \geq 1$ that $K^{(j)}$ is many-one reducible to $K^{(\omega)}$.*
2. *Show that $K^{(\omega)}$ is not Turing reducible to $K^{(j)}$ for any $j \geq 1$.*

4

Introduction to Complexity Theory

4.1   Complexity Classes and Complexity Measures   74

4.2   Prerequisites   77

The remaining chapters of this book are concerned with complexity theory. The goal of complexity theory is to provide mechanisms for classifying combinatorial problems and measuring the computational resources necessary to solve them. Complexity theory provides an explanation of why certain problems have no practical solutions and provides a way of anticipating difficulties involved in solving problems of certain types. The classification is quantitative and is intended to investigate what resources are necessary (lower bounds) and what resources are sufficient (upper bounds) to solve various problems.

This classification should not depend on a particular computational model but rather should measure the intrinsic difficulty of a problem. The basic model of computation for our study is the multitape Turing machine, but the measurement mechanisms are essentially machine-independent, up to the exactitude required. Cobham's thesis and the expanded version of Church's thesis summarize the fact that all reasonable general models of computation give rise to essentially the same classification. Let's recapitulate: We will be interested primarily in the class of problems that can be computed in polynomial time (Cobham's thesis), and any computational device that operates in polynomial time can be simulated by a Turing machine that runs in polynomial time (expanded version of Church's thesis). Thus, especially for polynomial time, the theory we provide is a robust one whose definition does not depend on a single machine or its technical features.

Many of the techniques of Chapters 2 and 3 will serve us well as we proceed. However, the most difficult and interesting facets of complexity theory appear exactly where the older mathematical theories lend no guiding hand and where new methods, particular to this study, must be developed.

Complexity theory today addresses issues of contemporary concern: cryptography and data security, probabilistic computation (those that depend on random number generators), parallel computation, circuit design, quantum computing, biological computing, development of efficient algorithms. Moreover, complexity theory is interested not in the merely computable but in problems that are *efficiently* computable. Algorithms whose running times are n^2 in the size of their inputs can be implemented to execute efficiently even for fairly large values of n, but algorithms that require an exponential running time can be executed only for small values of n. It is common today to identify efficiently computable problems with those that have polynomial-time algorithms.

A complexity measure quantifies the use of a particular computational resource during execution of a computation. The two most important measures, and the two most common measures, are *time*, the time it takes a program to execute, and *space*, the amount of storage used during a computation. However, other measures are considered as well, and we will introduce other resources as we proceed.

Complexity theory forms a basis for the classification and analysis of combinatorial algorithms. To illustrate this, consider the Hamiltonian Circuit problem, the problem of determining whether an arbitrary graph possesses a Hamiltonian circuit. Currently it is not known whether this problem has a feasible solution, and all known solutions are equivalent to a sequential search of all paths through the graph, testing each in turn for the Hamiltonian property. Since complexity will be measured by time and/or space in Turing-machine computations, it becomes clear why it is important to be able to efficiently encode data structures such as graphs into words over Σ so that what is intuitively the size of the graph differs from the length of the input by no more than a polynomial. Then, we must demand that the theory is capable of classifying the intrinsic complexity of this problem in a precise way and is capable of elucidating the difficulty in finding an efficient solution to this problem.

To summarize the discussion so far, we conclude that the use of the multitape Turing machine as the basic model of computation is robust over all possible models of computation and is robust via standard encodings for all standard data types.

Nondeterminism will play an important role in this study. We do not design nondeterministic machines to be executed, as are ordinary computing devices. Rather, one should understand nondeterministic Turing machines to be a useful mode for classification of computational problems. For example, whereas it is not known whether there is a deterministic polynomial-time-bounded Turing machine to solve (an encoding of) the Hamiltonian Circuit problem, it is easy to design a nondeterministic polynomial-time-bounded Turing machine that solves this problem. This is what makes it possible to give an exact classification of the Hamiltonian Circuit problem. Indeed, this problem is known to be NP-complete, which places it among hundreds of other important computational problems whose deterministic complexity is still open.

We will return to nondeterminism and to a precise definition of NP-complete in Chapter 6.

4.1   Complexity Classes and Complexity Measures

In order to define time complexity, we consider on-line Turing machines. An *online* Turing machine is a multitape Turing machine whose input is written on one of the work tapes, which can be rewritten and used as an ordinary work tape. The machine may be either deterministic or nondeterministic. Let M be an on-line Turing machine, and let T be a function defined on the set of natural numbers. M is a $T(n)$ *time-bounded* Turing machine if for every input of length n, M makes at most $T(n)$ moves before halting. If M is nondeterministic, then every computation of M on words of length n must take at most $T(n)$ steps. The language $L(M)$ that is accepted by a deterministic $T(n)$ time-bounded M has *time complexity* $T(n)$.

By convention, the time it takes to read the input is counted, and every machine is entitled to read its input. This takes $n + 1$ steps. So when we say a computation has time complexity $T(n)$, we really mean $\max(n + 1, \lceil T(n) \rceil)$.

Denote the length of a word x by $|x|$. We might be tempted to say that a nondeterministic Turing machine is $T(n)$ time-bounded if, for every input word $x \in L(M)$, the number of steps of the shortest accepting computation of M on x is at most $T(|x|)$. In Chapter 5 we will see that the formulations are equivalent for the specific time bounds that we write about. But they are not equivalent for arbitrary time bounds.

A complexity class is a collection of sets that can be accepted by Turing machines with the same resources. Now we define the time-bounded complexity classes: Define DTIME($T(n)$) to be the set of all languages having time complexity $T(n)$. Define NTIME($T(n)$) to be the set of all languages accepted by nondeterministic $T(n)$ time-bounded Turing machines.

In order to define space complexity, we need to use off-line Turing machines. An *off-line* Turing machine is a multitape Turing machine with a separate read-only input tape. The Turing machine can read the input but cannot write over the input. Let M be an off-line multitape Turing machine and let S be a function defined on the set of natural numbers. M is an $S(n)$ *space-bounded* Turing machine if, for every word of length n, M scans at most $S(n)$ cells over all storage tapes. If M is nondeterministic, then every computation must scan no more than $S(n)$ cells over all storage tapes. The language $L(M)$ accepted by a deterministic $S(n)$ space-bounded Turing machine has *space complexity* $S(n)$.

Observe that the space the input takes is not counted. Every Turing machine is permitted to use at least one work cell, so when we say that a problem has space complexity $S(n)$, we always mean $\max(1, \lceil S(n) \rceil)$. For example, space complexity $\log(n)$ can never be 0.

One might be tempted to say that a nondeterministic Turing machine is $S(n)$ space-bounded if, for every word of length n that belongs to $L(M)$, there is an accepting computation that uses no more than $S(n)$ work cells on any work tape. As is the case for nondeterministic time, we will show in the next chapter that the two formulations are equivalent for the time bounds that interest us.

Now, we define the space-bounded complexity classes: Define $\mathrm{DSPACE}(S(n))$ to be the set of all languages having space complexity $S(n)$. Define $\mathrm{NSPACE}(S(n))$ to be the set of all languages accepted by nondeterministic $S(n)$ space-bounded Turing machines.

The study of time complexity begins with the paper [HS65] of Hartmanis and Stearns. The title of this paper contains the first usage of the phrase "computational complexity." The study of space complexity begins with the paper [HLS65] of Hartmanis, Lewis, and Stearns. These seminal papers introduced some of the issues that remain of concern even today. These include time/space trade-offs, inclusion relations, hierarchy results, and the efficient simulation of nondeterministic computations.

We will be primarily concerned with classes defined by logarithmic, polynomial, and exponential functions. As we proceed to relate and discuss various facts about complexity classes in general, we will see their impact on the following list of *standard* complexity classes. These classes are well studied in the literature; each contains important computational problems. The classes are introduced with their common notations.

1. $\mathrm{L} = \mathrm{DSPACE}(\log(n))^*$
2. $\mathrm{NL} = \mathrm{NSPACE}(\log(n))$
3. $\mathrm{POLYLOGSPACE} = \bigcup \{\mathrm{DSPACE}((\log n)^k) \mid k \geq 1\}$
4. $\mathrm{DLBA} = \bigcup \{\mathrm{DSPACE}(kn) \mid k \geq 1\}$
5. $\mathrm{LBA} = \bigcup \{\mathrm{NSPACE}(kn) \mid k \geq 1\}$
6. $\mathrm{P} = \bigcup \{\mathrm{DTIME}(n^k) \mid k \geq 1\}$
7. $\mathrm{NP} = \bigcup \{\mathrm{NTIME}(n^k) \mid k \geq 1\}$
8. $\mathrm{E} = \bigcup \{\mathrm{DTIME}(k^n) \mid k \geq 1\}$
9. $\mathrm{NE} = \bigcup \{\mathrm{NTIME}(k^n) \mid k \geq 1\}$
10. $\mathrm{PSPACE} = \bigcup \{\mathrm{DSPACE}(n^k) \mid k \geq 1\}$
11. $\mathrm{EXP} = \bigcup \{\mathrm{DTIME}(2^{p(n)}) \mid p \text{ is a polynomial}\}$
12. $\mathrm{NEXP} = \bigcup \{\mathrm{NTIME}(2^{p(n)}) \mid p \text{ is a polynomial}\}$

The study of the computational complexity of specific computational problems on specific models of computation is called *concrete complexity*. The

*All logarithms in this book are binary.

concrete-complexity literature provides a rich source of examples of problems in our standard list. The following is merely an introduction to a vast subject.

NL contains the problem of determining for arbitrary directed graphs G and vertices u and v, whether there is a path from u to v. This problem is not known to belong to L. The class L contains the restriction of this problem to the case that no vertex has more than one directed edge leading from it. [Jon73, Jon75]. P is identified with the class of feasibly computed problems. The corresponding nondeterministic class NP will be discussed in a later chapter. We will easily see that P is a subset of NP, but it is not known whether P is equal to NP, and many consider the question of whether these two classes differ to be the most important open question of either mathematics or computer science. Chapters 6 and 7 will focus almost entirely on this question.

The class $\bigcup\{\text{NSPACE}(kn) \mid k \geq 1\}$ is denoted LBA because it is known to be identical to the class of languages accepted by linear-bounded automata, otherwise known as the context-sensitive languages [Myh60, Kur64]. This explains the notation for the corresponding deterministic class as well.

The class E characterizes the complexity of languages accepted by writing push-down automata [Mag69], and NE characterizes the complexity of a well-known computational problem in finite model theory [JS74]. PSPACE contains many computational games, such as generalized HEX [ET76]. These results are beyond the scope of this text.

4.1.1   Computing Functions

Occasionally we will need to discuss the computational complexity of computing functions. We are already familiar with partial computable functions and the Turing machines that compute them. However, for our study of complexity theory, let us agree on the following particular formalism. A Turing-machine *transducer* M is a multitape Turing machine, either deterministic or nondeterministic, with a distinguished write-only output tape and with accepting and rejecting states in the usual manner. A transducer M computes a value y on an input string x if there is an accepting computation of M on x for which y is the final contents of M's output tape. In general, such transducers compute partial multivalued functions—partial because transducers do not typically accept all input strings, and multivalued because different accepting computations of a nondeterministic transducer may produce different output values. We will see important examples of this phenomena in Chapter 5. For now, we will not be concerned with partial functions.

Let f be a function defined on Σ^*. A deterministic Turing-machine transducer M *computes* f if, for all x, M on input x halts in its accepting state with $f(x)$ written on the output tape. A nondeterministic Turing-machine transducer M *computes* f if (i) there is an accepting computation of M on x, and (ii) every accepting computation of M on x has $f(x)$ written on the output tape. Time-bounded transducers are defined as above. A transducer M is $S(n)$ space-bounded if M is an off-line transducer (i.e., M has a separate read-only input tape) that never uses more than $S(n)$ storage cells on any computation on an input word of length n. The space the input and output words take is not counted.

4.2 Prerequisites

Before proceeding, let us review the main points that students should know from the earlier chapters:

- Students should know that multitape Turing machines and RAMs have identical computing power.

- Students should know how to represent data structures as words over a finite alphabet with no more than a polynomial blowup in size.

- Students should know the capabilities of Turing machines (for example, understand that a finite table can be stored in a Turing machine's finite control).

- Students should be comfortable with the universal Turing machine and believe that there exists a compiler that will translate any algorithm written in pseudo-code into a Turing machine.

In addition, complexity theory will borrow the methods of relative computability that we learned in the last chapter.

Finally, we invite students to read some discussion of Cobham's thesis such as the excellent one in the first paragraph of Garey and Johnson's monograph [GJ79].

5

Basic Results of Complexity Theory

5.1   Linear Compression and Speedup   80

5.2   Constructible Functions   86

5.3   Tape Reduction   90

5.4   Inclusion Relationships   97

5.5   Separation Results   107

5.6   Translation Techniques and Padding   111

5.7   Relations between the Standard Classes—Continued   115

5.8   Additional Homework Problems   120

We begin our study of complexity theory by examining the fundamental properties of complexity classes. These results apply to all complexity classes and show that the definitions of these classes are invariant under small changes in the time or space bounds of the Turing machines that define them. We will prove general relationships between time- and space-bounded complexity classes. These consist of inclusions between some classes and separations of other classes. Then we will apply the methods and results of these general relationships to important specific cases in order to establish relationships between the central standard complexity classes we defined in the previous chapter. In order to begin this study we need to understand some simple assertions that involve the behavior of functions at limits, so let's review these now.

Let f be a function that is defined on the set of all natural numbers, and recall that by definition

$$\sup_{n \to \infty} f(n) = \lim_{n \to \infty} \text{l.u.b.} \{ f(m) | m \geq n \}$$

and
$$\inf_{n\to\infty} f(n) = \lim_{n\to\infty} \text{g.l.b.}\{f(m)|m \ge n\}.$$

Then the limit $\lim_{n\to\infty} f(n)$ is defined to exist if and only if $\inf_{n\to\infty} f(n) = \sup_{n\to\infty} f(n)$, in which case,
$$\lim_{n\to\infty} f(n) = \inf_{n\to\infty} f(n) = \sup_{n\to\infty} f(n).$$

Example 5.1   *Consider the function $f(n)$ defined by*
$$f(n) = \begin{cases} 1/n & n \text{ is even,} \\ n & n \text{ is odd,} \end{cases}$$

Observe that $\text{l.u.b.}\{f(n), f(n+1), \ldots\} = \infty$ *for every n. Hence,*
$$\sup_{n\to\infty} f(n) = \lim_{n\to\infty} \text{l.u.b.}\{f(m)|m \ge n\} = \infty.$$

For any n, $\text{g.l.b.}\{f(n), f(n+1), \ldots\} = 0$. *So,* $\inf_{n\to\infty} f(n) = 0$. *Thus, the limit* $\lim_{n\to\infty} f(n)$ *does not exist.*

Example 5.2   *Consider the function $f(n)$ defined by $f(n) = n/(n+1)$. We have*
$$\text{l.u.b.}\{n/(n+1), (n+1)/(n+2), \ldots\} = 1,$$

for all n, and
$$\text{g.l.b.}\{n/(n+1), (n+1)/(n+2), \ldots\} = n/(n+1),$$

from which we arrive at
$$\lim_{n\to\infty} 1 = \lim_{n\to\infty} n/(n+1) = 1.$$

Thus, the limit exists, and $\lim_{n\to\infty} f(n) = 1$.

We will need to understand the assertion
$$\inf_{n\to\infty} f(n) = \infty.$$

Let $g(n) = \text{g.l.b.}\{f(n), f(n+1), \ldots\}$. Then the following are immediate:
$$\inf_{n\to\infty} f(n) = \infty \Leftrightarrow \lim_{n\to\infty} \text{g.l.b.}\{f(n), f(n+1), \ldots\} = \infty$$
$$\Leftrightarrow \lim_{n\to\infty} g(n) = \infty$$
$$\Leftrightarrow (\forall c > 0)(\exists N)(\forall n \ge N)(g(n) > c).$$

Then $(\forall c > 0)(\exists N)(\forall n \ge N)(f(n) > c)$, because $f(m) \ge g(n)$ for all $m \ge n$. Thus,
$$\inf_{n\to\infty} f(n) = \infty \quad \text{implies} \quad \lim_{n\to\infty} f(n) = \infty.$$

We can use this assertion to define "little-oh" notation. Namely,
$$g(n) \in o(f(n)) \Leftrightarrow \inf_{n\to\infty} f(n)/g(n) = \infty$$
$$\Leftrightarrow (\forall c > 0)(\exists N)(\forall n \ge N)(cg(n) < f(n)).$$

Example 5.3 $\log n \in o(n)$ and $n \in o(n \log n)$. *The second statement holds as, given a constant* $c > 0$, *we can choose* N *such that* $\log N > c$. *Then* $c \log n < n \log n$ *for any* $n > N$.

Homework 5.1   *Prove that* $\log n \in o(n)$ *and that* $n \in o(n^{1+\epsilon})$ *for any* $\epsilon > 0$.

5.1   Linear Compression and Speedup

The proofs of the results in the next few sections involve clever and sometimes tricky algorithms. The algorithms tell us how one Turing machine can efficiently simulate another when it has slightly less computational power, either having less space or less time. In Section 5.3 we consider the question of efficient simulations of k-tape Turing machines by one-tape and two-tape tape Turing machines. Since complexity classes are defined in terms of multitape Turing machines—not in terms of one-tape or two-tape machines—one might view this as a digression from our main purpose, which is to elucidate properties of complexity classes. However, the results proved will turn out to be important in later sections of this chapter.

The first results are of the following form: If a language can be accepted with resource $f(n)$, then it can be accepted with resource $cf(n)$ for any $c > 0$. These results justify use of "big-oh" notation for complexity functions. To review this notation, $g(n) \in O(f(n))$ if there is a constant $c > 0$ such that, for all n, $g(n) \leq cf(n)$. We define the class $\text{DTIME}(O(T(n))$ as follows:

$$\text{DTIME}(O(T(n)) = \bigcup \{\text{DTIME}(g(n)) \mid g(n) \in O(T(n))\}.$$

$\text{DSPACE}(O(S(n)))$, $\text{NTIME}(O(T(n)))$, and $\text{NSPACE}(O(S(n)))$ are defined similarly. It follows readily that $\text{DTIME}(O(T(n)) = \bigcup \{\text{DTIME}(cT(n)) \mid c > 0\}$. Similar identities hold for the other classes.

The first example of a theorem of this form is the *space compression theorem* [HLS65]. This theorem asserts that if L is accepted by a k-tape $S(n)$ space-bounded Turing machine, then for any $c > 0$, L is accepted by a k-tape $cS(n)$ space-bounded Turing machine. If the $S(n)$ space-bounded Turing machine is nondeterministic, then so is the $cS(n)$ space-bounded Turing machine. In the following theorem, we combine space compression with tape reduction—the result is a one-tape $cS(n)$ Turing machine. The proof is essentially the same simple simulation that we used in the proof of Theorem 2.2. We repeat it in part to note that it applies to nondeterministic Turing machines as well as to deterministic ones. As a corollary, it follows that $\text{DSPACE}(S(n)) = \text{DSPACE}(O(S(n)))$ and $\text{NSPACE}(S(n)) = \text{NSPACE}(O(S(n)))$.

Theorem 5.1   **(Space Compression with Tape Reduction)** *For every* k-tape $S(n)$ *space-bounded off-line Turing machine* M *and constant* $c > 0$, *there exists a one-tape*

track 1	a_{11}	a_{12}	a_{13}		a_{1d}	
track 2	a_{21}	$\uparrow a_{22}$	a_{23}		a_{2d}	
track k	a_{k1}	a_{k2}	a_{k3}		a_{kd}	

FIGURE 5.1. A single cell of N.

$cS(n)$ *space-bounded off-line Turing machine* N *such that* $L(M) = L(N)$. *Furthermore, if* M *is deterministic, then so is* N.

Proof. Let M be a k-tape $S(n)$ space-bounded off-line Turing machine, and let $c > 0$. Choose an integer d such that $2 \leq cdk$. As in the proof of Theorem 2.2, view the single work tape of N as consisting of k tracks, one track for each work tape of M. (This is pictured in Fig. 5.1.) The difference is that now each cell of N contains a "composite symbol" that represents a k by d matrix, where the ith row contains d tape symbols of the ith tape of M, and possibly an indicator $\uparrow$ of the head position of the ith tape head. Formally, the tape alphabet of N is sufficiently large so that each tape symbol of N uniquely denotes such a k by d matrix of M's tape and with head indicators.

Since d symbols of each of M's work tapes are encoded in a single cell of N, N uses at most $\lceil S(n)/dk \rceil$ cells to encode all of M's work tapes.

N simulates a move of M as follows: Beginning at the leftmost cell containing a head marker, N "sweeps right" until it has visited all cells containing head markers and then "sweeps left" to its start position. A *neighborhood* of M consists of those cells of M that either are scanned by some tape head or are adjacent to such a scanned cell. On the sweep right, N records all the current neighborhoods of M in its finite control. On the left sweep, it updates the neighborhoods to reflect the changes that M would have made.

It is clear that N uses no more than

$$\lceil S(n)/dk \rceil \leq 2(S(n)/dk) \leq cS(n)$$

cells. □

Corollary 5.1 $\mathrm{DSPACE}(S(n)) = \mathrm{DSPACE}(O(S(n)))$ *and* $\mathrm{NSPACE}(S(n)) = \mathrm{NSPACE}(O(S(n)))$.

Since a "linear bounded automaton" is just a one-tape n space-bounded Turing machine, it follows from this corollary that the formal language class DLBA = DSPACE(n), and LBA = NSPACE(n).

Linear speedup of time is possible, too, but not quite as readily as is linear compression of space.

Theorem 5.2   **(Linear Speedup [HS65])** *If L is accepted by a k-tape T(n) time-bounded Turing machine M, k > 1, and if n ∈ o(T(n)), then for any c > 0, L is accepted by a k-tape cT(n) time-bounded Turing machine N. Furthermore, if M is deterministic, then so is N.*

Proof. Let M be a k-tape $T(n)$ time-bounded Turing machine, where $k \geq 2$, let $c > 0$, and assume that $n \in o(T(n))$.

Choose m so that $mc \geq 16$. The ith tape of N will encode the contents of the ith tape of M using composite symbols (i.e., using a large tape alphabet), and eight moves of N will simulate at least m moves of M.

To begin, N scans the input of M and copies the input onto a storage tape, encoding m symbols of M into one symbol of N. After this, N moves the head of the storage tape containing the input back to the left end. This routine takes

$$n + \lceil n/m \rceil$$

moves. Henceforth, N will use its original input tape as a storage tape and use the tape containing the compressed input as an input tape.

N simulates moves of M as follows: Define a *neighborhood* of N to be those cells of N currently being scanned together with their adjacent cells. Let us say that the head of tape i is currently scanning cell j. First, N makes four moves (left to $j - 1$, right to j, right to $j + 1$, left to j) to determine the contents of its current neighborhood. Using its finite control, N determines the contents of all of M's cells represented by this neighborhood and determines what the contents will be the very next time, say t_0, that the head of tape i is not scanning one of the cells represented by the region $j - 1, j, j + 1$. If M accepts its input before any tape head of M moves outside the region corresponding to the current neighborhood of N, then N accepts immediately. Similarly, if M halts, so does N. Otherwise, N uses four more moves to update the contents of its neighborhood to correspond correctly with the contents of M's cells at time t_0, and N completes its sequence of eight moves by positioning its heads over the cells that represent the region M is in at time t_0. (For example, suppose N is to change its neighborhood on tape i from $j - 1, j, j + 1$ to $j + 1, j + 2, j + 3$ with the head scanning $j + 2$. Then N updates cells $j - 1, j, j + 1$ by moving left one cell from j and then updating $j - 1, j, j + 1$ in that order, and then moves to $j + 2$.)

M must make at least m moves in order to move out of a region, so N takes eight moves to simulate at least m moves of M.

Now we calculate the running time of N. Let this be denoted by T_N. We have

$$T_N \leq n + \lceil n/m \rceil + 8\lceil T(n)/m \rceil.$$

Since $\lceil x \rceil \leq x + 1$, for all x,

$$T_N \leq n + n/m + 8T(n)/m + 9.$$

By the hypothesis that $n \in o(T(n))$, $(\forall d)(\exists N_d)(\forall n \geq N_d)(dn < T(n))$. That is,

$$(\forall d)(\exists N_d)(\forall n \geq N_d)(n < T(n)/d).$$

Also, for all $n \geq 9$, $n + 9 \leq 2n$. Thus, for all $d > 0$ and all $n \geq \max(9, N_d)$,

$$T_N \leq 2T(n)/d + T(n)/md + 8T(n)/m$$
$$= T(n)[2/d + 1/md + 8/m]$$
$$\leq T(n)[32/16d + c/16d + 8c/16] \text{ (because } cm \geq 16).$$

We want to choose d so that $32/16d + c/16d + 8c/16 \leq c$: Because

$$32/16d + c/16d + 8c/16 \leq c \Leftrightarrow 32 + c + 8cd \leq 16cd$$
$$\Leftrightarrow 32 + c \leq 8cd$$
$$\Leftrightarrow (32 + c)/8c \leq d$$
$$\Leftrightarrow 4/c + 1/8 \leq d,$$

it suffices to choose d in accordance with the last inequality. Then, for all $n \geq \max(9, N_d)$, N makes at most $cT(n)$ moves.

To recognize words in $L(M)$ whose length is less than $\max(9, N_d)$, store these words in the finite control on N. □

Corollary 5.2 *If $n \in o(T(n))$, then*

$$\mathrm{DTIME}(T(n)) = \mathrm{DTIME}(O(T(n)))$$

and

$$\mathrm{NTIME}(T(n)) = \mathrm{NTIME}(O(T(n))).$$

The condition $n \in o(T(n))$ stipulates that $T(n)$ grows faster than every linear function. For this reason, the linear speedup theorem does not apply if $T(n) = cn$ for some constant c. Instead, we have the following result.

Corollary 5.3 *For all $\epsilon > 0$,*

$$\mathrm{DTIME}(O(n)) = \mathrm{DTIME}((1 + \epsilon)n)$$

and

$$\mathrm{NTIME}(O(n)) = \mathrm{NTIME}((1 + \epsilon)n).$$

Proof. The same simulation applies. Let M be a k-tape cn time-bounded Turing machine, where $k > 1$ and $c > 0$. Let $\epsilon > 0$. Recall from the proof of the linear speedup theorem that $T_N \leq n + n/m + 8T(n)/m + 9$. Using the hypothesis, we derive the following estimates to T_N:

$$T_N \leq n + n/m + 8T(n)/m + 9$$
$$\leq n + n/m + 8cn/m + 9$$
$$= n[1 + (1 + 8c)/m + 9/n]$$
$$< (1 + \epsilon)n$$

if n and m are chosen so that $(1 + 8c)/m < \epsilon/2$ and $9/n < \epsilon/2$. Thus, the result holds for all $n > 18/\epsilon$, and with $m > 2(1 + 8c)/\epsilon$ as an additional condition.

For $n \leq 18/\epsilon$, store the words in $L(M)$ in the finite control of N. □

This result cannot be improved for deterministic linear-time complexity classes, because Rosenberg [Ros67] showed that

$$\text{DTIME}(n) \neq \text{DTIME}(2n).$$

However, a stronger result is known for nondeterministic linear-time complexity classes: A Turing machine that accepts inputs of length n in time $n + 1$ (the time it takes to read the input) is called *real time*. Nondeterministic Turing machines that accept in time $n + 1$ are called *quasi-real time*. The class of quasi-real-time languages is NTIME$(n+1)$. Book and Greibach [BG70] showed that NTIME$(n+1) = \text{NTIME}(O(n))$. This result is a corollary of the next theorem.

Theorem 5.3   **([BG70])**   *Let M be a k-tape $T(n)$ time-bounded Turing machine, $T(n) \geq n$. Let $c > 0$. Then there is a nondeterministic $(k + 3)$-tape Turing machine N such that $L(M) = L(N)$ with the property that for every word $x \in L(M)$, $|x| = n$, there is an accepting computation of N that accepts x in time*

$$\max(n + 1, cT(n)).$$

Proof.   Choose an integer d (according to specifications to be given later). As before, one symbol of N will compress d symbols of M. For $i = 2, \ldots, k$, tape i will contain in compressed form the contents of tape i of M. Tape $k + 1$ will contain in compressed form an initial segment of the input string of M. Tapes $k + 2$ and $k + 3$ will contain certain guesses of the input string. Remember that the simulation in the proof of the linear speedup theorem, Theorem 5.2, first writes the input of M onto one of its tapes in compressed form, which requires $n + \lceil n/d \rceil$ steps, and then enters a process that uses eight moves of N to simulate d moves of M. This simulation will use nondeterminism and even parallel processing to cleverly reduce the time of these processes.

N simulates M in two phases, and each phase consists of two simultaneous processes. In the initial phase execute the following processes 1 and 2 in parallel:

1. Nondeterministically copy a prefix x_1 of the input word x onto tape $k + 1$ in compressed form. (This takes $|x_1|$ steps.)

2. N writes onto tapes $k + 2$ and $k + 3$ some guessed string y from the input alphabet of M in compressed form. Then the heads of $k + 2$ and $k + 3$ move synchronously leftward over y and nondeterministically stop while scanning y.

For any word w from the tape alphabet of M, let $\overline{w}$ denote the compressed version of w. The initial phase ends when both processes halt. At this point, on tape 1, the input tape, is $x = x_1 x_2$, where x_1 is the initial segment of x that is copied in compressed form onto tape $k + 1$. On tapes $k + 2$ and $k + 3$ are $\overline{y} = \overline{y_1}\,\overline{y_2}$. Note that x_1, y_1, or y_2 may be empty. Fig. 5.2 illustrates the current situation.

| tape 1 | x_1 | x_2 | |

| tape $k+1$ | $\overline{x}_1$ | | |

| tape $k+2$ | $\overline{y}_1$ | $\overline{y}_2$ | |

| tape $k+3$ | $\overline{y}_1$ | $\overline{y}_2$ | |

FIGURE 5.2. The initial phase.

The final phase consists of the following processes executed in parallel:

3. The input head scans the rest of the input (i.e., x_2) comparing it to $\overline{y}_2$, the compressed copy of y_2, on tape $k + 2$. It is important to note that both input heads began at the left end of x_2 and y_2, respectively. If $x_2 \neq y_2$ is discovered, N halts without accepting. Otherwise, process 3 stops when it confirms that $x_2 = y_2$.

4. Use $\overline{x}_1$ on tape $k + 1$ and $\overline{y}_1$ on tape $k + 3$ to check whether $x_1 = y_1$. If $x_1 \neq y_1$ is discovered, then N rejects. Otherwise, the head of $k + 3$ is placed at the beginning of y, and the "8-move simulation" of the linear speedup theorem begins.

Observe that process 4 may be executing the "8-move simulation" even while step 3 is still verifying the input on tape $k + 3$. Clearly, $x \in L(M)$ if and only if there is a computation of N for which $x_2 = y_2$, $x_1 = y_1$, and N accepts x.

Assume that $d \geq 3$. Let $n = |x|$, and consider an accepting computation of N for which $|x_1| = \lceil 3n/d \rceil$. Recall that process 1 took $|x_1| = \lceil 3n/d \rceil$ steps. Since process 2 actually wrote $\overline{x}$, process 2 took $\lceil n/d \rceil$ steps to guess y and $\lceil |y_2|/d \rceil$ steps to position heads $k + 2$ and $k + 3$. Thus, the initial phase takes

$$\max(|x_1|, (n + |y_2|)/d + O(1)) = |x_1|$$

steps for sufficiently large n.

Process 3 takes $\leq |x_2|$ steps. Process 4 takes $\leq \lceil |x_1|/d \rceil$ steps to check that $x_1 = y_1$, and, of course, the 8-move simulation takes $\lceil 8T(n)/d \rceil$ steps. So, process 4 takes $\leq \lceil |x_1|/d \rceil + \lceil 8T(n)/d \rceil$ steps. Thus, the final phase takes

$$1 + \max(|x_2|, |x_1|/d + 8T(n)/d + O(1))$$

steps. (Note that it takes one step at the end to enter an accepting or nonaccepting state.)

Now, let us calculate, for sufficiently large n, the total time T_N:

$$T_N \leq |x_1| + 1 + \max(|x_2|, |x_1|/d + 8T(n)/d + O(1))$$
$$\leq 1 + \max(n, |x_1| + |x_1|/d + 8T(n)/d + O(1))$$
$$\leq 1 + \max(n, 3n/d + |x_1|/d + 8T(n)/d + O(1))$$
$$\text{(because } |x_1| \leq \lceil 3n/d \rceil)$$

$$\leq 1 + \max(n, 12T(n)/d + O(1)).$$

The last inequality holds because $|x_1| \leq n \leq T(n)$.
Thus, we choose $d > 12/c$ in order to obtain

$$\max(n + 1, cT(n))$$

for all sufficiently large n. $\square$

Corollary 5.4 $\text{NTIME}(n + 1) = \text{NTIME}(O(n))$.

Proof. We know already that $\text{NTIME}(O(n)) = \text{NTIME}(2n)$. Let $c = 1/2$. If M is any $2n$ time-bounded Turing machine, Theorem 5.3 gives a nondeterministic Turing machine N that accepts a word x if and only if *some* computation of N accepts x within $\max(n + 1, n) = n + 1$ steps. This by itself does not yield our result because we need to know that *all* computations of N terminate in $n+1$ steps. We can obtain this condition for the special case that $T(n) = 2n$ and $c = 1/2$. In fact, observing that the input head of N moves to the right only, let us stipulate that the input head moves one cell to the right every step and that the computation of N halts when the input head reads the first blank after the input word. This stipulation does not affect N's computation on the correct nondeterministically guessed accepting computation. Thus, $L(N) = L(M)$ and N runs in time $n + 1$.
$\square$

5.2   Constructible Functions

A function $S(n)$ is *space-constructible* if there is an $S(n)$ space-bounded Turing machine M such that for each n there is some input of length n on which M uses exactly $S(n)$ cells. A function $S(n)$ is *fully space-constructible* if, in addition, on every input of length n, M uses exactly $S(n)$ cells.

A function $T(n)$ is *time-constructible* if there is a $T(n)$ time-bounded Turing machine M such that for each n there is some input of length n on which M runs for exactly $T(n)$ steps. A function $T(n)$ is *fully time-constructible* if, in addition, on every input of length n, M runs for exactly $T(n)$ steps.

The usefulness of constructible functions will become clear as we proceed. The following homework exercise demonstrates that the functions in which we are interested primarily (those that are either space bounds or time bounds for the complexity classes that we named in the previous chapter) are constructible.

Homework 5.2   *Show the following:*

1. *the functions*

   $$\log(n), n^k, 2^n, \text{ and } n!$$

   are space-constructible and, with the exception of $\log n$, *time-constructible;*
2. *if* $S_1(n)$ *and* $S_2(n)$ *are space-constructible, then so are* $S_1(n)S_2(n)$, $2^{S_1(n)}$, *and* $S_1(n)^{S_2(n)}$;

3. *if $T_1(n)$ and $T_2(n)$ are time-constructible, then so are are $T_1(n)T_2(n)$, $2^{T_1(n)}$, and $T_1(n)^{T_2(n)}$.*

Homework 5.3   *Show that space-constructible implies fully space-constructible for space bounds $S(n)$ such that $S(n) \geq n$. Hint: On an input word of length n, use a separate tape to cycle through all input words of length n.*

5.2.1   Simultaneous Simulation

Here we will show that the decisions we made when defining nondeterministic complexity classes do not matter for the classes that we are most interested in. At the same time, we will illustrate the usefulness of constructible functions. First we show that if $S(n)$ is a fully space-constructible function, then, in the definition of NSPACE($S(n)$), it does not matter whether we insist that all paths are $S(n)$ space-bounded or whether only some path must be $S(n)$ space-bounded. More precisely, we claim that the following proposition holds.

Proposition 5.1   *If $S(n)$ is fully space-constructible, then $L \in$ NSPACE($S(n)$) if and only if there is a nondeterministic Turing machine N that accepts L such that for every word x of length n that belongs to L, there is an accepting computation of N on input x that uses no more than $S(n)$ cells on any work tape.*

Proof. The proof from left to right is trivial: Namely, if $L \in$ NSPACE($S(n)$), then, by definition, there is a nondeterministic Turing machine N that accepts L that uses at most $S(n)$ tape cells in every computation. Thus, the restriction that N uses no more than $S(n)$ cells on words x of length n that belong to L certainly holds.

Now assume that L is accepted by a nondeterministic Turing machine for which this property holds. We will prove that $L \in$ NSPACE($S(n)$) by showing that there is another nondeterministic Turing machine N' that accepts L that uses no more than $S(n)$ space on every computation: Using the proof technique of Theorem 5.1 (enlarge the tape alphabet to replace k tapes by one tape with k tracks), there is a one-tape Turing machine N that accepts L such that the same property holds. Define N' so that on an input word x of length n, it first runs the space constructor on x and marks on its work tape all the cells that the space constructor visits on this input. Then N' simulates N on input x within the marked region of the work tape. However, if N' ever attempts to leave the marked region, then it halts without accepting. Thus, since the space constructor is $S(n)$ space-bounded, so is N'. If N reaches an accepting state without leaving the marked region, then N' accepts. Since the space constructor marks $S(n)$ cells and since, for every word x of length n that belongs to L, there is an accepting computation of N on input x that uses no more than $S(n)$ cells, N' accepts L. $\square$

If $T(n)$ is fully time-constructible, then we can make the analogous claim for NTIME($T(n)$) but we need a more complicated analysis. Recall that a function

$T(n)$ is fully time-constructible if there is a $T(n)$ time-bounded Turing machine M that on every input of length n runs for exactly $T(n)$ steps. A Turing machine that runs for exactly $T(n)$ steps on every input of length n is called a "$T(n)$-clock," and we denote this by C_T.

Let $T(n)$ be a fully time-constructible function and let M be an arbitrary Turing machine. In several applications we will want to construct a Turing machine $M' = M \| C_T$ that simultaneously simulates M and a $T(n)$-clock C_T. M' should have the property that it is $T(n)$ time-bounded and that it accepts an input word x if and only if M accepts x within $T(|x|)$ steps. The difficulty in constructing M' is that C_T and M might access the input word differently. That is, at some ith step $(i > 0)$ of a computation C_T might expect its read/write head to be acting on a different symbol of the input word than M is currently acting on. The simplest solution to this problem is to have two copies of the input word available. M' begins its computation with the input word x in cells 1 through $|x|$ on tape 1 with the head scanning cell 1. Tape 2 is blank and its head is also scanning cell 1. M' begins its computation by copying x from tape 1 to tape 2, moving both heads from left to right, and then returns both heads to the starting position. This takes $2(|x| + 1)$ steps. Then M' begins its simultaneous simulation of C_T and M. Thus, in order to simulate $T(n)$ moves of M, M' may require $2(|x| + 1) + T(n)$ steps. Since by convention $T(n) \geq n + 1$, we see that for some constant $c > 0$, M' is $cT(n)$ time-bounded. If $n \in o(T(n))$, then Theorem 5.2 yields a Turing machine M'' that is $T(n)$ time-bounded and that accepts the same language as M'. If $T(n)$ is bounded by a linear function, then Corollary 5.4 yields a machine M'' that accepts the same language as M' and that runs in time $n + 1$. In either case, since M' accepts a word x if and only if M accepts x within $T(|x|)$ steps, so does M''. Suppose that $T(n)$ is a fully time-constructible function such that either $n \in o(T(n))$ or $T(n)$ is bounded by a linear function, and suppose that N is a nondeterministic Turing machine that accepts a language L such that for every word x of length n that belongs to L, the number of steps in the shortest accepting computation of N on input x is at most $T(n)$. Let $N' = N \| C_T$. Then, the Turing machine N'' that results either from Theorem 5.2 or Corollary 5.4 is $T(n)$ time-bounded and accepts an input word x if and only if some computation of N accepts x within $T(|x|)$ steps. That is, N'' accepts L.

All the time bounds in which we are interested satisfy one of the conditions, either $n \in o(T(n))$ or $T(n)$ is bounded by a linear function. For these, the construction that we just described works fine. However, fully time-constructible functions that do not satisfy either of these properties exist.

Homework 5.4   *Give examples of fully time-constructible functions $T(n)$ that do not satisfy these properties.*

The following theorem asserts the result we want for all fully time-constructible functions. This result is probably known, but it was communicated to the authors by Regan [Reg].

Theorem 5.4 *If $T(n)$ is fully time-constructible, then $L \in \mathrm{NTIME}(T(n))$ if and only if there is a nondeterministic Turing machine N that accepts L such that for every word x of length n that belongs to L, the number of steps in the shortest accepting computation of N on input x is at most $T(n)$.*

Proof. As was the case for Proposition 5.1, the proof of this result from left to right is trivial. We describe the proof from right to left. Noting that the extra cost incurred in the fundamental simultaneous simulation is the cost of copying the input to a new tape, the idea of the proof is to use the technique in the proof of Theorem 5.3 to guess and verify a copy of the input in compressed form while the simultaneous simulation is taking place. Specifically, let M be a nondeterministic Turing machine that accepts L such that, for every word x of length n that belongs to L, the number of steps in the shortest accepting computation of M on input x is at most $T(n)$. We will show that $L \in \mathrm{NTIME}(T(n))$. Let $C = C_T$ be a Turing-machine "clock" that runs exactly $T(n)$ steps on every input of length n. Let $c = 1/3$ and, as in the proof of Theorem 5.3, choose $d > 12/c$ (i.e., choose $d > 36$). Now we will implement a variation of the construction in the proof of Theorem 5.3 in order to define a new machine N in which one symbol of N will compress d symbols of M. N simulates M and C simultaneously in compressed form, in two stages and possibly a little bit more.

Let x be an input word to N. In stage 1, N uses three new tapes to guess the compressed input word $\overline{x}$. With one addition, N does this exactly as before. The addition is that N also writes its guess of the input word on tape $k+4$. Thus, at the end of stage 1, tape $k+1$ contains a prefix $\overline{x_1}$ of the input word in compressed form and tapes $k+2$, $k+3$, and $k+4$ contain a string $\overline{y_1 y_2}$.

In stage 2, N runs the following processes simultaneously:

1. As before, N uses tapes 1, $k+1$, $k+2$, and $k+3$ to verify that the guess $\overline{y_1 y_2}$ is correct.
2. After verifying that $\overline{x_1} = \overline{y_1}$, N begins the "8-move simulation" of the linear speedup theorem of M with the compressed input string on tape $k+3$ and N begins the "8-move simulation" of the linear speedup theorem of C with the same compressed input string on tape $k+4$.

We stipulate that stage 2 of N ends when the input head reaches the first blank after reading the input. That is, stage 2 ends when its first process is complete. Recall that this takes exactly $n+1$ steps.

If the simulation of C halts by the end of stage 2, then, because $c = 1/3$, $T(|x|) \le 3|x|$. Thus, in this case, N halts. If M accepts x and N has guessed well, then N will have found an accepting computation of M. Now comes the little bit more: Otherwise, N continues the "8-move simulations" of both C and M until C halts, and then N halts. Observe, in this case, that N is simultaneously simulating M and C for $T(n)$ steps. As in the previous case, if M accepts x and N has guessed well, then N will have found an accepting computation of M. Moreover, the running time of N is this case is only $cT(|x|)$.

Finally, let us observe that N runs for no more than $T(n)$ steps on every input of length n, and this completes the proof. ☐

A central and unifying theme in complexity theory is the problem of determining the exact power of nondeterminism. For most of the time bounds and space bounds we study, the question is open, but for linear time the following results are known. Since DTIME(n) is a proper subset of DTIME($2n$), and DTIME($2n$) ⊆ NTIME($2n$) = NTIME(n), it follows that DTIME(n) ≠ NTIME(n). In 1983, Paul, Pippenger, Szemerédi obtained the striking and deep result that DTIME($O(n)$) ≠ NTIME($O(n)$).

5.3   Tape Reduction

In this section we present results on tape reduction for time-bounded Turing machines. The first theorem is proved using the same "k tracks for k tapes" technique as in the space reduction theorem.

Theorem 5.5   **([HS65])** *Let M be a k-tape $T(n)$ time-bounded Turing machine such that $n \in o(T(n))$. There is a one-tape $T^2(n)$ time-bounded Turing machine N such that $L(N) = L(M)$. Furthermore, if M is deterministic, then so is N.*

Proof. We use the one-tape simulation given in the proof of the space compression theorem: N has one tape; this tape is viewed as consisting of k tracks, with one composite symbol of N representing k symbols of M.

Since all heads of M begin at the leftmost cell of M's tapes, after i moves of M, the heads of M can be at most i cells apart. Recall that a "move" of N consists of a sweep left followed by a sweep right. We see that it takes at most $2(i + 1)$ steps of N to simulate the $(i + 1)$st move of M. Thus, for every positive integer t, it takes

$$\sum_{i=1}^{t} 2i = O(t^2)$$

moves of N to simulate t moves of M.

At this point, we see that M can be replaced by an equivalent $O(T^2(n))$ one-tape Turing machine. However, we may apply the linear speedup theorem to M before applying the above simulation so that the resulting one-tape Turing machine N is $T^2(n)$ time-bounded. ☐

This is the best result possible, for it is known [HU79] that the language

$$L = \{wcw^r \mid w \in \{0, 1\}^* \},$$

where c is a symbol not belonging to $\{0, 1\}^*$, cannot be accepted by any one-tape Turing machine of time complexity $T(n)$ unless $\sup_{n \to \infty} T(n)/n^2 > 0$.

Homework 5.5   *Show that L can be recognized by a deterministic two-tape Turing machine in linear time.*

On the one hand, Theorem 5.5 is an important result because it is part of the illustration that computing models are equivalent within polynomial time. On the other hand, because of the quadratic slowdown, one-tape Turing machines are frequently considered of limited interest. If we restrict ourselves to two tapes, there is a classic simulation of k tapes by a two-tape Turing machine due to Hennie and Stearns [HS66], where the simulation is slower by a logarithmic factor. The following result of Pippenger and Fischer [PF79] yields a two-tape "oblivious" Turing machine with the same time bound as the result of Hennie and Stearns. The proof is long, but the algorithm is clever and the result is important.

Definition 5.1   *A Turing machine is* oblivious *if the sequence of head moves on the Turing machine's tapes is the same for all input words of the same length. That is, for $t \geq 1$, the position of each of the heads after t moves on an input word x depends on t and $|x|$, but not on x.*

Oblivious Turing machines idealize certain kinds of oblivious algorithms, for example, searching a file sequentially, which depends on the size of the file but not its contents.

Theorem 5.6   **([PF79])** *If L is accepted by a k-tape $T(n)$ time-bounded Turing machine M, then L is accepted by an oblivious two-tape Turing machine N in time $O(T(n) \log T(n))$. Furthermore, if M is deterministic, then so is N.*

Before describing the proof, we state the following corollary, which is the result of Hennie and Stearns [HS66].

Corollary 5.5   *If L is accepted by a k-tape $T(n)$ time-bounded Turing machine M, then L is accepted by a two-tape Turing machine N' in time $T(n) \log T(n)$. Furthermore, if M is deterministic, then so is N'.*

The proof of the corollary is immediate. As $n \in o(T(n) \log T(n))$, we obtain N' by applying to N the linear speedup theorem, Theorem 5.2. Of course, N' is no longer oblivious. In this chapter we will require only the corollary. However, the fact that N is oblivious will be useful for the study of families of Boolean circuits.*

Homework 5.6   *The proof of the next theorem constructs a Turing machine with a two-way infinite tape. Show that if a language L is accepted in time $T(n)$ by a Turing machine M with a two-way infinite tape, then L is accepted in time $T(n)$ by a Turing machine with a one-way infinite tape.*

---

*We will learn about Boolean circuits in Part II of this book, which the authors are currently writing.

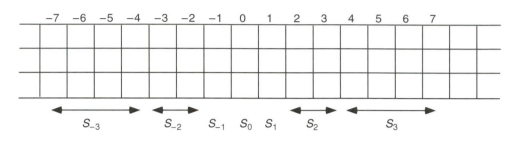

FIGURE 5.3. Three tracks of N grouped into segments.

Proof. We assume that M contains two-way infinite tapes, and so will N. One tape of N will consist of tracks that encode the k tapes of M. The other tape of N will support various bookkeeping and auxiliary memory activities. Let us focus on tape 1 of N. Tape 1 has $3k$ tracks, three tracks for each tape of M. We introduce a new symbol # that does not belong to M's tape alphabet Γ. # will be used as a marker. Each cell of tape 1 of N holds a composite symbol that represents $3k$ symbols of $\Gamma \cup \{\#\}$. The cells of tape 1 are labeled by the integers. Unlike all previous simulations, N does not simulate M by moving head markers; rather, N moves data. In particular, the storage symbols that are scanned by M's heads are always in cell 0. When the head of one of M's tapes moves left (say), the entire contents of this tape, on its tracks in tape 1 of N, are shifted right, so that the scanned symbol on M's tape is in cell 0 of N's tape 1. This, by itself, would still result in an $O(T^2(n))$ simulation. The clever idea that improves the running time is to divide the information on the tape into blocks. Blocks near the origin (cell 0) are small, but they double in size as they get farther from the origin. The information in the small blocks that are close to the origin will be moved often, but the data in larger blocks that are far from the origin will rarely be moved.

First we divide the tape into segments S_i. The length of each segment grows exponentially in size, with $\|S_i\| = \|S_{-i}\| = 2^{i-1}$ for $i \geq 1$. There is a marker between each segment, but it does not actually appear until the segment is used. Segment S_0 is cell 0 of N. Segment S_1 is cell 1 of N. Segment S_2 consists of cells 2 and 3 of N. In general, segment S_j consists of cells

$$[2^{j-1}, 2^j) = \{2^{j-1}, 2^{j-1} + 1, \ldots, 2^j - 1\},$$

and segment S_{-j} consists of $(-2^j, -2^{j-1}]$. This is illustrated in Fig. 5.3.

Now we are ready to say what the blocks are. Consider the three tracks of N's tape 1 that represent some work tape T of M. Given a segment S_i, let block B_i^1 be the lower track of S_i, let block B_i^2 be the middle track of S_i, and let block B_i^3 be the upper track of S_i. A segment, therefore, is the union of its three blocks. A block is called *empty* if it contains only #'s and is called *full* if it contains no #. A segment is *empty* if each of its blocks is empty and is *full* if each of its blocks is full. We define a segment to be *clean* if the number of its full blocks is either one or two.

Initially, when N begins its simulation, tracks 2 and 3 contain the marker #
and track 1 contains the contents of T. Thus, when N scans the symbol a of M
for the first time, it reads the composite symbol $(a, \#, \#)$. Initially all blocks are
either full or empty, and all segments are clean.

We will define a procedure sim that simulates one step of the computation
of M on an input of length n. Because M is $T(n)$ time-bounded, N stops operating after it executes sim $T(n)$ times. N's operation, however, is more complicated than this. In order to move data in blocks efficiently, we need to use empty
blocks as buffers. For this reason certain segments need to be clean prior to executions of sim. Execution of sim might not leave segments clean, so we have
to define a procedure clean(k) with an integer parameter k. Clean(k) cleans segments S_{-k} and S_k. For each t, $1 \leq t < T(n)$, the tth execution of sim is followed
by clean$(1), \ldots,$ clean(l_t), for $l_t = \max\{m \mid 2^{m-1} \text{ divides } t\}$, prior to the next
execution of sim. Think of the simulation as a sequence of *stages*, where, for
$1 \leq t < T(n)$, stage t consists of the tth execution of sim followed by execution of clean$(1), \ldots,$ clean(l_t). We manage this requirement by using one track
on tape 2 to count executions of sim in binary. Observe that it easy to determine
from this value which clean(k) procedures need to be performed: Just count the
number of rightmost zeros and add 1. Note also that these actions on tape 2 are
oblivious.

We assume as induction hypotheses that the following conditions hold:

- Conditions 1 to 3 hold at the beginning of each execution of either sim or
  clean(k), $k \geq 1$.

  1. Each block is full or empty.
  2. The contents of each block represent consecutive cells of T. If $i < j$,
     then a block in segment S_i represents cells to the left of those in any
     block in S_j. If $i \geq 0$, then B_i^1 represents cells to the left of B_i^2, and
     B_i^2 represents cells to the left of B_i^3. If $i < 0$, then the opposite holds,
     that is, B_i^3 represents cells to the left of B_i^2, and B_i^2 represents cells
     to the left of B_i^1.
  3. The head of N scans cell 0, which is segment S_0. Block B_0^1 contains
     the symbol that M's head is scanning on tape T. Block B_0^3 is empty.

- For $1 \leq t < T(n)$, at the beginning of the tth execution of sim, segments

  $$S_{-l_{(t-1)}}, \ldots, S_{l_{(t-1)}}$$

  are clean.

- An execution of clean(k) visits at most segments $S_{-(k+1)}, \ldots, S_{(k+1)}$ and
  increases or decreases the number of full blocks of $S_{-(k+1)}$ and $S_{(k+1)}$ by at
  most 1.

Note that the induction hypotheses hold before the first execution of sim.

Sim operates as follows. Suppose that the current state of M is q, that the head of tape T is scanning symbol a, and that $\delta_M(q, a) = (q', a', D)$. N has state q stored in its finite control before this execution of sim and replaces this with q'. If $D = L$, then N needs to move data to the right, and if $D = R$, then N needs to move data to the left. Nevertheless, it it will be easy to see that sim can perform its tasks obliviously. Suppose that $D = L$. By the induction hypotheses, segments S_{-1}, S_0, and S_1 are clean. N copies the symbol in block B_0^2 into B_0^3, and then writes a' into B_0^2. Next, N writes the symbol in the full block of S_{-1} that is closest to the origin into B_0^1, and replaces the symbol in that block with #. (That is, if B_{-1}^j, $1 \leq j \leq 3$, is the only full block in segment S_{-1} that is full, or if B_{-1}^j and $B_{-1}^{j'}$ are both full and $1 \leq j < j' \leq 3$, then N writes the symbol in B_{-1}^j into B_0^1, and writes # into B_{-1}^j.) Finally, to ensure that S_0 is clean after execution of sim, if segment S_0 is now full, then N needs to move the symbol in B_0^3 into segment S_1. This is easy to accomplish because S_1 contains at least one empty block. If B_1^1 is empty, then N moves the contents of B_0^3 into B_1^1 (i.e., copies the symbol in B_0^3 into B_1^1 and writes # into B_0^3). Otherwise, N moves data in S_1 upward in order to free up block B_1^1. (This is easy to do. Either B_1^2 is empty or it is full, and students should consider both cases.) If $D = R$, then N moves similarly to shift data to the left. This completes the description of sim, except that in order to have the procedure oblivious, the head will simulate the actions that need to take place for both $D = L$ and $D = R$, but N will perform only the actions that are correct. Observe that S_{-1}, S_0, and S_1 are the only segments that are visited during execution of sim. After execution, S_0 is clean, but S_{-1} and S_1 might not be clean.

Now we explain clean(k). Using a separate track on tape 2, N counts the distance to the first cell of S_k. When it completes its work at S_k, it moves to the first cell of S_{-k}, cleans that segment, and then returns to the origin. The actions that take place at S_k depend on whether the segment is already clean, empty, or full. However, in order to make the procedure oblivious, the head simulates all cases. If S_k is clean, nothing is done. If all blocks of S_k are empty, then the procedure *moves* the contents of the full block of S_{k+1} that is closest to S_k into blocks B_k^1 and B_k^2. Let us note some details: We prove as a separate claim below that clean(k) can carry out the actions that it needs to, so there is a full block B_{k+1}^j to move. B_{k+1}^j contains twice the number of cells as the blocks of S_k, so this action leaves S_k with two full blocks. Finally, we stress that moving symbols from a block leaves the block empty. If all blocks of S_k are full, then N concatenates the contents of blocks B_k^2 and B_k^3 and moves them into B_{k+1}^1. In order to do this, if B_{k+1}^1 is empty, then N copies the contents of B_{k+1}^1 into B_{k+1}^2. Otherwise, N first copies the contents of B_{k+1}^2 into B_{k+1}^3 and then copies the contents of B_{k+1}^1 into B_{k+1}^2.

To copy the contents of a block from one segment into another, N copies the data to a separate track of tape 2 (just as they would appear in tape T) and then copies from tape 2 to the target segment. The three tracks of tape 2 that we have described and the different actions that take place on these tracks occur during the execution of different procedures, so all head movements on tape 2 are oblivious.

It is straightforward to see that the relevant induction hypotheses hold after execution of clean(k). Now we will show that clean(k) can perform the steps that it needs to:

Claim 1   *For each t, $1 \le t < T(n)$, if* clean(k) *is executed at stage t, then*

> *(i) if S_k (S_{-k}) is empty, then S_{k+1} ($S_{-(k+1)}$) contains a full block, and*
>
> *(ii) if S_k (S_{-k}) is full, then S_{k+1} ($S_{-(k+1)}$) contains an empty block.*

Proof. Since all segments are clean before N begins its simulation, the conditions clearly hold at time $t = 1$. Suppose that $t \ge 1$, that N executes clean(k) at stage t, and that clean(k) successfully carries out it actions at this stage. We need to prove that conditions (i) and (ii) hold the next time that clean(k) is executed.

Note that $k \le l_t$. If $k < l_t$, then N executes clean($k + 1$) immediately after executing clean(k), so S_{k+1} will be clean the next time that N executes clean(k). Therefore, assume that $k = l_t$. By definition of l_t, $t = m2^{k-1}$, where m is odd. N next executes clean(k) at stage

$$t_1 = t + 2^{k-1}$$
$$= m2^{k-1} + 2^{k-1}$$
$$= (m + 1)2^{k-1}.$$

(However, $m + 1$ is even, so N executes clean($k + 1$) at stage t_1 also.) We need to show that conditions (i) and (ii) hold when N attempts to clean S_k at stage t_1. Consider the actions that take place when N cleans S_k at stage t that might interfere with conditions (i) and (ii) holding at stage t_1. If S_k is full prior to execution of clean(k) at stage t, then, after execution, S_k has one full block and two empty blocks, and S_{k+1} might be full. This can be a problem only if S_k is full at stage t_1, but that cannot happen: It requires at least 2^k executions of sim to fill two blocks of S_k, but N simulates only 2^{k-1} moves of M between stages t and t_1. The other possibility that we must eliminate is that S_k and S_{k+1} are both empty at stage t_1. If S_{k+1} is empty at stage t_1, it is because S_k is empty at stage t, for which reason N moves one full block from S_{k+1} into two full blocks of S_k. Thus, in this case, after execution of clean(k) at stage t, S_k has two full blocks. Now, just as in the previous case, we see that it is impossible for S_k to be empty at stage t_1: It requires at least 2^k simulations of sim to empty two blocks of S_k.

The argument for S_{-k} is identical, so the proof of the claim is complete.   □

Our discussion demonstrates that N accepts L and that N is oblivious. Now we must determine N's running time. Each execution of sim takes time $O(1)$ and sim executes $T(n)$ times. An execution of clean(k) takes $O(2^k)$ steps, because moving takes a number of steps proportional to the number of symbols moved. As we have seen already, there must be at least 2^{k-1} stages between consecutive executions of clean(k). (If clean(k) executes as stage t, then $k \leq l_t$, so N executes clean(k) next at stage $t + 2^{k-1}$.) Also, N does not perform clean(k) for the first time until stage 2^{k-1}. Thus, for each k, N executes clean(k) at most $T(n)/2^{k-1}$ times, and each costs $O(2^k)$. The largest value of k such that N executes clean(k) is

$$m = \log T(n) + 1.$$

Thus, the number $T_N(n)$ of moves N makes is given as follows:

$$T_N(n) \leq \sum_{i=1}^{m} \frac{T(n)O(2^i)}{2^{i-1}}$$
$$\leq c2T(n)[\log T(n) + 1]$$
$$\leq 4cT(n) \log T(n),$$

where c is a constant. This completes the proof. $\qquad\square$

Homework 5.7 *Let M be a Turing machine, the details of which are unnecessary to specify, except to say that on one of its tapes M always moves left, replaces the symbol a that it currently scans by the symbol a', and remains in the same state. Give N's simulation for this tape of the first four stages. Present your answer as a sequence of drawings.*

The next result [BGW70] shows that a two-tape nondeterministic machine can simulate a k-tape machine with a time loss of only a multiplicative constant. The proof we give here is due to Seiferas, Fischer, and Meyer [SFM78].

Theorem 5.7 **([BGW70])** *If L is accepted by a k-tape $T(n)$ time-bounded nondeterministic Turing machine M, then there are a constant $c > 0$ and a two-tape nondeterministic Turing machine N that accepts L such that for each word $x \in L$, the number of steps in the shortest computation of N on x is at most $cT(n)$.*

Proof. Define the "display" of a configuration of a k-tape Turing machine M to be a $k + 1$-tuple consisting of the current state and the k tape symbols scanned in the configuration. The display of a configuration determines whether the configuration is an accepting one and if it is not, determines what actions of M are legal as the next move. We design N to behave as follows: N nondeterministically guesses on its second tape an alternating sequence of displays and legal actions by M. Observe that this sequence describes a legal computation by M on the given input if and only if the symbols that are actually scanned on each tape when the actions are taken agree with the guessed displays. This can be checked independently for each tape in turn by letting the first tape of N play the role of the tape to be checked while running through the guessed sequence of displays and actions.

Clearly, each check takes time proportional to the length of the guessed sequence. Since there are k checks, the total running time of N is proportional to the length of the guessed check. $\qquad\square$

5.4   Inclusion Relationships

Now we survey the known inclusion relationships between time-bounded and space-bounded, deterministic, and nondeterministic classes.

Our first theorem requires no proof.

Theorem 5.8   *For every function f,*

$$\mathrm{DTIME}(f) \subseteq \mathrm{DSPACE}(f)$$

and

$$\mathrm{NTIME}(f) \subseteq \mathrm{NSPACE}(f).$$

A Turing machine might enter an infinite loop and still use only bounded space. Nevertheless, the next theorem shows that if a language L is accepted by an $S(n)$ space-bounded Turing machine, where $S(n) \geq \log(n)$, then L is accepted by an $S(n)$ space-bounded Turing machine that halts on every input. The proof depends on the observation that within space $S(n)$ a Turing machine can enter at most an exponential in $S(n)$ possible distinct configurations. A machine enters an infinite loop by repeating one of these configurations, thus making loop detection possible.

Lemma 5.1   *Let M be a one-tape $S(n)$ space-bounded Turing machine, where $S(n) \geq \log n$. Define the* length *of a configuration I of M to be the length of the work tape of M in configuration I. There exists a constant k such that for each n and each l, $\log n \leq l \leq S(n)$, the number of different configurations of M having length l on any input of length n is at most k^l. In particular, the number of different configurations of M on any input of length n is at most $k^{S(n)}$.*

Proof. Assume that M has s states and t tape symbols. A configuration I of M of length l consists of

    (i)   the input head position (at most $n + 1$),
    (ii)   the tape head position (at most l),
    (iii)   the current state (at most s), and
    (iv)   the tape contents (at most t^l).

Thus, M has at most $(n + 1)slt^l$ different configurations.

We claim that there is a constant k such that for all $n \geq 1$ and $\log n \leq l \leq S(n)$,

$$k^l \geq (n+1)slt^l.$$

We will not prove the claim in detail, but simply note that the key is the following sequence of inequalities: Suppose c and d are constants;

$$\begin{aligned}
n^c d^l &= 2^{c \log n} d^l \\
&= 2^{c \log n} 2^{d_1 l}, \quad \text{for some } d_1 \\
&= 2^{c \log n + d_1 l} \\
&\leq 2^{cl + d_1 l}, \quad \text{since } \log n \leq l \\
&= k^l, \quad \text{for some } k.
\end{aligned}$$

Using Lemma 5.1, the following theorem is obtained easily.

Theorem 5.9 **([HU69])** *If L is accepted by an $S(n)$ space-bounded Turing machine, $S(n) \geq \log n$, then L is accepted by an $S(n)$ space-bounded Turing machine that halts on every input.*

Proof. Let M be a one-tape $S(n)$ space-bounded off-line Turing machine that accepts L. Let k be the constant guaranteed by Lemma 5.1. We design a Turing machine N to simulate M but to shut off after $k^{S(n)}$ moves. N simulates M on one track and at the same time counts in base k on another track, thereby using no more than $S(n)$ space to count to $k^{S(n)}$. More generally, for each length $\log n \leq l \leq S(n)$, N uses no more than space l to count to k^l.

N initially assigns $\log n$ space to the counter. Whenever M scans a new cell beyond the cells containing the counter, increase the counter length by 1. Suppose M repeats some configuration. Then, this must occur with M using only some l cells, where $l \leq S(n)$. Thus, by Lemma 5.1, this looping will eventually be detected because the counter will not be large enough to hold the count. Since M is $S(n)$ space-bounded, the largest the counter can be is $S(n)$, which is large enough to hold the count of all of M's accepting computations. Thus, $L(N) = L(M)$. $\square$

Corollary 5.6 $\mathrm{DSPACE}(S(n)) \subseteq \bigcup \{\mathrm{DTIME}(c^{S(n)}) \mid c \geq 1\}$,
for $S(n) \geq \log(n)$.

The next result improves one of the assertions of Theorem 5.8.

Theorem 5.10 $\mathrm{NTIME}(T(n)) \subseteq \mathrm{DSPACE}(T(n))$.

Recall the breadth-first search in the proof of Theorem 2.3: To prove Theorem 5.10, we need to to observe that if we are given a $T(n)$ time-bounded nondeterministic Turing machine, then the deterministic Turing machine that performs the breadth-first search simulation is $T(n)$ space-bounded.

Proof. Let L be accepted by k-tape Turing machine N in time $T(n)$. As in the proof of Theorem 2.3, let b be the largest number of choices given by N's transition function. Assign addresses to each node of N's computation tree as we did earlier. Since each computation path of N on an input of length n is bounded by $T(n)$, all computation paths will terminate within $T(n)$ steps, and every address has length less than or equal to $T(n)$.

Define M to be an off-line Turing machine with at least $k + 1$ tapes and possibly one more. In order for the breadth-first search algorithm to terminate correctly, it needs to recognize two cases: when N has an accepting path, and when all paths terminate in a nonaccepting configuration. The first case is straightforward. The algorithm uses a Boolean flag to detect the second case. The flag is initialized to 0. When the breadth-first search visits the address of a nonterminating configuration, then the flag is changed to 1. After M visits all nodes at a given level in the computation tree, it continues to the next level if the value of the flag is 1 and terminates in the reject state if the flag is set to 0. (The details of how the flag is implemented are not important. We could keep this stored in the finite control of M or on a separate tape. Let's not allow implementation details get in the way of understanding or appreciating the algorithm. With this in mind, we continue as follows.) Turing machine M uses tape $k + 1$ to record N's location in the computation tree. The computation proceeds as follows:

1. Initially the input tape contains the input word w, all other tapes are empty, and the flag is set to 0.

2. M copies the input w to tape 1.

3. M simulates N on tapes 1 through k using the string on tape $k + 1$ to determine which choices to make. If this string does not provide M with a valid simulation, then M aborts this branch and goes to step 4. Otherwise, the string on tape $k + 1$ provides M with a valid simulation. If this simulation reaches an accepting configuration, then M halts and accepts. If the simulation reaches a nonaccepting halting configuration, then M aborts this branch and goes to step 4. If the simulation terminates in a nonhalting configuration, then M sets the flag to 1, aborts this branch, and goes to step 4.

4. Let x be the current string on tape $k + 1$, let $l = |x|$, and let $x + 1$ denote the lexicographically next string after x. If the length of $x + 1$ is greater than l and the flag is set to 0, then M halts and rejects, for in the case there are no computation paths of length greater than l. If the length of $x + 1$ is greater than l and the flag is set to 1, then M sets the flag to 0, replaces the string on tape 3 with $x + 1$, and returns to step 2. If the length of $x + 1$ is equal to l, then M replaces the string on tape 3 with $x + 1$ and returns to step 2.

It is clear that M correctly simulates N. Since N is $T(n)$ time-bounded, tapes 1 through k use no more than $T(n)$ cells. Furthermore, since all computation paths terminate within $T(n)$ steps, tape $k+1$ uses no more than $T(n)$ cells. Therefore (using Corollary 5.1), $L \in \text{DSPACE}(T(n))$.   □

Corollary 5.7 $\text{NP} \subseteq \text{PSPACE}$.

The following theorem is a corollary of Theorem 5.10, because there are at most $b^{T(n)}$ distinct computation paths and each path takes at most $T(n)$ steps. Nevertheless, it is instructive to give a proof that is based on a depth-first search of the computation tree, because this will introduce ideas that we will continue to use in later proofs.

Theorem 5.11 $\text{NTIME}(T(n)) \subseteq \bigcup \{\text{DTIME}(c^{T(n)}) \mid c \geq 1\}$.

Proof. Let L be accepted by M in time $T(n)$. Assume that M is a k-tape on-line nondeterministic Turing machine with s states and t tape symbols. A configuration of M consists of

    (i) the current state (at most s),

    (ii) the position of each tape head (at most $(T(n)+1)^k$), and

    (iii) the tape contents (at most $t^{kT(n)}$).

Thus, M has at most $s(T(n)+1)^k t^{kT(n)}$ different configurations. A computation similar to the one in the proof of Lemma 5.1 shows that there exists a constant d such that

$$s(T(n)+1)^k t^{kT(n)} \leq d^{T(n)}$$

for all $n > 0$.

We design a Turing machine N to behave as follows. Let I_0 denote the initial configuration of M. N executes the following procedure in order to make a list of all configurations that M can reach from I_0:

> place I_0 on the list;
> **repeat**
>   **for** each configuration I on the list **do**
>   place all configurations I' on the list
>   that M can reach in one move
>   and that are not already on the list
>   **until** for each I on the list, no such I' exists.

This procedure can be carried out in time $O((\text{length of the list})^2)$ on a RAM, so for some constant c, we can design N to carry out this procedure in time (length of the list)^c. The length of the list is $\leq d^{T(n)} * $ (the length of a configuration), and the length of a configuration is bounded by some polynomial in $T(n)$. Finally, $O(1)^{T(n)} T(n)^{O(1)} = O(1)^{T(n)}$.

N is to accept its input if and only if it places an accepting configuration on the list. Since N makes no more than $O(1)^{T(n)}$ moves on any input, the result is proved.   □

Observe that N in this way computes the transitive closure $\vdash_M^*$ of M's next-move relation $\vdash_M$.

Theorem 5.12 **([Coo71a])** *Let $S(n) \geq \log n$. Let M be a nondeterministic off-line Turing machine such that for every word $x \in L(M)$ there is an accepting computation of M on x that scans at most $S(n)$ cells on any work tape. There is a deterministic on-line Turing machine N such that $L(N) = L(M)$ and there is a constant c such that for every $x \in L(N)$, N on input x makes at most $c^{S(n)}$ moves.*

Corollary 5.8 **([Coo71a])** *If S is fully time-constructible and $S(n) \geq \log(n)$, then*

$$\text{NSPACE}(S(n)) \subseteq \bigcup \{\text{DTIME}(c^{S(n)}) \mid c \geq 1\}.$$

Homework 5.8 *Prove the corollary. (Observe, for each constant c, that $c^{S(n)}$ is fully time-constructible when S is. Also, observe that $n \in o(c^{S(n)})$, so the construction in Section 5.2.1 can be made to work.)*

Proof. Much as in the proof of the previous theorem, we want to construct N so that N can find all configurations I that are reachable from I_0, the initial configuration of M. Since M on input x has an $S(n)$ space-bounded computation if M accepts x, it suffices to consider only those configurations whose work-tape strings have length bounded by $S(n)$. The problem is, we are not assuming that S is space-constructible, so we may not be able to compute $S(n)$. Instead, N uses a parameter l stored on one of its work tapes to guess at $S(n)$. Initially, $l = 1$. In general, if N finds all configurations I such that $I_0 \vdash_M^* I$ for which M's work tapes are l-bounded, and if none of these is accepting, then l is incremented by 1. The process may run forever, but if M accepts x, then N will find an accepting I for some $l \leq S(n)$.

Let $V_{x,l}$ denote the set of all configurations of M on input x with work tapes restricted to length l. Assume the configurations in $V_{x,l}$ are ordered in some canonical way, and consider the $\|V_{x,l}\| \times \|V_{x,l}\|$ Boolean matrix $A_{x,l}$ that represents the next-move relation $\vdash_M$ of M restricted to configurations in $V_{x,l}$. In other words, for $1 \leq i, j \leq \|V_{x,l}\|$, $A_{x,l}(i, j) = 1$ if and only if $I_i \vdash_M I_j$.

It is well known (assuming you know the Floyd–Warshall algorithm [War62]) that transitive closure of an $n \times n$ matrix can be computed in time $O(n^3)$ on a RAM. Hence, N can compute $A_{x,l}^*$ in $\|V_{x,l}\|^{O(1)}$ steps.

Clearly, M accepts an input word x if and only if there are $l \leq S(n)$ and $j \leq \|V_{x,l}\|$ such that I_j is an accepting configuration and $A_{x,l}^*(0, j) = 1$. Thus, if M accepts x, then N accepts x within

$$\sum_{l=1}^{S(n)} \|V_{x,l}\|^{O(1)}$$

steps. Finally, there is a constant d such that for all l, $\|V_{x,l}\| \leq d^{S(n)}$. Thus,

$$\sum_{l=1}^{S(n)} \|V_{x,l}\|^{O(1)} = O(1)^{S(n)},$$

which proves our result.   □

The theorems we have studied thus far are proved by reasonably straightforward simulations. The next theorem involves a deep recursion in the simulation. The result is due to Savitch [Sav70] and is widely known as Savitch's theorem. Our formulation of the proof is due to Hopcroft and Ullman [HU79].

Theorem 5.13   **(Savitch [Sav70])** *If S is fully space-constructible and $S(n) \geq \log(n)$, then*

$$\text{NSPACE}(S(n)) \subseteq \text{DSPACE}(S^2(n)).$$

This is an important result. Observe that a standard depth-first search simulation, as in the previous theorems, would only provide an exponential upper bound.

Corollary 5.9

$$\text{PSPACE} = \bigcup \{\text{DSPACE}(n^c) \mid c \geq 1\}$$
$$= \bigcup \{\text{NSPACE}(n^c) \mid c \geq 1\}$$

and

$$\text{POLYLOGSPACE} = \bigcup \{\text{DSPACE}(\log(n)^c) \mid c \geq 1\}$$
$$= \bigcup \{\text{NSPACE}(\log(n)^c) \mid c \geq 1\}.$$

For this reason, we did not define nondeterministic versions of PSPACE and POLYLOGSPACE as standard complexity classes.

Corollary 5.10

$$\text{NSPACE}(n) \subseteq \text{DSPACE}(n^2)$$

and

$$\text{NL} \subseteq \text{POLYLOGSPACE}.$$

Proof of Theorem 5.13. Let S be a fully space-constructible function such that $S(n) \geq \log(n)$, and let $L = L(M)$, where M is an $S(n)$ space-bounded one-tape nondeterministic Turing machine with s states and t tape symbols. Using Lemma 5.1, recall that there is a constant c so that $c^{S(n)}$ is greater than or equal to the number of configurations for an input of length n. If M accepts an input word w, $|w| = n$, then a shortest accepting computation will not have any configura-

FUNCTION TEST(I_1, I_2, i): Boolean;
var I': configuration;
begin
if ($i = 0$) and ($I_1 = I_2$ or $I_1 \vdash_M I_2$)
    then return true;
if $i \geq 1$
    then for each I' of length at most $S(n)$ **do**
        if TEST($I_1, I', i - 1$) and TEST($I', I_2, i - 1$)
            then return true;
return false;
end;

FIGURE 5.4. The recursive procedure TEST.

tion repeated. Thus, if M accepts w, there is an accepting computation of length $\leq c^{S(n)}$.

Let $m = \lceil \log c \rceil$. The value $c^{S(n)}$ in binary notation has length at most

$$\lceil \log c^{S(n)} \rceil \leq S(n) \lceil \log c \rceil = mS(n).$$

Also, $2^{mS(n)} \geq c^{S(n)}$.

Let w be an input word of length n. Recall that we defined the length of a configuration I to mean the length of the work tape of M in configuration I. If M accepts w, then there is a sequence of at most $2^{mS(n)}$ moves from the initial configuration I_0 to some accepting configuration I_f of length at most $S(n)$. Moreover, each intermediate configuration must have length at most $S(n)$.

In Fig. 5.4 we introduce a computable function

TEST(I_1, I_2, i) : Boolean;

that returns true if and only if there is a sequence of at most 2^i moves from I_1 to I_2 such that each intermediate move has length at most $S(n)$. Then we can determine membership of w in L by the following procedure that makes calls to TEST:

    for each accepting configuration I_f
        of length at most $S(n)$ **do**
        if TEST($I_0, I_f, mS(n)$)
            then accept;
    reject;

We claim that these procedures can be implemented by an $S^2(n)$ space-bounded deterministic Turing machine. First, let us observe that each of the configurations I_1, I_2, and I' requires no more than $O(S(n))$ space. This is certainly true of the storage tape and head positions. Since we are assuming that $\log n \leq S(n)$, the input head position can be written in binary in no more than

$S(n)$ space. Also, since $i \leq mS(n)$, i in binary takes $\leq O(S(n))$ space. So the active variables in a call to TEST takes space $O(S(n))$.

TEST can be implemented by a stack of activation records for the calls. The activation record contains the values of all global and local variables at the current incarnation of the recursion. Although students of computer science should be familiar with the implementation of recursive procedures, let's visit the implementation of TEST, because we want to see that the depth of the stack is never more than $mS(n)$. The initial call to TEST has $i = mS(n)$, each successive call decrements the value of i by 1, and no call is made with $i = 0$. Each call to TEST generates two new recursive calls to TEST. However, we do not make the second call until the first call is returned, and we make the second call only if the first call is positive.

Implement the recursive procedure as follows: Use a tape of the Turing machine we are constructing as a stack. To execute $\text{TEST}(I_1, I_2, i)$, if $i \geq 1$, then begin an enumeration of the configurations I' of length at most $S(n)$. Given such a configuration I', to call TEST from within the current incarnation, write the activation record, which consists of the calling arguments I_1, I_2, I', and i onto the stack. Continue recursively from there. On return from this recursive call, if the return is positive, and if this is the first call to TEST from the current incarnation, then make the second call. Now, it should be clear how to proceed. It should be clear that the value of i in successive activation records on the stack decreases by 1 and therefore that the depth of the stack never exceeds $mS(n)$.

We showed above that each activation record has size $O(S(n))$. Thus, the total stack size is $O(S^2(n))$. Finally, $O(S^2(n))$ space can be compressed to $S^2(n)$, and this proves the theorem. □

The following corollary is a generalization of Theorem 5.13. Note that we do not even assume that $S(n)$ is space-constructible.

Corollary 5.11   *Let $S(n) \geq \log(n)$. If L is accepted by a nondeterministic Turing machine with simultaneous bounds of space $S(n)$ and time $T(n)$, then L is accepted by a deterministic Turing machine that accepts every word in L within space $S(n) \log T(n)$.*

Proof. For each $s \geq 1$, let $C(s)$ be the set of all configurations I of M of length $\leq s$. For $I_1, I_2 \in C(s)$, and $t \geq 1$, define $\text{TEST}(I_1, I_2, t, s)$ if and only if there is a computation of M from I_1 to I_2 of length $\leq 2^t$ such that each intermediate configuration belongs to $C(s)$.

Recursive implementation of TEST is as above; however, if the process ever tries to exceed a stack depth of $\log t$, then stop. Observe that the total stack size does not exceed $s \log t$.

We determine membership in L by the following procedure that contains nested loops:

for $t = 1, 2, \ldots$
      for $s = 1, \ldots, t$
            for each accepting configuration I_f
               of length at most s
               if TEST$(I_0, I_f, \log t, s)$
                   then accept;
reject;

If M accepts x, then there is an accepting computation that uses space at most $s = S(n)$ and time at most $t = T(n)$. For these values of s and t, the procedure will return and accept—and will use no more than $S(n) \log T(n)$ space. $\qquad\square$

Observe that our assertion applies only to words x that belong to L; we make no claim about words that do not belong to L.

The following example illustrates an application of Corollary 5.11. Although in the sequel we will not be concerned with languages that can be recognized by simultaneous resource-bounded Turing machines, let us define

N-SPACE-TIME$(S(n), T(n))$

to be the set of languages L that are accepted by a nondeterministic Turing machine with *simultaneous* bounds of space $S(n)$ and time $T(n)$. (One could define corresponding deterministic classes similarly.)

Example 5.4   N-SPACE-TIME$(n, n^2) \subseteq$ DSPACE$(n \log n)$.

Corollary 5.11 yields a deterministic Turing machine that accepts every word in L within space $n \log n$. Even though the corollary does not provide any bound on words that do not belong to L, $n \log n$ is a fully space-constructible function. Thus, we can ensure that no more than $n \log n$ space is used on every input word.

5.4.1   Relations between the Standard Classes

Figs. 5.5 and 5.6 show the inclusion relations that emerge by application of the results just presented. In these figures, a complexity class C is included in complexity class D if there is a path from C to D reading upward.

The following consequences follow from Corollary 5.6: L $\subseteq$ P, PSPACE $\subseteq$ EXP, and DLBA $\subseteq$ E.

Corollary 5.7 states that NP $\subseteq$ PSPACE.

By Corollary 5.9, we know that LBA $\subseteq$ PSPACE. Corollary 5.10 states that NL $\subseteq$ POLYLOGSPACE.

Corollary 5.8 is used to conclude that NL $\subseteq$ P and LBA $\subseteq$ E.

All other inclusions in the figures are straightforward.

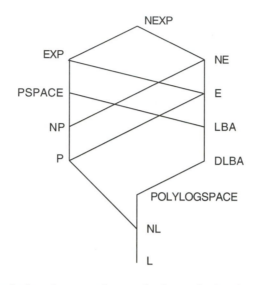

FIGURE 5.5. Inclusions between the standard complexity classes, perspective I.

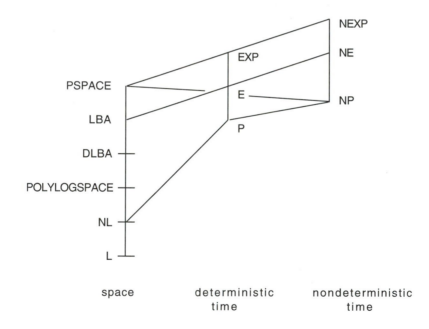

FIGURE 5.6. Inclusions between the standard complexity classes; perspective II.

5.5   Separation Results

In this section we consider which of these classes are the same and which are not equal. First though, we present an improvement of Theorem 5.9 due to Sipser that does not require the assumption that $S(n) \geq \log n$. The reader might observe that we could have presented this theorem earlier. However, the main results of the previous section cannot take advantage of Theorem 5.14 because they require Lemma 5.1.

Theorem 5.14   **([Sip78])**   *For every one-tape off-line deterministic Turing machine M, there is a Turing machine N such that for all input strings x:*

1. *N accepts if and only if M accepts;*
2. *N uses no more space than does M; and*
3. *N does not loop using a finite amount of tape.*

Proof. Let M be a one-tape off-line Turing machine. We assume without loss of generality that when M accepts an input string it completely erases its work tape, returns the heads to their starting points, and then halts in a unique accepting state. Thus, M has a unique accepting configuration. N will execute a procedure to determine whether M's starting configuration reaches the accepting configuration by a computation that uses at most space l, where $l \geq 1$. Think of the configurations of M using at most space l to be the nodes of a finite directed graph. The edges of the graph "point backward one step in M's computation." That is, if (I, J) is an edge in the digraph, then I and J are configurations of M and $J \vdash_M I$. Because M is deterministic, the component of this graph that contains the accepting configuration is a tree rooted at the accepting configuration. Our procedure begins at the accepting configuration and performs a depth-first search of this tree to determine if the starting configuration is a member. We will say that the procedure is searching *backward* if it is moving backward through a computation (a sequence of configurations) of M; that is, if it is searching down the tree (from the root toward a leaf). For any configuration I', there may be several configurations I such that $I \vdash_M I'$. These are ordered in some canonical way and N selects them one at a time in the usual depth-first search manner. If, however, there is no way to search backward from a current configuration I', either because I' has no predecessor or because the predecessors use space $l + 1$, then a leaf of the tree is reached and the search instead proceeds *forward*. N easily implements a forward search by simulating execution of M one step from the current configuration.

A difficulty arises in using the above reverse-search procedure because N has no advance knowledge of the amount of space used by M, so N will need to execute the procedure iteratively for $l = 1, 2, 3, \ldots$ until an accepting computation is found. If M accepts its input, then this uses exactly as much space as M. However, if M does not accept, then this will run forever (risking the possibility that N uses more space than M). To prevent this, N ensures that M uses at least space $l + 1$ before beginning an $l + 1$ search. N does so by cycling through all configurations using space l and selecting those that are about to use a $(l + 1)$st cell on the next step. (N's read-only input tape contains the same input word as M, so N simulates a move of M from a configuration I of M by writing the contents of I on its work tape, moving its heads to the positions given by I, and entering the state of I. Then N makes the move that M's next-move relation indicates. N can cycle through all configurations of M that use space l by ordering these configurations in some canonical way. After testing a configuration I of length l, N can enter the successor configuration by moving its heads, changing state, or incrementing the word of length l that is written on the work tape in accordance with the canonical ordering.) For each configuration that uses space l and that is about to use an $(l + 1)$st cell on the next step, N performs the reverse search for the initial configuration. If none of these reverse searches is successful, then N rejects since it knows that M does not use space $l + 1$. If, however, one of these succeeds, then N continues its iteration and performs an $l + 1$ search from the accepting configuration as before.   □

Corollary 5.12   *If L is accepted by an $S(n)$ space-bounded Turing machine, then L is accepted by an $S(n)$ space-bounded Turing machine that halts on every input.*

Our first separation result, the *space hierarchy theorem*, asserts that if two space bounds differ by even a small amount, then the corresponding complexity classes differ. The second separation result, the *time hierarchy theorem*, requires that the time functions differ by a logarithmic factor. There are technical reasons for this. The intuition that makes results for time harder to obtain than for space is straightforward though. Time marches relentlessly forward, but space can be reused.

Theorem 5.15   **(Space Hierarchy Theorem [HLS65])**   *Let $S(n)$ be fully space-constructible. There is a language $L \in \mathrm{DSPACE}(S(n))$ such that for every function $S'(n)$, if $S'(n) \in o(S(n))$, then $L \notin \mathrm{DSPACE}(S'(n))$.*

For each one-tape Turing machine M, let w_M denote the result of encoding M as a word over a two-letter alphabet (Section 3.2). Here, however, we assume the two-letter alphabet is $\{0, 1\}$. It is possible to pad codes w_M with arbitrarily many extraneous bits in order to obtain a code w for M of every sufficiently large length. To do this, we let the string $w = 0^i 111 w_M$, for each $i \geq 0$, be a pad of the code w_M. If w is a code (padded or otherwise) for some Turing machine, we let M_w denote the Turing machine encoded by w. However, given a Turing machine M, w_M will denote the minimum-length, unpadded, code for M.

The simplest way to obtain a language L that does not belong to $\mathrm{DSPACE}(S'(n))$, in direct analogy to the set $\overline{K}$, which we earlier showed is not accepted by *any* Turing machine, is to define $L = \{w_M \mid M$ does not accept w_M and M is $S'(n)$ space-bounded$\}$. Using diagonalization, L does not belong to $\mathrm{DSPACE}(S'(n))$. However, this language does not satisfy the condition of belonging to DSPACE($S(n)$). (It is not even decidable.) To solve this difficulty, the proof to follow defines a language L so that for *each* $S'(n)$ space-bounded Turing machine M, L will contain *some sufficiently large* code w of M if and only if M does not accept w.

Proof. Let C be a one-tape Turing machine that uses exactly $S(n)$ space on every input of length n. We will design a two-tape off-line Turing machine D, whose tape alphabet is the same as C, to behave as follows on an input word w: If w is a code of some one-tape Turing machine M, then first D simulates C on input w on both tapes, marking every cell that it visits. In this manner, D marks $S(|w|)$ cells on both tapes. Then D copies w_M onto one of the tapes, assuming that it is possible. If not, D halts and rejects. On the other tape, using the copy of w_M and the input word w, D attempts to simulate M on input w within the marked region. (It should be clear why D needs a copy of w_M in order to perform its simulation. To see this, recall that D is an off-line Turing machine. So it is not possible to write on the input tape.) If D ever attempts to leave the marked region, D halts and rejects. D accepts w if and only if it can complete its simulation within the allotted space and M halts without accepting w.

Clearly, $L(D)$ is in DSPACE($S(n)$). Let $S'(n)$ be any function such that $S'(n) \in o(S(n))$. Now we show that $L(D)$ is *not* in DSPACE($S'(n)$). Suppose that $L(D) \in$ DSPACE($S'(n)$) and, using Corollary 5.12, that M is an $S'(n)$ space-bounded Turing machine with t tape symbols that halts on all its inputs (because M does not loop on a finite amount of space) and that accepts $L(D)$. Recall that strings of length $\lceil \log t \rceil$ can represent the t tape symbols of M. It follows that D can simulate M on input any code w of M in space $\lceil \log t \rceil S'(|w|) + |w_M|$. Since $S'(n) \in o(S(n))$, we know that

$$(\forall c > 0)(\exists N > 0)(\forall n > N)(cS'(n) < S(n)).$$

Thus,

$$(\exists N > 0)(\forall n > N)(\lceil \log t \rceil S'(n) + |w_M| < S(n)). \tag{5.1}$$

Choose N so that Equation 5.1 is satisfied, and let w be a code of M of length greater than N. Then, on input w, D has sufficient space to simulate M. However, by definition, D accepts w if and only if M does not accept w. Thus, $L(D) \neq L(M)$, which is what we wanted to prove. Thus, $L(D) \notin$ DSPACE($S'(n)$). □

Let $\subset$ denote *proper* inclusion.

Corollary 5.13   L $\subset$ POLYLOGSPACE, POLYLOGSPACE $\subset$ DLBA, *and* DLBA $\subset$ PSPACE.

Proof. We prove only the second assertion, for the others are straightforward.

$$\text{POLYLOGSPACE} = \bigcup \{\text{DSPACE}((\log n)^k) \mid k \geq 1\}$$
$$\subseteq \text{DSPACE}(n^{\frac{1}{2}})$$
$$\subset \text{DLBA.} \qquad\qquad\qquad \square$$

Corollary 5.14   LBA $\subset$ PSPACE.

Proof.

$$\begin{aligned}
\text{LBA} &= \text{NSPACE}(n), && \text{by Corollary 5.1} \\
&\subseteq \text{DSPACE}(n^2), && \text{by Theorem 5.13} \\
&\subset \text{DSPACE}(n^3), && \text{by Theorem 5.15} \\
&\subseteq \text{PSPACE}.
\end{aligned}$$
$\square$

The proof of Theorem 5.15 requires that $S(n)$ is fully space-constructible. It is possible to prove this result assuming only that $S(n)$ is space-constructible, but, since the space bounds in which we are interested are fully space-constructible, we will not burden ourselves with the technical intricacies that the extension requires.

Theorem 5.16   **(Time Hierarchy Theorem [HS65])** *Let T be a fully time-constructible function and assume that there exists a function $T'(n)$ so that*

$$T'(n)\log(T'(n)) \in o(T(n)).$$

Then there is a language $L \in \text{DTIME}(T(n))$ such that for every function $T'(n)$ such that $T'(n)\log(T'(n)) \in o(T(n))$, $L \notin \text{DTIME}(T'(n))$.

Proof. Now the goal is to construct a Turing machine D so that D is $T(n)$ time-bounded and simultaneously, for each T', diagonalizes over all T' time-bounded Turing machines. More exactly, $L(D)$ will belong to $\text{DTIME}(T(n))$, but for every T' and every language $L' \in \text{DTIME}(T'(n))$, D will diagonalize over some Turing machine that accepts L. Let us observe that if a word w is a code of a multitape Turing machine M_w, then w must encode the number k of tapes of M_w. The details of how are not important.

We adapt the construction in Section 5.2.1: We design D so that on an input word w, D simultaneously does the following: (1) D executes a Turing machine that fully time-constructs $T(|w|)$; and (2) if w is a code of a two-tape Turing machine M_w, then D attempts to simulate M_w on input w. D completes its simulation of M_w on input w only if it can do so within $T(|w|)$ steps. If the simulation is successful within $T(|w|)$ steps, then D accepts w if and only if M_w does not accept w. (If w is not the code of a two-tape Turing machine or the simulation is not successful, then D rejects w.)

Recall from Section 5.2.1 that D runs for at most $2(n+1) + T(n)$ steps on inputs of length n. (Therefore, $L(D) \in \text{DTIME}(O(T(n)))$.) We are assuming that $T'(n)$ is a function with the property that $T'(n)\log(T'(n)) \in o(T(n))$. Then, since for all n, $n + 1 \leq T'(n)$, it follows that $n + 1 \in o(T(n))$. Thus, Theorem 5.2, the linear speedup theorem, applies, from which we conclude that $L(D) \in \text{DTIME}(T(n))$.

Now let show that $L(D)$ is not in $\text{DTIME}(T'(n))$ if $T'(n) \log(T'(n)) \in o(T(n))$. Suppose otherwise. Then, by Corollary 5.5, there is a two-tape Turing machine M such that $L(M) = L(D)$ and M runs in time $T'(n) \log(T'(n))$. As in the proof of the previous theorem, choose n sufficiently large so that M has a code w of length n and such that

$$\lceil \log t \rceil T'(n) \log(T'(n)) \leq T(n),$$

where t is the number of M's tape symbols. On this input w, D completes its simulation of M and D accepts w if and only if M rejects w. Thus, we have a contradiction; $L(M) \neq L(D)$. So, $L(D)$ is not in $\text{DTIME}(T'(n))$. $\square$

Corollary 5.15   *For every constant $c > 0$, $\text{DTIME}(n^c) \subset \text{DTIME}(n^{c+1})$ and $\text{DTIME}(2^{cn}) \subset \text{DTIME}(2^{(c+1)n})$.*

Corollary 5.16 $\text{P} \subset \text{E}$ *and* $\text{E} \subset \text{EXP}$.

5.6   Translation Techniques and Padding

Using Savitch's theorem and the space hierarchy theorem, it is easy to see that $\text{NSPACE}(n^2)$ is properly included in $\text{DSPACE}(n^5)$, so we may conclude immediately that $\text{NSPACE}(n^2)$ is properly included in $\text{NSPACE}(n^5)$. Using the following theorem, we can show that $\text{NSPACE}(n^2)$ is properly included in $\text{NSPACE}(n^3)$. The theorem states that inclusions "translate" upward. The proof is based on the simple idea of padding, which we illustrate with the observation that if L is a language in $\text{DSPACE}(n^2)$, then the language of "padded" words

$$\{w 10^{|w|^2 - |w| - 1} \mid w \in L\}$$

is in $\text{DSPACE}(n)$.

Lemma 5.2   *Let $S(n)$ and $f(n)$ be fully space-constructible functions, where $S(n) \geq n$ and $f(n) \geq n$. For a language L, define*

$$p(L) = \{x 10^i \mid x \in L \text{ and } |x 10^i| = f(|x|)\}.$$

Then $L \in \text{NSPACE}(S(f(n))) \Leftrightarrow p(L) \in \text{NSPACE}(S(n))$.

Proof. Let $L \in \text{NSPACE}(S(f(n)))$ and let M be a nondeterministic $S(f(n))$ space-bounded Turing machine that accepts L. We need to define an $S(n)$ space-bounded Turing machine N to accept $p(L)$. On an input $x 10^i$, N marks $|x 10^i|$ cells. Then N identifies x and within the marked cells N attempts to mark $f(|x|)$ cells. If N discovers that $f(|x|)$ is less than $|x 10^i|$, or if attempting to mark $f(|x|)$ cells wants to use more than $|x 10^i|$ cells, then N halts without accepting, for the two lengths are not equal. Next, N uses these cells to mark $S(f(|x|))$ cells. Since $S(n) \geq n$, we have $S(f(n)) \geq f(n)$; so N uses at most $S(f(|x|))$ cells for this. Then N simulates a computation of M on x and accepts its input if and only if the computation is accepting and stays within the marked cells. It is clear that N accepts $p(L)$ and, letting $n = |x10^i|$, since $|x10^i| = f(|x|)$, it is clear that N operates in space $S(n)$.

To prove the converse, suppose $p(L) \in \text{NSPACE}(S(n))$ and let M be a nondeterministic $S(n)$ space-bounded Turing machine that accepts $p(L)$. We define an $S(f(n))$ space-bounded Turing machine N that accepts L: On an input word x, N marks $f(|x|)$ cells and then writes $x10^i$ on the marked cells, where $|x10^i| = f(|x|)$. Then N simulates a computation of M on $x10^i$ and accepts its input if and only if the computation is accepting. A computation of M on $x10^i$ uses space at most $S(|x10^i|) = S(f(|x|))$. Thus, N accepts L and N is $S(f(n))$ space-bounded.   □

Theorem 5.17   *Let $S_1(n)$, $S_2(n)$, and $f(n)$ be fully space-constructible functions, where $S_1(n) \geq n$, $S_2(n) \geq n$ and $f(n) \geq n$. Then*

$$\text{NSPACE}(S_1(n)) \subseteq \text{NSPACE}(S_2(n)) \text{ implies}$$

$$\text{NSPACE}(S_1(f(n))) \subseteq \text{NSPACE}(S_2(f(n))).$$

Proof. Let $L \in \text{NSPACE}(S_1(f(n)))$. By Lemma 5.2, $p(L) \in \text{NSPACE}(S_1(n))$. So $p(L) \in \text{NSPACE}(S_2(n))$. Use the Lemma again to conclude that $L \in \text{NSPACE}(S_2(f(n)))$.   □

Similar arguments show analogous results for DSPACE, DTIME, and NTIME.

Example 5.5 $\text{NSPACE}(n^2)$ *is properly included in* $\text{NSPACE}(n^3)$.

Suppose that $\text{NSPACE}(n^3) \subseteq \text{NSPACE}(n^2)$. *Apply Theorem 5.17 with* $f(n) = n^2$ *to get* $\text{NSPACE}(n^6) \subseteq \text{NSPACE}(n^4)$, *and with* $f(n) = n^3$ *to get* $\text{NSPACE}(n^9) \subseteq \text{NSPACE}(n^6)$. *Then combine these inclusions to derive the following:*

$$\text{NSPACE}(n^9) \subseteq \text{NSPACE}(n^6)$$
$$\subseteq \text{NSPACE}(n^4)$$
$$\subseteq \text{DSPACE}(n^8), \text{ by Theorem 5.13,}$$
$$\subset \text{DSPACE}(n^9)$$
$$\subseteq \text{NSPACE}(n^9),$$

which is a contradiction. Thus, our assumption that $\text{NSPACE}(n^3)$ *is included in* $\text{NSPACE}(n^2)$ *is false.*

Using a similar line of reasoning, Ibarra [Iba72] proved that $\text{NSPACE}(n^r) \subset \text{NSPACE}(n^{r+\epsilon})$ for all $\epsilon > 0$ and $r \geq 0$. We will not prove this result because a tight hierarchy theorem for nondeterministic space will follow immediately from a result, Theorem 5.21, that we will obtain in a later section. Nevertheless, translation techniques remain important, as the next example, due to Hopcroft and Ullman [HU79], demonstrates.

Example 5.6   *We use the analog of Theorem 5.17 for deterministic time to show that*

$$\text{DTIME}(2^n) \subset \text{DTIME}(n2^n).$$

This does not follow from Theorem 5.16 because

$$\inf_{n \mapsto \infty} \frac{2^n \log 2^n}{n 2^n} = \inf_{n \mapsto \infty} \frac{n 2^n}{n 2^n} = 1.$$

Suppose $\text{DTIME}(n2^n) \subseteq \text{DTIME}(2^n)$. *Apply the translation theorem with* $f(n) = 2^n$ *to get*

$$\text{DTIME}(2^n 2^{2^n}) \subseteq \text{DTIME}(2^{2^n})$$

and with $f(n) = n + 2^n$ *to get*

$$\text{DTIME}((n + 2^n) 2^{n+2^n}) \subseteq \text{DTIME}(2^{n+2^n}).$$

Combining these inclusions, we arrive at

$$\text{DTIME}((n + 2^n) 2^n 2^{2^n}) \subseteq \text{DTIME}(2^{2^n}).$$

However,

$$\inf_{n \mapsto \infty} \frac{(n + 2^n) 2^n 2^{2^n}}{2^{2^n} \log 2^{2^n}} = \inf_{n \mapsto \infty} \frac{(n + 2^n) 2^n 2^{2^n}}{2^{2^n} 2^n}$$
$$= \inf_{n \mapsto \infty} (n + 2^n) = \infty.$$

Thus, $\text{DTIME}((n + 2^n) 2^n 2^{2^n}) \subseteq \text{DTIME}(2^{2^n})$ *is false, from which it follows that our assumption* $\text{DTIME}(n2^n) \subseteq \text{DTIME}(2^n)$ *is false.*

There are hierarchy theorems for nondeterministic time, and these are harder to obtain than for nondeterministic space because Savitch's theorem, Theorem 5.13, is not available. The results that are known use translation techniques in exceedingly clever ways. Observe that straightforward diagonalization does not work because we do not know how to detect in time $T(n)$ when a nondeterministic $T(n)$ time-bounded Turing machine does not accept its input. Cook [Coo73] obtained the first hierarchy theorem for nondeterministic time, and Seiferas, Fischer, and Meyer [SFM78] wrote a thorough study of such hierarchy theorems. The strongest hierarchy theorem for nondeterministic time that is currently known is due to Žák [Ž83]. Žák proved that if T_1 and T_2 are fully time-constructible functions such that $T_1(n + 1) \in o(T_2(n))$, then $\text{NTIME}(T_2(n))$ contains a set that is not in $\text{NTIME}(T_1(n))$.

5.6.1 Tally Languages

A *tally* string is a word over the alphabet $\{1\}^*$, and a tally language is a subset of $\{1\}^*$. We have seen already that natural numbers n can be represented succinctly as a word $n(w)$ in 2-adic notation. Unlike such an acceptable representation, the tally string $1^{n(w)}$ is a verbose representation of the information $n(w)$ that w represents. Here we will exploit this observation in order to obtain another interesting translation result. For $L \subseteq \Sigma^*$, let $\text{Tally}(L) = \{1^{n(w)} \mid w \in L\}$.

Theorem 5.18   **([Boo74])** NE $\subseteq$ E *if and only if every tally language in* NP *belongs to* P.

Proof. Let Σ be a two-letter alphabet and let L denote a language in Σ^*. The proof proceeds by establishing the following four claims:

1. $L \in \text{NE} \Rightarrow \text{Tally}(L) \in \text{NP}$;
2. $\text{Tally}(L) \in \text{P} \Rightarrow L \in \text{E}$;
3. $\text{Tally}(L) \in \text{NP} \Rightarrow L \in \text{NE}$;
4. $L \in \text{E} \Rightarrow \text{Tally}(L) \in \text{P}$.

Assume that the claims are correct. Let $L \in \text{NE}$ and assume that every tally language in NP belongs to P. By claim 1, $\text{Tally}(L) \in \text{NP}$, so $\text{Tally}(L) \in \text{P}$. Then, by claim 2, $L \in \text{E}$. Thus, NE $\subseteq$ E. To prove the converse, let T be a tally language in NP and assume that NE $\subseteq$ E. Let $L = \{w \in \Sigma^* \mid 1^{n(w)} \in T\}$. By claim 3, $L \in \text{NE}$, so $L \in \text{E}$. Then, by claim 4, $\text{Tally}(L) = T \in \text{P}$. Thus, every tally language in NP belongs to P.

Proof of claim 1. Let $L \in \text{NE}$, and let M_1 be a 2^{cn} time-bounded nondeterministic multitape Turing machine that accepts L. From M_1 we construct a Turing machine M_2 that operates as follows: Given an input string 1^m, M_2 writes onto a storage tape the unique word w such that $n(w) = m$. M_2 does this by adding 1 in dyadic notation for each symbol 1 read as input. Then M_2 simulates M_1's computation on w and M_2 accepts $1^{n(w)}$ if and only if M_1 accepts w. Thus, $L(M_2) = \text{Tally}(L(M_1)) = \text{Tally}(L)$. We need to calculate the running time of M_2 as a function of the length of its input word, i.e., as a function of m. The number of steps taken by M_2 is $O(m \log m + 2^{c|w|})$. For some constant c_2, $|w| \leq c_2 \log m$, so M_2 runs in time $O(m \log m + m^{c_3})$ for some constant c_3. Since M_1 is nondeterministic, so is M_2, and M_2 runs in polynomial time. Thus, $\text{Tally}(L) \in \text{NP}$, which establishes claim 1.

Homework 5.9   *Prove claims 2, 3, and 4.*

And this completes the proof.   □

Corollary 5.17   P $=$ NP *implies* E $=$ NE.

Homework 5.10   *Prove the following:* NP $\subseteq$ E *if and only if for every* $L \in \text{NP}$, $\text{Tally}(L) \in \text{P}$.

5.7 Relations between the Standard Classes—Continued

All known inclusions between the standard classes have been given. Book [Boo72, Boo76] has shown that none of the complexity classes POLYLOGSPACE, DLBA, and LBA is equal to either P or NP. However, to this date, it is not known which of these classes contains a language that does not belong to the other. The following theorem shows that DLBA $\neq$ P, and we leave the others as exercises. The lemma uses a padding argument.

Lemma 5.3   *If* DSPACE$(n) \subseteq$ P, *then* PSPACE $=$ NP $=$ P.

Proof. It suffices to show, for each integer $k > 1$, that DSPACE$(n^k) \subseteq$ P. Let $L \in$ DSPACE(n^k) and define the language $p(L)$ as follows:

$$p(L) = \{w10^m \mid w \in L \text{ and } |w10^m| = |w|^k\}.$$

Since $L \in$ DSPACE(n^k), it follows that $p(L) \in$ DSPACE(n). Thus, by hypothesis, $p(L) \in$ P. However, this implies that $L \in$ P as well, because to recognize L, simply pad each input word w to $w10^m$ and use the polynomial-time algorithm for $p(L)$ to determine whether $w10^m \in p(L)$. $\square$

Theorem 5.19   **([Boo72])**   DLBA $\neq$ P.

Proof. Recall that DLBA $=$ DSPACE(n). If DSPACE$(n) =$ P, then by Lemma 5.3, PSPACE $=$ P. Combining these, we have PSPACE $\subseteq$ DSPACE(n). However, by the space hierarchy theorem, Theorem 5.15, this inclusion is false. Thus, our assumption that DSPACE$(n) =$ P is false. $\square$

Homework 5.11   *Show that* LBA $\neq$ P *and that* DLBA $\neq$ NP.

Equality (or inequality) of all other inclusion relationships given in Figs. 5.5 and 5.6 is unknown. Amazingly, proper inclusion of each inclusion in the chain

$$L \subseteq NL \subseteq P \subseteq NP \subseteq PSPACE$$

is an open question even though the ends of the chain are distinct (L $\neq$ PSPACE). Similarly, equality of each inclusion in the chain

$$P \subseteq NP \subseteq PSPACE \subseteq EXP$$

is open, yet P $\neq$ EXP.
Also, it is not known whether any of the inclusions in the chain

$$DLBA \subseteq LBA \subseteq E \subseteq NE$$

are proper.

5.7.1   Complements of Complexity Classes: The Immerman–Szelepcsényi Theorem

It is always important to know whether complexity classes are closed under natural operations. Here we discuss closure under complements. The complement of a language L over the finite alphabet Σ is the language $\overline{L} = \Sigma^* - L$. For any complexity class $\mathcal{C}$, $co\text{-}\mathcal{C} = \{\overline{L} \mid L \in \mathcal{C}\}$.

It is easy to see that $\text{DTIME}(T(n)) = co\text{-}\text{DTIME}(T(n))$ for any time bound $T(n)$. If M is a deterministic $T(n)$ time-bounded Turing machine, we can easily define a deterministic $T(n)$ time-bounded N that accepts $\overline{L(M)}$. N simply accepts if and only if M halts in a nonaccepting state, but in every other respect N behaves exactly as M.

The above trick of reversing the roles of accepting and nonaccepting states is insufficient for showing that deterministic space-bounded complexity classes are closed under complements, because space-bounded Turing machines may enter infinite loops. However, it follows immediately from Sipser's theorem, Theorem 5.14, that this difficulty can be eliminated. Thus, as a corollary of Theorem 5.14 it follows that $\text{DSPACE}(S(n)) = co\text{-}\text{DSPACE}(S(n))$ for all S.

It is not known whether nondeterministic time-bounded complexity classes are closed under complements, and we will discuss the question of whether NP = co-NP in the next chapter.

In 1987 Immerman [Imm88] and Szelepcsényi [Sze88] independently proved that nondeterministic $S(n)$ space-bounded complexity classes are closed under complements for $S(n) \geq \log(n)$. It follows immediately that context-sensitive languages are closed under complements, thus settling a question raised by Kuroda in 1964 [Kur64]. We prove this theorem next.

Theorem 5.20   *For any $S(n) \geq \log(n)$, $\text{NSPACE}(S(N)) = co\text{-}\text{NSPACE}(S(n))$.*

First we will prove Theorem 5.20 with the additional assumption that $S(n)$ is fully space-constructible. Then we will indicate how to remove this condition.

The proof consists of two lemmas. The first lemma says that the exact number of configurations that are reachable from an initial configuration of an $S(n)$ space-bounded nondeterministic Turing machine can be computed in $\text{NSPACE}(S(n))$. The second lemma says that once this number is calculated, rejection as well as acceptance can be detected.

Given an $S(n)$ space-bounded Turing machine M, $S(n) \geq \log(n)$, define the function COUNT_M as follows: For any input word x of M, $\text{COUNT}_M(x) = $ the number of configurations of M that are reachable from I_0^x, the initial configuration of M on input x.

Lemma 5.4   *There is a nondeterministic $S(n)$ space-bounded Turing machine transducer N that computes COUNT_M.*

Proof. By Lemma 5.1, there is a constant k such that the number of different configurations of M on any input of length n is $\leq k^{S(n)}$. Thus, for any input x

of length n, $\text{COUNT}_M(x)$ can be written in space $O(S(n))$. Define the relation $\text{REACH}_M(x, I, d)$, where I is a configuration of M that uses space $S(n)$ and $d \leq k^{S(n)}$ by

$\text{REACH}_M(x, I, d) \equiv I$ is reachable from I_0^x in at most d steps.

The set of yes-instances of the relation $\text{REACH}_M(x, I, d)$ can be accepted non-deterministically in space $S(n)$ by guessing a computation C of at most d steps from I_0^x, and accepting if and only if I is the final configuration of C.

Let $N(x, d)$ denote the number of configurations that are reachable from I_0^x in at most d steps. We show by induction on d that $N(x, d)$ can be computed non-deterministically in space $S(n)$. This will prove the lemma for $\text{COUNT}_M(x) = N(x, k^{S(n)})$. Obviously, $N(x, 0) = 1$. A naive approach to computing $N(x, d+1)$ would be to cycle through all configurations that use space $S(n)$ and to increment a counter for each configuration that is found to be reachable from I_0^x in at most $d + 1$ steps (i.e., for which $\text{REACH}_M(x, I, d + 1)$). It is possible that the non-deterministic algorithm that implements $\text{REACH}_M(x, I, d + 1)$ does not execute an accepting computation even though the relation is true. Thus, this approach cannot be correct. Observe that a configuration TARGET is reachable from I_0^x in at most $d + 1$ steps if and only if there is a configuration TEST such that $\text{REACH}_M(x, \text{TEST}, d)$ and TARGET $=$ TEST or TEST leads to TARGET in one step. By induction hypothesis we know the number $N(x, d)$ of different configurations such that $\text{REACH}_M(x, \text{TEST}, d)$ holds. In order to have a correct procedure, we only need to know that TEST is one of these. To summarize, we cycle through all configurations TARGET that use space $S(n)$. For each, we cycle through all configurations TEST, and for each such that $\text{REACH}_M(x, \text{TEST}, d)$, we increment a counter if TARGET $=$ TEST or TEST leads to TARGET in one step.

The procedure to compute $N(x, d + 1)$ is given in Fig. 5.7. In this procedure, if I is a configuration that uses space $S(n)$, we let $I + 1$ denote the next configuration in the lexicographic ordering of all configurations that use space $S(n)$. In order to properly initialize the program, let $\perp$ denote the predecessor of the lexicographically smallest configuration that uses space $S(n)$, and let us stipulate that $\text{REACH}_M(x, \perp, d)$ is false for all x and d.

Since each configuration uses space $S(n)$, the counters never exceed $k^{S(n)}$, and REACH_M is accepted in nondeterministic space $S(n)$, it follows that the procedure can be implemented by a nondeterministic $S(n)$ space-bounded Turing machine transducer.

To see that the procedure is correct, in an accepting computation each execution of the inner loop terminates without causing the procedure to halt. Thus, either TARGET is reachable and C is incremented, or we can be sure that TARGET is not reachable because all $N(x, d)$ values of TEST have been found. □

Lemma 5.5 *There is a nondeterministic $S(n)$ space-bounded Turing machine N' that, given input words x and $\text{COUNT}_M(x)$, accepts if and only if M does not accept x.*

$C := 0$; {C is a counter that will hold $N(x, d + 1)$ }
for each configuration TARGET that uses space $S(n)$ **do**
{cycle through all such configurations in lexicographic order}

    begin

    $D := 0$

    {D is a counter that will increment to $N(x, d)$ }

    TEST := $\perp$;

    repeat

        TEST := TEST $+ 1$;

        if REACH$_M(x,$ TEST$, d)$ **then**

            $D := D + 1$;

    until $(D = N(x, d))$ or (REACH$_M(x,$ TEST$, d)$ and

        (TARGET = TEST or TEST leads to TARGET in one step))

        or (all configurations that use space $S(n)$ have been tested) ;

    if REACH$_M(x,$ TEST$, d)$ and (TARGET = TEST or

        TEST leads to TARGET in one step)

        then $C := C + 1$; { REACH$_M(x,$ TARGET$, d + 1)$ }

        else if $(D \neq N(x, d))$ **then**

            halt without accepting;

            {all configurations that us space $S(n)$ have been

            tested but the nondeterministic implementations of

            REACH$_M$ have not found $N(x, d)$ reachable configurations }

    end

$N(x, d + 1) := C$

FIGURE 5.7. Procedure to compute $N(x, d + 1)$.

Proof. Cycle through all configurations that use space $S(n)$. For each such configuration TARGET, nondeterministically determine whether TARGET is reachable from I_0^x (i.e., whether REACH$_M(x,$ TARGET$, k^{S(n)})$) and whether TARGET is an accepting configuration. If this iterative procedure finds an accepting configuration of M on x, then it should halt without accepting. Every time the procedure finds a configuration TARGET for which

$$\text{REACH}_M(x, \text{TARGET}, k^{S(n)})$$

is true, it iterates a counter. If the counter eventually reaches COUNT$_M(x)$, and none of these COUNT$_M(x)$ configurations is accepting, then the procedure accepts its input, for in this case it has discovered that none of M's reachable configurations on input x has an accepting configuration.

    The procedure is given in greater detail in Fig. 5.8. As in the proof of Lemma 5.4, there is an $S(n)$ space-bounded nondeterministic Turing machine N' that implements the procedure. Suppose M accepts. Then at least one of the

$D := 0$; {D is a counter that will increment to $\text{COUNT}_M(x)$ }
$\text{TARGET} := \bot$;
repeat
    $\text{TARGET} := \text{TARGET} + 1$;
    if $\text{REACH}_M(x, \text{TARGET}, k^{S(n)})$ **then**
        $D := D + 1$;
until $(D = \text{COUNT}_M(x))$
    $\cdot$ or $(\text{REACH}_M(x, \text{TARGET}, k^{S(n)})$ and TARGET is an accepting configuration)
    or (all configurations that use space $S(n)$ have been tested);
if $\text{REACH}_M(x, \text{TARGET}, k^{S(n)})$ and TARGET is an accepting configuration
    then halt without accepting {because M accepts x}
    else if $D = \text{COUNT}_M(x)$
        then {all reachable configurations of M have
            been found and none of them is accepting}
            accept and halt
        else {all configurations have been tested but the nondeterministic tests
            did not find all $\text{COUNT}_M(x)$ reachable configurations}
            halt without accepting

FIGURE 5.8. Procedure to accept $\overline{L(M)}$, given COUNT_M.

$\text{COUNT}_M(x)$ reachable configurations is accepting, so N' rejects. On the other hand, if M does not accept, then none of the $\text{COUNT}_M(x)$ reachable configurations is accepting, so in this case N' accepts. $\qquad\square$

The proof of Theorem 5.20, with the assumption that $S(n)$ is fully space-constructible, follows immediately from the lemmas. We only need to observe that the value $\text{COUNT}_M(x)$ computed in Lemma 5.4 uses no more than $O(S(n))$ space.

Now that we have mastered the proof, do not assume that $S(n)$ is fully space-constructible. Instead we will initialize a counter S for the space bound to $\log(n)$ and increment the space bound as needed. We need to show that we never exceed $S(n)$ and we need to see that if our algorithm claims that no reachable configuration (within space S) is accepting, then, in fact, the input word x does not belong to $L(M)$. The technique follows:

At some stage of the inductive counting, S has some value and we nondeterministically compute the number of configurations that are reachable within the space bound S and within some d steps. Call this $N(x, S, d)$. (Remember that the procedure to compute $N(x, S, d)$ is nondeterministic; that if the procedure computes a value, the value it computes is correct; and that if no value is returned, the procedure halts.) Suppose that $N(x, S, d)$ is not 0. Then nondeterministically compute $N(x, S + 1, d + 1)$ and $N(x, S, d + 1)$. If the difference is nonzero, i.e., M uses space $S + 1$ to reach configurations in $d + 1$ steps that it cannot reach using space S, then continue the process with $S = S + 1$; that is, continue with $N(x, S + 1, d + 1)$. Otherwise, do not increment S; that is, continue with $N(x, S, d + 1)$.

Since no computation path of M on any input x of length n uses more than $S(n)$ space, our procedure does not exceed the space bound $S(n)$, except by a constant. Second, if no computation of M on input x is accepting, then this process will discover that. The point is that for all $S \leq S(n)$ and all $d \leq k^{S(n)}$, all possible routes to reachable configurations are checked.

Counting plays an important role in many aspects of complexity theory, which the interested student can learn more about from the survey article by Schöning [Sch90].

Theorem 5.21   *If S_2 is fully space-constructible, $S_1(n) \in o(S_2(n))$ and $S_1 \geq \log n$, then there is a language in $\mathrm{NSPACE}(S_2(n))$ that is not in $\mathrm{NSPACE}(S_1(n))$.*

Recall that the proof of the hierarchy theorem for deterministic space, Theorem 5.15, required us to show that looping in finite space can be detected. More precisely, if w is the code for some $S_1(n)$ space-bounded deterministic Turing machine, the diagonalizing $S_2(n)$ space-bounded Turing machine D needs to determine whether M_w halts *without accepting* w. This is the information that Theorem 5.20 provides for nondeterministic space.

Proof.   Given any Turing machine M_w, let M_w^c denote the nondeterministic Turing machine that is constructed in the proof of Theorem 5.20. Thus, M_w^c uses no more space on any input word than M_w, and M_w^c accepts an input x if and only if $x \notin L(M_w)$. As in the proof of Theorem 5.15, design a nondeterministic Turing machine D to mark $S_2(|w|)$ cells on two tapes, and if D ever attempts to leave the marked region, then D halts and rejects. Next, if w is a code, then D simulates M_w^c on input word w. D accepts w if and only if it completes its simulation within the allotted space and M_w^c accepts w. As a consequence, in the case that D completes its simulation of M_w^c within its allotted space, observe that D accepts w if and only if M_w does not accept w. This is the point we needed to demonstrate; the rest of the proof proceeds exactly as in the proof of Theorem 5.15.

There is one detail that we thus far have glossed over. D must simulate M_w^c from the code for M_w. Thus D must implement the algorithms that comprise the proof of Theorem 5.20. It should be clear that D does so without using any more space on any input word than M_w. $\square$

5.8   Additional Homework Problems

Homework 5.12   *If one of the following classes is included in another, state which and explain why. If one of the inclusions is a proper inclusion, then state that and explain why. Find as many inclusions and proper inclusions as possible:* $\mathrm{DTIME}(n^2)$, $\mathrm{DSPACE}(n^8)$, $\mathrm{NTIME}(n^2)$, $\mathrm{NSPACE}(n^5)$.

Homework 5.13   *Do the same for the following classes:* $\text{DTIME}(2^n)$, $\text{DTIME}(3^n)$, $\text{NSPACE}(2^n)$, $\text{DSPACE}(5^n)$.

Homework 5.14   *Show that if* $\text{L} = \text{NL}$, *then* $\text{DLBA} = \text{LBA}$. *Use a padding argument.*

Homework 5.15   *Define*

$$\text{ESPACE} = \bigcup \{\text{DSPACE}(k^n) \mid k \geq 1\}$$

and

$$\text{NESPACE} = \bigcup \{\text{NSPACE}(k^n) \mid k \geq 1\}.$$

Prove that $\text{ESPACE} = \text{NESPACE}$.

Homework 5.16   *Prove that* NP *is not included in* $\text{DTIME}(n^k)$ *for any fixed* $k \geq 1$.

Nondeterminism and NP-Completeness

6.1   Characterizing NP 123

6.2   The Class P 124

6.3   Enumerations 126

6.4   NP-Completeness 128

6.5   The Cook–Levin Theorem 130

6.6   More NP-Complete Problems 136

6.7   Additional Homework Problems 142

Several different additions to the basic deterministic Turing-machine model are often considered. These additions add computational power to the model and so allow us to compute certain problems more efficiently. Often these are important problems with seemingly no efficient solution in the basic model. The question then becomes whether the efficiency the additional power provides is really due to the new model or whether the added efficiency could have been attained without the additional resources.

The original and most important example of this type of consideration is nondeterminism. For each of the standard nondeterministic complexity classes we have been considering, it is an open question whether the class is distinct from its deterministic counterpart. We will concentrate our study of nondeterminism on the class NP, for this is the most important nondeterministic complexity class. Recall that

$$NP = \bigcup \{NTIME(n^k) \mid k \geq 1\}$$

is the class of languages that can be solved nondeterministically in polynomial time. NP plays a central role in complexity theory as many important problems from computer science and mathematics that are not known to be solvable deterministically in polynomial time are in NP. The most central and well-known open problem in complexity theory is whether P = NP. All that is known about NP with respect to deterministic time is that NP $\subseteq$ EXP. A given problem in NP might be solvable in deterministic polynomial time, or it might require exponential time, but a middle ground is conceivable as well: A function g *majorizes* a function f if there exists $N > 0$ such that, for all $n \geq N$, $g(n) \geq f(n)$. The function $n^{\log n} = 2^{\log^2(n)}$ is subexponential but majorizes all polynomials. Thus, a given problem in NP might be solvable in, and require, deterministic time $n^{\log n}$. These are general remarks only; unfortunately, little is actually known.

6.1 Characterizing NP

Recall that a nondeterministic Turing machine is one with a multivalued transition function, and recall that such a machine M accepts an input word x if there is a computation path of M on x that terminates in an accepting state.

Homework 6.1 *Given a Turing machine M, recall that an accepting computation of M is defined to be a sequence of configurations $I_0, I_1, \ldots, I_n$ such that I_0 is an initial configuration, I_n is an accepting configuration, and for each $i < n$, $I_i \vdash_M I_{i+1}$. Thus, a computation is a word over the finite alphabet that defines M. Consider the binary relation R defined as follows:*

$$R(x, y) \Leftrightarrow [x \text{ is an input word to } M \text{ and } y \text{ is} \qquad (6.1)$$
$$\text{an accepting computation of } M \text{ on } x].$$

Show that $\{(x, y) | R(x, y)\}$ is in the complexity class L.

The following theorem gives an important machine-independent characterization of NP.

Theorem 6.1 *A set A belongs to NP if and only if there exist a polynomial p and a binary relation R that is decidable in polynomial time such that for all words in Σ^*,*

$$x \in A \Leftrightarrow \exists y [|y| \leq p(|x|) \wedge R(x, y)]. \qquad (6.2)$$

Proof. Assume that $A \in$ NP, and let M be a nondeterministic polynomial time-bounded Turing machine that accepts A. Since L $\subseteq$ P, it follows from Homework 6.1, that the relation R defined in Equation 6.1 satisfies Equation 6.2.

Conversely, if there exist a polynomial p and a polynomial-time recognizable relation R such that Equation 6.2 holds, then a nondeterministic Turing machine N will accept A in the following two-stage manner: On input x, (1) N nondeterministically writes a string y on its work tape whose length is at most $p(|x|)$; (2) N deterministically verifies in polynomial time that $R(x, y)$ holds. Thus, $A \in$ NP. $\qquad \square$

Given a set A in NP together with a corresponding polynomial p and relation R for which Equation 6.2 holds, for any word x in A, a string y such that $R(x, y)$ holds is called a *witness* or *proof* that x belongs to A. Let us reflect on Turing machine N's two-stage process. Informally, stage (1) comprises a "guess" of a witness y to the fact that $x \in A$, and stage (2) comprises a deterministic "verification" that y is a correct guess. Theorem 6.1 demonstrates that "guessing" and "verifying" completely characterize nondeterminism. We can make these observations a bit more formal as follows: Define a *verifier* for a language A to be an algorithm V such that

$$A = \{x \mid \exists y[V \text{ accepts } \langle x, y \rangle]\}.$$

A *polynomial-time verifier* is a verifier that runs in polynomial time in the length of x. Then, the following elegant and useful characterization of NP follows immediately from Theorem 6.1.

Corollary 6.1   NP *is the class of all languages A having a polynomial-time verifier.*

The proof follows by taking V to be the polynomial-time algorithm that accepts the relation $R(x, y)$ in Equation 6.2. Since the length of the witness y is a polynomial in the length of x, V runs in polynomial time in the length of x.

Example 6.1   *Recall (Example 3.1) that the Hamiltonian Circuit problem is the problem of determining whether a graph has a Hamiltonian circuit. It is easy to show that the Hamiltonian Circuit problem belongs to NP: A nondeterministic Turing machine in polynomial time can, given as input a graph G, guess a sequence of vertices, and then accept if and only if it verifies that the sequence is a Hamiltonian circuit.*

It is just as easy to show that the Hamiltonian Circuit problem belongs to NP by using Corollary 6.1: A verifier V for this problem should, given as input a graph G and a path p in G, accept if p is a Hamiltonian circuit, and reject otherwise.

6.2 The Class P

Before continuing with our detailed discussion of nondeterminism, since the question of whether P = NP drives so much of this development, let us say a few words about the class P. Recall that we identify P with the problems that are feasibly computable and that we do so based on the evidence supporting Church's and Cobham's theses. The simple distinction that makes theory of computing crucial to computing practice, and independent of the current state of technology, is seen by comparing a typical polynomial running time with an exponential one on modest-size input strings: An algorithm whose running time is n^3 on strings of length 100 takes one billion (100^3) steps. However, an algorithm whose running time is 2^n would require 2^{100} steps, which is greater than the number of atoms in the universe. Contrary to naive intuition, improvements in hardware technology make this difference more dramatic, not less. As hardware gets faster, computers can handle larger input instances of problems having polynomial-time algorithms, but the number of steps required for an exponential-time algorithm remains unfathomably large.

We present two typical decision problems that belong to P. One's experience as a student of computer science presents many more (everything that you compute). Our examples here are quite simple, but our intent is to illustrate that it is not usually apparent whether a problem has an efficient algorithm, and finding good algorithms is a challenging intellectual endeavor.

First we show that the following GRAPH ACCESSIBILITY PROBLEM (GAP) problem belongs to P.

GRAPH ACCESSIBILITY PROBLEM (GAP)
>   **instance** A digraph $G = (V, A)$, and vertices s and t in V
>   **question** Is there a path from s to t?

It is obvious that GAP belongs to NP: Just guess a sequence of vertices p beginning with s and ending at t. However, the following straightforward algorithm shows that this problem is in P:

1. input G, s, and t;
2. mark node s;
3. **repeat**
>   **for all** nodes b of G
>>   **if** there is an arc (a, b), where a is marked
>>>   **then** mark b
>   **until** no new nodes are marked;
4. **if** t is marked **then** accept **else** reject.

Clearly, the algorithm is correct. We only need to see that it operates in polynomial time: Steps 2 and 4 execute once. Let m be the number of nodes in G. The repeat-until loop marks at least one new node every time it executes. Thus, step 3 runs no more than m times. Searching all nodes takes m steps. Marking a node takes constant time. So the algorithm runs in $O(m^2)$ steps. Recalling how we encode graphs as an input string, the length of the input is a polynomial in m. Thus, the algorithm can be implemented on a Turing machine in time a polynomial in the length of the input.

Homework 6.2   *Show that* GAP *belongs to* NL.

The next example demonstrates that the set of relatively prime pairs of integers

$$RELPRIME = \{(x, y) \mid x \text{ and } y \text{ are relatively prime}\}$$

belongs to P. We learned in Section 1.7 that the Euclidean Algorithm computes $\gcd(x, y)$. Thus, all that we need to do is demonstrate that this algorithm runs in polynomial time. Recall that the Euclidean Algorithm proceeds by computing a sequence of remainders $r_1, r_2, \ldots$.

Claim 1   *For each $j \geq 1$, $r_{j+2} < \frac{1}{2} r_j$.*

Proof. If $r_{j+1} \leq \frac{1}{2} r_j$, then $r_{j+2} < r_{j+1} \leq \frac{1}{2} r_j$ immediately. Suppose that $r_{j+1} > \frac{1}{2} r_j$. Then the next division gives $r_j = 1 \cdot r_{j+1} + r_{j+2}$, so $r_{j+2} = r_j - r_{j+1} < \frac{1}{2} r_j$. □

Hence, every two steps cut the size of the remainder at least in half. Therefore, there are at most $2 \log x$ divisions. That is, the loop executes $O(\log x)$ times. Since $\log x$ is essentially the length of x, the loop executes $O(n)$ times, where n is the length of the input, and this completes our demonstration.

6.3 Enumerations

Definition 6.1   *A class of sets $\mathcal{C}$ is* effectively presentable *if there is an effective enumeration $\{M_i\}_i$ of Turing machines such that every Turing machine in the enumeration halts on all inputs and $\mathcal{C} = \{L(M_i) \mid i \geq 0\}$.*

The key feature in this definition is that the Turing machines halt on all inputs, so an effectively presentable class must be a class of decidable sets. Let $\{DM_i\}_i$ be the standard effective enumeration of all deterministic Turing machines from Chapter 3, and let $\{NM_i\}_i$ be a standard effective enumeration of all nondeterministic Turing machines. (We can obtain this easily by encoding nondeterministic Turing machines in the same way that we encoded deterministic Turing machines.) We want to start with these enumerations and develop effective presentations of the languages in P and NP, respectively. A naive approach would be to scan the machines in each list, select those that are polynomial time-bounded, and discard the others. However, this is not possible, for we are stymied by the following theorem.

Theorem 6.2   *There is no effective enumeration of the class of all deterministic Turing machines that operate in polynomial time. That is,*

$$S = \{i \mid DM_i \text{ operates in polynomial time}\}$$

in not a computably enumerable set.

The analogous result holds for nondeterministic machines as well. Intuitively, the problem is that one cannot decide whether a Turing machine is polynomial time-bounded.

Proof. The set $L_U = \{\langle i, w \rangle \mid \text{Turing machine } DM_i \text{ on input } w \text{ converges}\}$ is a computably enumerable, undecidable set. Thus, the complement of L_U, the set

$$D = \{\langle i, w \rangle \mid DM_i \text{ on input } w \text{ diverges}\}$$

is not computably enumerable, because it is the complement of a computably enumerable, undecidable set.

Now, we will give an effective procedure that, given a Turing machine code i and input word w, produces a Turing machine $F(i, w)$ such that $\langle i, w \rangle \in D$ if and only if $F(i, w)$ operates in polynomial time. It follows that any effective enumeration of the class of all deterministic Turing machines that operate in polynomial time would yield one for D.

$F(i, w)$ on an input word x is to operate as follows: Simulate DM_i on w for at most $|x|$ steps. If DM_i on w does not halt within $|x|$ steps, then accept input x. Otherwise, let $F(DM_i, w)$ run forever on x.

If DM_i diverges on input w, then $F(i, w)$ will accept every word x in linear time. If DM_i converges on input w, then it will do so after some N steps. So $F(i, w)$ will run forever, and therefore not operate in polynomial time, on all inputs of length greater than N. Thus, $\langle i, w \rangle \in D \Leftrightarrow F(i, w)$ operates in polynomial time.

The proof is essentially complete. For each Turing-machine code i and input word w, define $f(i, w)$ to be the code for the Turing machine $F(i, w)$. Then

$$\langle i, w \rangle \in D \Leftrightarrow f(i, w) \in S.$$

Observe that f is a computable function. Thus, by Lemma 3.2, S in not c.e. $\quad\square$

Nevertheless, it is possible to enumerate a list of deterministic Turing machines, $\{P_i\}_i$, each of which is polynomial time-bounded, so that $\{L(P_i)|i \geq 0\} =$ P and a list of nondeterministic Turing machines,$\{NP_i\}_i$, each of which is polynomial time-bounded, so that $\{L(NP_i)|i \geq 0\} =$ NP. By the previous theorem, neither of these lists will contain *all* the polynomial time-bounded machines, but we don't care.

We will use the pairing function of Section 3.3. Observe that the function $< , >$ and its inverses τ_1 and τ_2 are computable in polynomial time and that $\langle x, y \rangle = z$ implies $x < z$ and $y < z$.

Let $p_j(n) = n^j + j$. Observing that each p_j is fully time-constructible, let C_j be a p_j-clock Turing machine. Let P_k (NP_k) be the Turing machine $DM_i||C_j$ ($NM_i||C_j$, respectively), where $k = \langle i, j \rangle$. Then, P_k is a polynomial-time-bounded Turing machine with p_j as its time bound. Furthermore, since $j < k$, p_k is a strict upper bound on the running time of P_k. Thus, each P_k is a polynomial-time-bounded Turing machine and each P_k operates in time p_k. Now we need to show that these classes of machines provide effective presentations of P and NP.

Theorem 6.3   P *and* NP *are effectively presentable:*

$$NP = \{L(NP_i)|i \geq 0\};$$
$$P = \{L(P_i)|i \geq 0\}.$$

Proof. We give the proof for NP only, as the argument for P is the same. Clearly,

$$L(NP_i)|i \geq 0\} \subseteq NP.$$

If $L \in \mathrm{NP}$, then there is some nondeterministic Turing machine NM_i that accepts L, and there is some polynomial p_j such that NM_i accepts L in time p_j. Thus, the Turing machine $NP_{\langle i,j \rangle} = NM_i \| C_j$ accepts L also. So, $\mathrm{NP} \subseteq \{L(NP_i) | i \geq 0\}$.

$\square$

Recall that a *function f is computable in time $T(n)$* if there is a deterministic multitape Turing-machine transducer with a distinguished output tape such that if x is any input of length n, then the Turing machine halts within $T(n)$ moves with $f(x)$ written on the output tape. A function f is *computable in polynomial time* if it is computable in time $p(n)$ for some polynomial p. A class of functions $\mathcal{F}$ is *effectively presentable* if there is an effective enumeration $\{M_i\}_i$ of Turing-machine transducers such that every Turing machine in the enumeration halts on all inputs and $\mathcal{F} = \{f \mid \text{for some } i \geq 0, f \text{ is computed by } M_i\}$. Using the same argument as above, it follows that the class of polynomial-time-computable functions is effectively presentable, and, for each k, the kth Turing-machine transducer in the enumeration operates in time p_k.

6.4   NP-Completeness

The concept of NP-completeness gives us a method of locating problems in NP whose deterministic complexity is as difficult as any problem in NP. One intuition for defining the notion of NP-completeness would be that a problem A in NP is NP-complete if any problem in NP could be computed efficiently using an efficient algorithm for A as a subroutine. In Section 3.9, without consideration of time-bounds, this intuition led us to define oracle Turing machines and Turing reductions. However, we will take a stronger condition, leaving this intuition as a necessary condition for NP-completeness, and we will return to consideration of time-bounded oracle Turing machines in Chapter 7. Instead, here we define a polynomial-time-bounded version of many-one reducibility. We say that a problem A in NP is NP-complete if every other problem in NP can be transformed into A by a polynomial-time-bounded function. Thus, A will be as difficult as any problem in NP for the simple reason that A encodes the information in every problem in NP. These remarks are informal, and precise definitions follow.

Definition 6.2   *A set A is* many-one reducible in polynomial time *to a set B (notation: $A \leq_m^P B$) if there exists a function f that is computable in polynomial time so that*

$$x \in A \Leftrightarrow f(x) \in B.$$

The function f transforms A into B. Polynomial-time many-one reducibility is the time-bounded restriction of *many-one reducibility* (Definition 3.3), which played an important role in our study of the computably enumerable sets. Polynomial-time many-one reducibility is frequently called "Karp reducibility" in honor of its usage in a seminal paper by Karp [Kar72] that demonstrated NP-completeness of a wide variety of important combinatorial problems. Observe that $\leq_m^P$ is a binary relation over Σ^*.

Homework 6.3   *Prove the following facts.*

      1. $\leq_m^P$ *is reflexive.*
      2. $\leq_m^P$ *is transitive.*
      3. $A \leq_m^P B$ *if and only if* $\overline{A} \leq_m^P \overline{B}$.
      4. $A \leq_m^P B$ *and* $B \in$ P *implies* $A \in$ P. *($\leq_m^P$ preserves membership in P.)*
      5. $A \leq_m^P B$ *and* $B \in$ NP *implies* $A \in$ NP. *($\leq_m^P$ preserves membership in NP.)*
      6.   *If* $A \in$ P, *then for all* B, $B \neq \Sigma^*$ *and* $B \neq \emptyset$, $A \leq_m^P B$.

In the following theorem we use statement 5 of Homework 6.3 to show that NP $\neq$ E. Unfortunately, the proof does not inform us whether NP $\not\subseteq$ E, E $\not\subseteq$ NP, or both.

Theorem 6.4   NP $\neq$ E.

Proof. We know that $\leq_m^P$ preserves membership in NP. We will use a padding argument to show that $\leq_m^P$ does not preserve membership in E. Let A be any set that belongs to DTIME(2^{n^2}) − E. Then let

$$B = \{w10^{|w|^2 - |w| - 1} \mid w \in A\}.$$

It is easy to see that the padded set B belongs to E. Define a function f by $f(w) = w10^{|w|^2 - |w| - 1}$, and observe that f is computable in polynomial time. Finally, observe that $w \in A \Leftrightarrow f(w) \in B$. Thus, $A \leq_m^P B$. Since $B \in$ E but $A \notin$ E, we see that $\leq_m^P$ does not preserve membership in E, so NP $\neq$ E.   □

Homework 6.4   NP $\neq$ NE.

Homework 6.5   *Show that there exist decidable sets A and B so that $A \leq_m^P B$ and $B \not\leq_m^P A$, and A, B, $\overline{A}$, and $\overline{B}$ are all infinite sets.*

Definition 6.3   *A set A is $\leq_m^P$-complete for* NP *(commonly called* NP-complete*) if*

      1. $A \in$ NP ,
      2.   *for every set $L \in$ NP, $L \leq_m^P A$.*

Let A be NP-complete. This definition captures the intuitive notion that every problem in NP is transformable into A. Furthermore, we see readily that any efficient algorithm for A could be used as a subroutine to efficiently determine membership in any set L in NP. An efficient procedure for determining whether x belongs to L is to compute $f(x)$ and then input $f(x)$ to a subroutine for determining membership in A. This observation yields the salient fact about NP-complete problems, which is that NP = P if and only if P contains an NP-complete problem. Thus, each NP-complete problem captures the complexity of the entire class.

Theorem 6.5   *If A is* NP-*complete, then A* ∈ P *if and only if* P = NP.

Proof. Let A be NP-complete and let $L \in$ NP. By definition, $L \leq_m^P A$. Since A belongs to P, so does L. Thus, NP $\subseteq$ P. The converse is trivial.   ☐

Now we prove, rather swiftly, that NP-complete languages exist. We do so by defining a *universal set* for NP. Define

$$\mathcal{U} = \{\langle i, x, 0^n \rangle | \text{ some computation of } NP_i \text{ accepts} \tag{6.3}$$
$$x \text{ in fewer than } n \text{ steps}\}.$$

Homework 6.6   *Show that* $\mathcal{U} \in$ NP.

Observe that it is necessary to write n is unary in Equation 6.3.

Theorem 6.6 $\mathcal{U}$ *is* NP-*complete.*

Proof. We know from Homework 6.6 that $\mathcal{U} \in$ NP, so we have to show that every set $S \in$ NP is $\leq_m^P$-reducible to $\mathcal{U}$. For each $S \in$ NP, there is some i such that $S = L(NP_i)$. Given $S = L(NP_i)$, define f so that for every word x,

$$f(x) = \langle i, x, 0^{p_i(|x|)} \rangle.$$

Clearly, f is computable in polynomial time. Also,

$$x \in S \Leftrightarrow NP_i \text{ accepts } x$$
$$\Leftrightarrow NP_i \text{ accepts } x \text{ in } p_i(|x|) \text{ steps}$$
$$\Leftrightarrow \langle i, x, 0^{p_i(|x|)} \rangle \in \mathcal{U}$$
$$\Leftrightarrow f(x) \in \mathcal{U}.$$

So $S \leq_m^P$ U.   ☐

Homework 6.7   *Explain why* $\{\langle i, x \rangle | NP_i \text{ accepts } x\}$ *is not* NP-*complete.*

Homework 6.8   *Show that*

$$\{\langle i, x, 0^n \rangle | \text{ some computation of } NM_i \text{ accepts } x \text{ in fewer than } n \text{ steps}\}$$

is NP-*complete.*

6.5   The Cook–Levin Theorem

Now we know that NP-complete sets exist, but the theory of NP-completeness is important outside the domain of complexity theory because of its practical signifi-cance. There exist hundreds of natural* NP-complete problems. These include the

---

*By "natural" we mean a problem whose definition has intrinsic independent interest, and one that does not arise by a complexity-theoretic construction.

Hamiltonian Circuit problem, various scheduling problems, packing problems, nonlinear programming, and many others. Many of these NP-complete problems are catalogued in Garey and Johnson's excellent guide to NP-completeness [GJ79]. The first to discover natural NP-complete problems were Cook [Coo71b] and Levin [Lev73]. Moreover, working independently, they were the first to formulate the notion and recognize its importance. Cook proved that the problem of determining, given a formula F of propositional logic, whether F is satisfiable, is NP-complete. The proof we will give of this result is a slight modification of the exposition of Garey and Johnson [GJ79].

The satisfiability problem SAT is the following problem of determining, for an arbitrary propositional formula F, whether F is satisfiable.

SATISFIABILITY (SAT)
>   **instance** A propositional formula F
>   **question** Is F satisfiable?

We will focus attention on the problem CNF-SAT of determining whether a cnf formula is satisfiable. A *cnf formula* is a propositional formula in conjunctive normal form. Recall that a formula is a cnf formula if it is a conjunction of clauses, and a clause is a disjunction of literals.

CNF-SAT
>   **instance** A cnf formula F
>   **question** Is F satisfiable?

The length N of an instance F of SAT is the length of an acceptable encoding of the instance as a word x over a finite alphabet. Suppose that F has n occurrences of variables. Since we represent each variable in binary (or dyadic), $N = O(n \log(n))$. Depending on whether there are multiple occurrences of variables, F might have 2^n different truth assignments. All known deterministic algorithms are equivalent to a sequential search of each of the assignments to see whether one of them leads to satisfaction (i.e., evaluates to the truth value True). Clearly, an exhaustive search algorithm for checking satisfaction takes 2^n steps. Thus, there is an exponential upper bound on the deterministic complexity of SAT.

Theorem 6.7   SAT *belongs to* NP.

The following nondeterministic algorithm for SAT, which follows the typical two-stage pattern that we described in Section 6.1, proves Theorem 6.7: (1) Guess an assignment to the Boolean variables of F. This takes $O(n)$ steps. (2) Verify that the assignment evaluates to True. A straightforward deterministic algorithm takes $O(N^2)$ time. Thus, SAT belongs to the class NP.

Homework 6.9   *Give an $O(N \log(N))$-time algorithm to determine whether an assignment satisfies an instance of SAT. Hint: The difficult part is to make the assignment to the variables. An input instance F is written on a Turing machine tape. Copy the liter-*

als in F onto another tape, but double-index each literal so that $u[i][j]$ ($\overline{u}[i][j]$)
denotes the fact that u_i ($\overline{u}_i$, respectively) is the jth occurrence of a literal in F.
Merge-sort the double-indexed literals on the first index. Then replace each vari-
able name by 1 or 0 in accordance with the assignment, but keep the indexing.
Finally, merge-sort again, this time on the second index in order to regain the
original ordering. Now, with one scan from left to right, it is possible to give each
literal in F its correct truth assignment.

Theorem 6.8   CNF-SAT *is an* NP-*complete problem.*

Proof. A formula belongs to CNF-SAT if and only if it is in conjunctive normal
form and belongs to SAT. Thus, CNF-SAT belongs to NP. We show that every
language L in NP is many-one reducible in polynomial time to CNF-SAT. Let L in
NP. By Theorem 6.1, there exist a polynomial q and a polynomial-time decidable
binary relation R that, for all words in Σ^*, satisfy

$$x \in L \Leftrightarrow \exists y[|y| \le q(|x|) \wedge R(x, y)]. \tag{6.4}$$

Without loss of generality, we may assume that $|y| = q(|x|)$. To see this, define
$R'(x, y)$ if and only if $R(x, z)$ for some prefix z of y. Then R' is decidable in
polynomial time and $R(x, y)$, where $|y| \le q(|x|)$, implies $R'(x, y0^{q(|x|)-|y|})$.

Let M be a deterministic single-tape Turing machine that decides R in polynomial time. Let r be a polynomial so that for all x and y, M runs in at most
$r(|x|+|y|+1)$ steps. Let $p(n) = r(n+q(n)+1)$. Then, for each string y, where
$|y| = q(|x|)$, M on input (x, y) runs no more than $p(|x|)$ steps. Clearly, $x \in L$
if and only if there is a string y, $|y| = q(|x|)$, such that M accepts the input pair
(x, y) in $p(|x|)$ steps. For any such string y, a computation of M uses at most tape
squares 1 through $p(n + 1)$.

Assume that M's set of states is $Q = \{q_0, q_1, \ldots, q_r\}$, where q_0 is the initial
state and $q_1 = q_{\text{accept}}$ is the unique accepting state. Let $\Gamma = \{s_0, \ldots, s_v\}$ be the
tape alphabet, and let $s_0 = B$ be the blank symbol.

Variable	Intended meaning	Range
$Q[i, k]$	At time i, M is in state q_k.	$0 \le i \le p(n)$ $0 \le k \le r$
$H[i, j]$	At time i, the read–write head is scanning tape square j.	$0 \le i \le p(n)$ $1 \le j \le p(n) + 1$
$S[i, j, k]$	At time i, the contents of tape square j is symbol s_k.	$0 \le i \le p(n)$ $1 \le j \le p(n) + 1$ $0 \le k \le v$

Table 6.1. Variables in $f_L(x)$ and Their Intended Meaning

Now we give the transformation f_L: Table 6.1 lists the set of variables U of $f_L(x)$ with their intended meanings. (Tables 6.1 and 6.2 are adapted from Garey and Johnson [GJ79]).

The set of variables U of $f_L(x)$ is given by Table 6.1. Note that these are just Boolean variables. The subscript notation is for convenience only, to help us remember the intended meaning of the various variables.

The formula $f_L(x)$ is the conjunction of six cnf formulas: $G_1, \ldots, G_6$. Each of these individual cnf formulas imposes a restriction on any satisfying assignment, as given in Table 6.2.

Given an accepting computation of M on x, it should be clear that if each individual cnf formula performs as intended, then a satisfying assignment to $f_L(x)$ will correspond to the accepting computation.

Now we describe the six cnf formulas. To make our formulas more readable, we begin by allowing the implication connective $\rightarrow$ in our formulas. The exact meaning of implication is given by the following truth-table:

$$\begin{array}{ccc} A & B & (A \rightarrow B) \\ 1 & 1 & 1 \\ 1 & 0 & 0 \\ 0 & 1 & 1 \\ 0 & 0 & 1 \end{array}$$

Formula G_1 is to mean that "At each time i, M is in exactly one state," so this can be expressed by the following formula:

$$(Q[i, 0] \vee Q[i, 1] \vee \cdots \vee Q[i, r])$$

Cnf formula	Restriction imposed
G_1	At each time i, M is in exactly one state.
G_2	At each time i, the read-write head is scanning exactly one tape square.
G_3	At each time i, each tape square contains exactly one symbol from Γ.
G_4	At time 0, the computation is in the initial configuration.
G_5	By time $p(n)$, M has entered the accepting state q_1.
G_6	For each time i, $0 \le i \le p(n)$, the configuration of M at time $i + 1$ follows by a single application of M's next-move relation from the configuration at time i.

Table 6.2. The Six Cnf Formulas.

Cnf formulas	Clauses
G_2	$(H[i, 1] \vee \cdots \vee H[i, p(n) + 1]), 0 \leq i \leq p(n)$ $(\overline{H[i, j]} \vee \overline{H[i, j']}), 0 \leq i \leq p(n), i \leq j < j' \leq p(n) + 1$
G_3	$(S[i, j, 0] \vee S[i, j, 1] \vee \cdots \vee S[i, j, v]), 0 \leq i \leq p(n), 1 \leq j \leq p(n) + 1$ $(\overline{S[i, j, k]} \vee \overline{S[i, j, k']}), 0 \leq i \leq p(n), 1 \leq j \leq p(n) + 1, 0 \leq k < k' \leq v$

Table 6.3. Clauses in G_2 and G_3.

$$\wedge (Q[i, 0] \to \overline{Q[i, 1]}) \wedge (Q[i, 0] \to \overline{Q[i, 2]}) \wedge \cdots \wedge (Q[i, 0] \to \overline{Q[i, r]})$$
$$\wedge \cdots \wedge (Q[i, r] \to \overline{Q[i, r - 1]}),$$

which is equivalent to

$$(Q[i, 0] \vee Q[i, 1] \vee \cdots \vee Q[i, r])$$
$$\wedge (\overline{Q[i, 0]} \vee \overline{Q[i, 1]}) \wedge (\overline{Q[i, 0]} \vee \overline{Q[i, 2]}) \wedge \cdots \wedge (\overline{Q[i, 0]} \vee \overline{Q[i, r]})$$
$$\wedge \cdots \wedge (\overline{Q[i, r]} \vee \overline{Q[i, r - 1]}).$$

Formulas G_2 and G_3 are similar to formula G_1, so these are the conjunction of the clauses listed in Table 6.3.

The cnf formula G_4 is to mean that "At time 0, M is in the initial configuration." Thus, G_4 is the conjunction of the following components:

(i) The input word $x = s_{k_1} \ldots s_{k_n}$ is written in squares 1 through n, square $n + 1$ contains the blank symbol, and a word y, $|y| = q(n)$, is written in squares $n + 2, \ldots, n + q(n) + 1$. The blank symbol is written in squares $n + q(n) + 2$ through $p(n) + 1$. This can be expressed as

$$S[0, 1, k_1] \wedge S[0, 2, k_2] \wedge \cdots S[0, n, k_n] \wedge S[0, n + 1, 0]$$
$$\wedge \overline{S[0, n + 2, 0]} \wedge \cdots \wedge \overline{S[0, n + q(n) + 1, 0]}$$
$$\wedge S[0, n + q(n) + 2, 0] \cdots \wedge S[0, p(n) + 1, 0].$$

(ii) The head scans square 1, which is expressed by the clause $H[0, 1]$.

(iii) The state is q_0, which is expressed by $Q[0, 0]$.

G_5 should state that at time $p(n)$, M is in the accepting state, which we assume is q_1, so G_5 is given by $Q[p(n), 1]$.

G_6 should mean that the configuration at time $i + 1$ should be obtained by a legal move of M from the configuration at time i. We need to express the changes that are made if the head is scanning square j at time i, and we need to express the fact that if the head is not scanning square j at time i, then the symbol in square j does not change. The latter is expressed by formulas of the form

$$S[i, j, l] \wedge \overline{H[i, j]} \to S[i + 1, j, l].$$

Thus, for each i, $0 \leq i < p(n)$, each j, $1 \leq j \leq p(n) + 1$, and each l, $0 \leq l \leq v$, G_6 contains clauses

$$(\overline{S[i, j, l]} \vee H[i, j] \vee S[i + 1, j, l]).$$

If the head at time i is scanning square j, then we need to know the current state and symbol scanned as well: Suppose that q_k is not the accepting state, and that in state q_k scanning symbol s_l, M writes $s_{l'}$, moves to square $j + \Delta$, and enters state $q_{k'}$. This is expressible by the formula

$$(H[i, j] \wedge Q[i, k] \wedge S[i, j, l])$$
$$\rightarrow (H[i + 1, j + \Delta] \wedge Q[i + 1, k'] \wedge S[i + 1, j, l']).$$

Thus, for every i, j, k, and l, $0 \leq i < p(n)$, $1 \leq j \leq p(n) + 1$, $0 \leq k \leq r$, $0 \leq l \leq v$, corresponding to the instruction "in state q_k scanning symbol s_l, write $s_{l'}$, move to square $j + \Delta$, and enter state $q_{k'}$," G_6 contains the conjunctions

$$(\overline{H[i, j]} \vee \overline{Q[i, k]} \vee \overline{S[i, j, l]} \vee H[i + 1, j + \Delta])$$
$$\wedge (\overline{H[i, j]} \vee \overline{Q[i, k]} \vee \overline{S[i, j, l]} \vee Q[i + 1, k'])$$
$$\wedge (\overline{H[i, j]} \vee \overline{Q[i, k]} \vee \overline{S[i, j, l]} \vee S[i + 1, j, l']).$$

For the accepting state q_1, we stipulate that

$$(H[i, j] \wedge Q[i, 1] \wedge S[i, j, l])$$
$$\rightarrow (H[i + 1, j] \wedge Q[i + 1, 1] \wedge S[i + 1, j, l]).$$

This case adds the following additional conjunctions to G_6:

$$(\overline{H[i, j]} \vee \overline{Q[i, 1]} \vee \overline{S[i, j, l]} \vee H[i + 1, j])$$
$$\wedge (\overline{H[i, j]} \vee \overline{Q[i, 1]} \vee \overline{S[i, j, l]} \vee Q[i + 1, 1])$$
$$\wedge (\overline{H[i, j]} \vee \overline{Q[i, 1]} \vee \overline{S[i, j, l]} \vee S[i + 1, j, l]).$$

This completes the construction of $f_L(x)$. To see that f_L can be computed in time some polynomial in $|x|$, we make two observations. One, the number of variables U and the size of $G_1, \ldots, G_6$ are no more than a polynomial in $|x|$. Second, only G_4 depends on input x, as the other clauses depend on M alone. Finding G_4, given x, is just a matter of filling values into a formula for G_4. A satisfying assignment corresponds uniquely to a value of y, $|y| = q(|x|)$, for which M accepts (x, y). Thus, $x \in L$ if and only if $f_L(x)$ is satisfiable. $\square$

We wish to make another observation about this important result. Let M be any nondeterministic polynomial-time-bounded Turing machine, and let $L = L(M)$. Let $q(n)$ be a polynomial bound on the running time of M. As in Homework 6.1, consider the relation $R(x, y)$ defined by "x is an input word to M and y is an accepting computation of M on x." Since computations are paddable, we may assume that M has an accepting computation on an input word x if and only if M has an accepting computation y on input x such that $|y| = q(|x|)$. Now consider the construction of f_L from R and q. Focus attention on G_4: Different satisfying assignments of $f_L(x)$ are due to the different values of y that at time 0 are written in squares $n + 2, \ldots, n + q(n) + 1$. Moreover, each satisfying assignment encodes, by assigning the value 1 to variables of the form $S[0, j, k]$, $n+2 \leq j \leq n+q(n)+1, 1 \leq k \leq v$, a unique value of y. Thus, every satisfying assignment of $f_L(x)$ encodes an accepting computation of M on x. In this case, the number of distinct accepting computations of M on x is equal to the number of different satisfying assignments of $f_L(x)$.

6.6 More NP-Complete Problems

Now that we know two NP-complete problems, additional NP-problems can be found using the following proposition.

Proposition 6.1   *If A is NP-complete, $A \leq_m^P B$, and $B \in$ NP, then B is NP-complete.*

Thus, given a language B, to show that B is NP-complete, we need to

(i) show that B belongs to NP, and

(ii) show that $A \leq_m^P B$, where it is already known that A is NP-complete.

Corollary 6.2   SAT *is NP-complete.*

Homework 6.10   *Use Proposition 6.1 to prove Corollary 6.2.*

In this section we will apply this technique in order to obtain other interesting NP-complete problems.* First, we digress to set down the following homework exercises, which concern the open question of whether NP is closed under complements.

Homework 6.11   *Prove the following:* co-NP $=$ NP *if and only if some* NP-*complete set has its complement in* NP.

Homework 6.12   *A set A in* co-NP *is $\leq_m^P$-complete for* co-NP *if for all $L \in$ co-NP, $L \leq_m^P A$. Show the following:*

1. *A is $\leq_m^P$-complete for* co-NP *if and only if $\overline{A}$ is $\leq_m^P$-complete for* NP.

2. *The problem of determining whether a formula of propositional logic is a tautology is $\leq_m^P$-complete for* co-NP.

We conclude that NP is closed under complements if and only if the set of all tautologies is in NP, which remains an open question.

---

*It should be apparent that we have been confusing "problem" with "language." Recall that we are free to do so because we identify a decision problem with the set of its yes-instances—those instances for which the answer to the question is "yes." Also, we are relying on the fact that there are polynomial-time encodings of the standard data structures into strings over the two-letter alphabet.

6.6.1   The Diagonal Set Is NP-Complete

Define

$$K = \{i \mid NP_i \text{ accepts } i \text{ within } |i| \text{ steps}\}.$$

We will show that K is NP-complete.

Homework 6.13   *Show that K belongs to NP.*

Theorem 6.9 K *is NP-complete.*

Proof. We will show that $\mathcal{U} \leq_m^P K$. Since, by Theorem 6.6, we know that $\mathcal{U}$ is NP-complete, this is all that is required.

Let M be a Turing machine that takes two strings x and y as input and that accepts x and y if and only if $x \in \mathcal{U}$. (Thus, M acts independently of y.) For each string x, consider the Turing machine M^x that operates as follows: M^x has x stored in its finite control. On an input string y, M^x simulates M on inputs x and y, and M^x accepts y if and only if M accepts x and y. Notice that M^x operates in constant time since M^x's computation on any input string y is independent of its input.

There is a procedure that for each input word x outputs the Turing machine M^x, and this procedure requires at most a polynomial in $|x|$ number of steps. (This procedure builds the code of M, and thus of $\mathcal{U}$, into the finite control of M^x—it does not run $\mathcal{U}$ on x.) Also, there is a procedure that takes as input a Turing machine M^x and outputs its index i in the standard enumeration $\{NM_i\}_i$ of all nondeterministic Turing machines. (As the index i is just a code for the Turing machine NM_i, this is true in general.) Finally, as M^x runs in constant time, $L(M^x) = L(NP_{\langle i,2 \rangle})$, where the pair $\langle i, 2 \rangle$ is an index in the enumeration $\{NP_i\}_i$ of nondeterministic Turing machines with clocks that effectively presents NP. Combining these procedures, we see that there is a function g that is computable in polynomial time so that for each word x, $g(x) = \langle i, 2 \rangle$ is an index in the enumeration $\{NP_i\}_i$ for which $L(M^x) = L(NP_{\langle i,2 \rangle})$. The salient fact about g is that

$$NP_{g(x)} \text{ accepts an input string } y \Leftrightarrow x \in \mathcal{U}.$$

We claim that $x \in \mathcal{U} \Leftrightarrow g(x) \in K$. First, observe that

$$x \in \mathcal{U} \Leftrightarrow L(NP_{g(x)}) = \Sigma^*, \text{ and}$$
$$x \notin \mathcal{U} \Leftrightarrow L(NP_{g(x)}) = \emptyset.$$

Thus,

$$x \in \mathcal{U} \Leftrightarrow NP_{g(x)} \text{ accepts } g(x)$$
$$\Leftrightarrow NP_{g(x)} \text{ accepts } g(x) \text{ in } |g(x)| \text{ steps}$$
$$\Leftrightarrow g(x) \in K.$$

Thus, g is an $\leq_m^P$-reduction from $\mathcal{U}$ to K, so K is NP-complete. $\square$

6.6.2   Some Natural NP-Complete Problems

3SAT is the restriction of CNF-SAT to instances for which every clause contains three literals

3SAT

> **instance** A cnf formula F such that each clause contains three literals
> **question** Is there a satisfying truth assignment for F?

Theorem 6.10   3SAT *is* NP-*complete.*

We know already that CNF-SAT belongs to NP, so 3SAT belongs to NP. Thus, to prove Theorem 6.10 it suffices to show that CNF-SAT $\leq^P_m$ 3SAT. Consider the mapping g whose input is an arbitrary conjunction of clauses F and whose output is given as follows: Replace each clause of F

$$(x_1 \vee \ldots \vee x_n) \tag{6.5}$$

with the following conjunction of clauses:

$$(x_1 \vee x_2 \vee y_1) \wedge (x_3 \vee \overline{y_1} \vee y_2) \wedge (x_4 \vee \overline{y_2} \vee y_3) \tag{6.6}$$
$$\wedge \cdots \wedge (x_{n-1} \vee x_n \vee \overline{y_{n-3}}),$$

where $y_1, \ldots, y_{n-3}$ are new variables that do not occur in VAR(F). We leave it to the reader to verify that the formula F is satisfiable if and only if the output formula $g(F)$ is satisfiable. The following observations will help in this task. Let t be an arbitrary assignment to VAR(F) and let t' be any assignment to VAR(F)$\cup\{y_1, \ldots, y_{n-3}\}$ that agrees with t on VAR(F). (That is, if u is a variable in VAR(F), then $t(u) = t'(u)$.) Then t satisfies the clause in Equation 6.6 if and only if t' satisfies the formula in Equation 6.5. Conversely, any assignment that satisfies Equation 6.5 must also satisfy Equation 6.6.

Since g is a polynomial-time reduction from CNF-SAT to 3SAT, we conclude that 3SAT is NP-complete.

Example 6.2   **($k = 4$)** *Let $x_1, \ldots, x_4$ be variables and let t be an assignment that assigns the value 1 to at least one of these variables, so that t satisfies the clause ($x_1 \vee x_2 \vee x_3 \vee x_4$). Then every extension of t to the variables $\{x_1, \ldots, x_4, y_1\}$ satisfies the formula*

$$(x_1 \vee x_2 \vee y_1) \wedge (x_3 \vee x_4 \vee \overline{y_1}).$$

Conversely, every satisfying assignment to this formula must assign the value 1 to at least one of the x_i, $1 \leq i \leq 4$.

Example 6.3   **($k = 5$)** *The same properties as in the previous example apply to the clause ($x_1 \vee x_2 \vee x_3 \vee x_4 \vee x_5$) and the corresponding conjunction of clauses*

$$(x_1 \vee x_2 \vee y_1) \wedge (x_3 \vee \overline{y_1} \vee y_2) \wedge (x_4 \vee x_5 \vee \overline{y_2}).$$

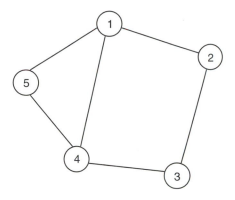

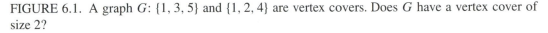

FIGURE 6.1. A graph G: $\{1, 3, 5\}$ and $\{1, 2, 4\}$ are vertex covers. Does G have a vertex cover of size 2?

Some of the most famous NP-complete problems are about graphs. The following problem, VERTEX COVER, is NP-complete and is an important tool for showing NP-completeness of other NP-complete problems. A *vertex cover* of a graph $G = (V, E)$ is a subset V' of V that, for each edge $(u, v) \in E$, contains at least one of the adjacent vertices u and v. The *size* of a vertex cover V' is the number of distinct vertices it contains. These notions are illustrated in Fig. 6.1.

VERTEX COVER
> **instance** A graph $G = (V, E)$ and a positive integer $k \leq \|V\|$
> **question** Is there a vertex cover of size $\leq k$ for G?

Theorem 6.11   VERTEX COVER *is* NP-*complete.*

Proof. It is easy to see that VERTEX COVER belongs to NP: Given a graph $G = (V, E)$, guess a set of vertices V', and check whether V' is a vertex cover. This test can be performed deterministically in polynomial time.

Now we show that 3SAT $\leq_m^P$ VERTEX COVER. We will describe a polynomial-time-bounded construction that maps an instance F of 3SAT to some graph $G = (V, E)$ and positive integer k such that F is satisfiable if and only if G has a vertex cover of size $\leq k$. The construction of G consists of the following three steps, each of which adds a different component to the graph:

1. Let $U = \text{VAR}(F)$. For each variable $u_i \in U$, put vertices u_i and $\overline{u_i}$ into V and put the edge $(u_i, \overline{u_i})$ into E. We call this the *truth-setting* component. Note that any vertex cover must contain at least one of u_i and $\overline{u_i}$.

2. Let C be the set of clauses in F; that is, $F = \bigwedge_{c_j \in C} c_j$. For each clause $c_j \in C$, put three vertices v_1^j, v_2^j, and v_3^j into V and three edges into E that join these vertices to make a triangle:

$$(v_1^j, v_2^j), (v_2^j, v_3^j), (v_3^j, v_1^j).$$

This is the *satisfaction-testing* component. Note that any vertex cover must contain at least two vertices from each triangle.

3. This step creates the *communications* component, which adds edges connecting the satisfaction-testing and truth-setting components. This is the only component that depends on which literals are contained in which clauses. Each clause $c_j \in C$ is a disjunction of literals $c_j = (x_j \vee y_j \vee z_j)$. For each such c_j, put the edges

$$(v_1^j, x_j), (v_2^j, y_j), (v_3^j, z_j)$$

into E.

This completes the definition of G. Define the constant k to be

$$k = \|U\| + 2\|C\|.$$

Clearly, the construction takes polynomial time.

We need to show that G has a vertex cover of size $\leq k$ if and only if F is satisfiable. Suppose V' is a vertex cover for G and $\|V'\| \leq k$; then, as we have noted, V' has at least one vertex for each variable (i.e., at least one of u_i and $\overline{u_i}$) and has at least two vertices for each clause (i.e., at least two vertices from each triangle). Thus, $\|V'\| = k$. Define an assignment $t : U \rightarrow \{0, 1\}$ by $t(u_i) = 1$ if $u_i \in V'$, and by $t(u_i) = 0$ if $u_i \notin V'$. We claim that this assignment satisfies each clause $c_j \in C$. Consider the triangle in the satisfaction-testing component that corresponds to c_j. Exactly two of the vertices of this triangle belong to V'. The third vertex does not belong to V', so the communications component edge between this vertex and a vertex in the truth-setting component must be covered by the vertex in the truth-setting component. By definition of the communications component, this means that c_j contains a literal $x \in \{u_i, \overline{u_i}\}$ and that $t(x) = 1$. Thus, t satisfies c_j.

Conversely, suppose that an assignment t satisfies each clause c_j in C. For each variable $u_i \in U$, either $t(u_i) = 1$ or $t(\overline{u_i}) = 1$. Place the vertex u_i into V' if $t(u_i) = 1$, and place the vertex $\overline{u_i}$ into V' if $t(\overline{u_i}) = 1$. Then V' contains one vertex of each edge in the truth-setting component. In particular, if $x \in \{u_i, \overline{u_i}\}$ is a literal in c_j that is assigned the value 1, then x is a vertex that is placed into V'. By definition of the communications component, one vertex of the triangle in the satisfaction-testing component that corresponds to c_j is covered by the edge that connects the triangle to the vertex x. For each clause c_j, place the other two vertices of the corresponding triangle into V'. It follows that $\|V'\| \leq k$ and that V' is a vertex cover. This completes the proof. ☐

Fig. 6.2 shows the graph that is obtained by applying the construction to the instance $(\overline{u_1} \vee u_2 \vee \overline{u_3}) \wedge (\overline{u_1} \vee \overline{u_3} \vee u_3)$ of 3SAT and shows the vertex cover that corresponds to the satisfying assignment $t(u_2) = 1$ and $t(u_1) = t(u_3) = 0$.

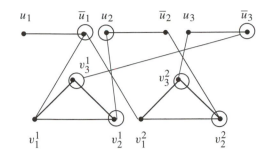

FIGURE 6.2. The instance of VERTEX COVER that results from the instance $(\overline{u_1} \vee u_2 \vee \overline{u_3}) \wedge (\overline{u_1} \vee \overline{u_2} \vee u_3)$ of 3SAT, with the vertex cover that corresponds to the satisfying assignment $t(u_2) = 1$ and $t(u_1) = t(u_3) = 0$.

For any graph G, recall from Example 2.3 that a *clique* is a complete subgraph of G. Now that we know that VERTEX COVER is NP-complete, it is rather easy to show that the following CLIQUE problem is NP-complete.

CLIQUE
> **instance** A graph $G = (V, E)$ and a positive integer $j \leq \|V\|$
> **question** Does G contain a clique of size j or more?

Theorem 6.12   CLIQUE *is* NP-*complete.*

Proof. It is easy to see that CLIQUE belongs to NP: To summarize the approach given in Example 2.3, given a graph G and integer $j \leq \|V\|$, guess a subgraph of G of size $\leq j$, and then determine whether it is a clique.

Now we show that VERTEX COVER $\leq_m^P$ CLIQUE. The *complement* of a graph $G = (V, E)$ is the graph $G^c = (V, E^c)$, where $E^c = \{(u, v) \mid u \in V, v \in V, \text{ and } (u, v) \notin E\}$. Given an instance of VERTEX COVER, a graph G, and positive integer $k \leq \|V\|$, the output of the polynomial-time reduction is G^c and integer $\|V\| - k$.

First we show that if V' is a vertex cover for G, then $V - V'$ is a clique of G^c. Let V' be a vertex cover for G, and let u and v belong to $V - V'$. Since every edge of G has at least one adjacent vertex in V', it follows that $(u, v) \notin E$. Thus, $(u, v) \in E^c$, and this proves the claim. It follows from the same line of reasoning that if V' is a clique in G^c, then $V - V'$ is a vertex cover for G. $\qquad\square$

Homework 6.14   *Show the natural reduction from* CLIQUE *to* VERTEX COVER.

We conclude this chapter with mention of two additional NP-complete problems: 3-DIMENSIONAL MATCHING and PARTITION.

3-DIMENSIONAL MATCHING
>   **instance** A set $M \subset W \times X \times Y$, where W, X, and Y are disjoint sets having the same number q of elements
>   **question** Is there a subset M' of M, called a *matching*, such that $\|M'\| = q$ and no two elements of M' agree in any coordinate?

PARTITION
>   **instance** A finite set A and a positive integer "size" $s(a)$ for each $a \in A$
>   **question** Is there a subset A' of A such that $\sum_{a \in A'} s(a) = \sum_{a \in A - A'} s(a)$?

The VERTEX COVER problem is used to show completeness of HAMIL-TONIAN CIRCUIT; i.e., VERTEX COVER $\leq_m^P$ HAMILTONIAN CIRCUIT.

We refer to a source such as Garey and Johnson's guide [GJ79] for the reductions showing that these problems are NP-complete and for in-depth study of NP-completeness. The intent of this section has been to provide a sense of the importance of NP-completeness as a tool for classifying seemingly intractable problems and to provide an understanding of the methods for proving NP-completeness. However, this is but one stopping point in our continuing development of complexity theory.

6.7   Additional Homework Problems

Homework 6.15   *Define the function maxclique by, for any graph G,*

$$maxclique(G) = \max\{k \mid G \text{ contains a clique of size } k\}.$$

Show that $P = NP$ if and only if the function maxclique is polynomial-time-computable.

Homework 6.16   *Show that some infinite subset of CLIQUE belongs to P.*

Homework 6.17   *Show that the set*

$$L = \{F \mid F \text{ is a propositional formula that has as least two satisfying assignments}\}$$

is NP-complete.

Homework 6.18   *Show that NTIME(n) contains an NP-complete language. (Hint: Use padding.)*

Homework 6.19   *Let S be a nonempty set and let C be a collection of nonempty subsets of S. A* hitting set *for C is a subset H of S such that H has a nonempty intersection with every set in C. Show that the following HITTING SET problem is NP-complete. (Hint: Reduce VERTEX COVER to HITTING SET.)*

HITTING SET

> **instance** *A nonempty set S, a collection of nonempty subsets C,*
> *and positive integer $k \geq 1$*
> **question** *Is there a hitting set for C of size at most k?*

Homework 6.20   *Define a partial function f by*

$$f(\phi) = \text{ some satisfying assignment of } \phi, \text{ if one exists,}$$

where ϕ is a formula of propositional logic (i.e., ϕ is an instance of the satisfiability problem). Show that f is polynomial-time-computable if and only if P = NP.

Homework 6.21   *Define a set $A \subseteq \Sigma^*$ to be p-selective [Sel79] if there is a polynomial-time-computable function $f : \Sigma^* \times \Sigma^* \to \Sigma^*$ such that*

> *(i) for all strings x and y, $f(x, y) = x$ or $f(x, y) = y$, and*
> *(ii) if $x \in A$ or $y \in A$, then $f(x, y) \in A$.*
> > *1. Show that every nonempty set in* P *is p-selective.*
> > *2. Show that if the set of all satisfiable formulas* SAT *is p-selective, then* SAT *belongs to* P.

Homework 6.22   *A probabilistic polynomial-time Turing machine [Gil77] N is a nondeterministic polynomial-time-bounded Turing machine, but the set of words that N accepts is defined differently. Assume that N's computation tree is binary. Assign a probability to each accepting path in N's computation tree by raising 1/2 to a power equal to the number of nondeterministic choices along it. For an input string x, let $\Pr(x)$ be the sum of the probabilities of all accepting paths. Then define $L(N)$ to be the set of all input strings x that are accepted with probability at least 1/2.*

> *1. Show that $L(N) \in$ PSPACE.*
> *2. Suppose, in addition, that $\Pr(x) = 0$ for all $x \notin L(N)$. Show that $L(N) \in$ NP.*

Homework 6.23   *Define a partial function f to be* honest *if there is a polynomial p such that for all $y \in range(f)$, there exists x such that $f(x) = y$ and $|x| \leq p(|f(x)|)$. Which of the following partial functions are honest?*

> *1. Let M be a deterministic polynomial-time-bounded Turing machine. Define $f(x) = y$ if M accepts x and y is an accepting computation of M on x.*
> *2. Let M be a nondeterministic polynomial-time-bounded Turing machine. Define $f(x) = y$ if x is an accepting computation of M and y is the input string that is accepted.*
> *3. Define $f(x) = 0^{\log|x|}$.*

Homework 6.24   *Let f be an honest, polynomial-time-computable partial function. We say that f is* invertible *if there exists a polynomial-time-computable partial function g so that for all $y \in range(f)$, $f(g(y)) = y$.*

1. *Prove that if* P = NP, *then every honest, polynomial-time-computable partial function f is invertible. Hint: Consider the following set pre-f, and observe that pre-f belongs to NP.*

$$pre\text{-}f = \{u\#y \mid \exists v[|v| \le p(|y|) \text{ and } f(uv) = y]\}.$$

2. *Prove that if every honest, polynomial-time-computable partial function is invertible, then* P = NP.

Homework 6.25   *Prove that if there exists an* NP-*complete tally language, then* P = NP. [Ber78]

7

Relative Computability

7.1   NP-Hardness 147

7.2   Search Problems 151

7.3   The Structure of NP 153

7.4   The Polynomial Hierarchy 162

7.5   Complete Problems for Other Complexity Classes 170

7.6   Additional Homework Problems 179

In this chapter we expand more broadly on the idea of using a subroutine for one problem in order to efficiently solve another problem. By doing so, we make precise the notion that the complexity of a problem B is related to the complexity of A—that there is an algorithm to efficiently accept B *relative to* an algorithm to efficiently decide A. As in Section 3.9, this should mean that an acceptor for B can be written as a program that contains subroutine calls of the form "$x \in A$," which returns True if the Boolean test is true and returns False otherwise. Recall that the algorithm for accepting B is called a *reduction procedure* and the set A is called an *oracle*. The reduction procedure is *polynomial time-bounded* if the algorithm runs in polynomial time when we stipulate that only one unit of time is to be charged for the execution of each subroutine call. Placing faith in our modified Church's thesis and in Cobham's thesis, these ideas, once again, are made precise via the oracle Turing machine.

Let M be an oracle Turing machine, let A be an oracle, and let T be a time-complexity function. We define an oracle Turing machine M with oracle A to be $T(n)$ *time-bounded* if, for every input of length n, M makes at most $T(n)$ moves before halting. If M is a nondeterministic oracle Turing machine, then every computation of M with A on words of length n must make at most $T(n)$ moves before halting. The language accepted by M with oracle A is denoted $L(M, A)$.

Let us consider once again the reduction procedure given in Fig. 3.2. For each input word x, the procedure makes a total of $|x|$ queries to the oracle set B. This reduction procedure can be implemented on an oracle Turing machine that operates in time cn^2 for some constant c. Suppose the input word is 110. The string 110 is the first query to B. The second query to the oracle is either 1101 or 1100, depending on whether or not 110 belongs to B. There is a potential of 2^n different queries as B ranges over all possible oracles.

Definition 7.1   *A set A is* Turing-reducible to B in polynomial-time *($A \leq_T^P B$) if there exists a* deterministic *polynomial-time-bounded oracle Turing machine M such that $A = L(M, B)$.*

Polynomial-time Turing reducibility is frequently called "Cook reducibility" in honor of its usage by Cook [Coo71b], who defined NP-completeness and proved that the satisfiability problem is NP-complete. Also, polynomial-time reducibility is the restriction to polynomial time of Turing reducibility (Definition 3.6).

Homework 7.1   *Prove the following facts.*

1. $\leq_T^P$ *is reflexive.*
2. $\leq_T^P$ *is transitive.*
3. $A \leq_T^P B$ *and* $B \in P$ *implies* $A \in P$.
4. *If* $A \in P$ *then, for all* B, $A \leq_T^P B$.
5. $\overline{A} \leq_T^P A$.
6. $A \leq_m^P B$ *implies* $A \leq_T^P B$.

Homework 7.2   *Prove the following: If $A \leq_T^P B$ and $B \in NP \cap co\text{-}NP$, then $A \in NP \cap co\text{-}NP$.*

Homework 7.3   *Prove that $\leq_T^P$ reducibility preserves membership in NP if and only if $NP = co\text{-}NP$.*

A *reducibility*, in general, is a reflexive, transitive binary relation defined on $\mathcal{P}(\Sigma^*)$. Let $\leq_r$ denote an arbitrary reducibility. It is immediate that $\leq_r \cap \leq_r^{-1}$ is an equivalence relation, which is denoted as $\equiv_r$. The equivalence classes of this relation are called *r-degrees*. Let us use $\leq_T^P$ to illustrate these notions. The relation $\equiv_T^P$ defined by $A \equiv_T^P B$ if and only if $A \leq_T^P B$ and $B \leq_T^P A$ is an equivalence relation. Two sets A and B such that $A \equiv_T^P B$ have the same $\leq_T^P$-degree. In this case, we say that they are $\leq_T^P$-equivalent or, informally, that they are "polynomially equivalent." For example, Homework 7.1 states that $\overline{A} \leq_T^P A$, for all A. Thus, A and $\overline{A}$ are polynomially equivalent. As another example, all $\leq_m^P$-complete sets for NP are $\leq_m^P$-equivalent.

Consider again the property that $\overline{A} \leq_T^P A$ for all A. We saw in Homework 6.3 that $\leq_m^P$ preserves membership in NP. If a reducibility were to satisfy both of these properties, then NP would be closed under complements. Indeed, we show next that sets are not in general $\leq_m^P$-reducible to their own complements. Thus, $\leq_m^P$ and $\leq_T^P$ are different reducibilities.

Theorem 7.1 *There is a decidable set A such that $\overline{A} \nleq_m^P A$ (and $A \neq \Sigma^*$ and $A \neq \emptyset$).*

Proof. Let $\{F_i\}_i$ be an effective presentation of the class of polynomial-time-computable functions. Let f_i denote the function computed by F_i. We define a set A so that, for each i,

$$\exists n \neg [0^n \in \overline{A} \Leftrightarrow f_i(0^n) \in A].$$

From this, it follows that, for each i, $\overline{A}$ is not many-one reducible to A by f_i.

A is defined inductively in a sequence of "stages." At stage 0, A is completely undefined. At stage i, $i > 0$, we assume for some n that A is already defined for all words of length less than n, and we call this set $A(n)$. That is, for every word w of length less than n, a decision has already been made concerning whether or not w belongs to A, and no decision has been made for any words of length n or higher.

We do the following at stage i: Compute $f_i(0^n)$. If $f_i(0^n) \in A(n)$, then define $A(n + 1) = A(n) \cup \{0^n\}$. (In this case both 0^n and $f_i(0^n)$ will belong to A.) Note that $A(n + 1)$ contains exactly one word of length n and that all other words of length n will not belong to A. However, if $f_i(0^n)$ does not belong to $A(n)$, either because its length is greater than or equal to n or because at an earlier stage it was excluded from A, then extend the definition of A to all words of length less than $m = 1 + \max\{n, |f_i(0^n)|\}$ as follows: Put 0^n and $f_i(0^n)$ into $\overline{A}$ and put all other words of length n through $m - 1$ into $A(m)$. (In this case, both 0^n and $f_i(0^n)$ will belong to $\overline{A}$.) This completes stage i.

At each stage A is defined on a larger initial segment of Σ^*, so A is eventually defined for every finite length. Both A and $\overline{A}$ are infinite sets, so $A \neq \Sigma^*$ and $A \neq \emptyset$. A is a decidable set because the inductive definition gives an effective procedure for determining membership in A. □

By carefully "padding out" the definition of A, we can make A belong to the complexity class E. This refinement is due to M. Machtey [LLS75].

7.1 NP-Hardness

In the previous chapter we studied NP-completeness, learned of the fundamental role of NP-complete sets, and examined several specific NP-complete problems. Now we will study sets that are as hard as NP, but do not necessarily belong to NP.

Definition 7.2 *A set A is NP-hard if, for every $L \in$ NP, $L \leq_T^P A$.*

There are two very important differences between this notion and NP-completeness. The first is that an NP-hard set does not need to belong to NP. The second is that we use Turing reducibility this time instead of many-one reducibility. Intuitively, a set is NP-hard if it is at least as difficult to recognize as every problem in NP. The proof of the following proposition is straightforward.

Proposition 7.1   *If A is NP-hard and $A \in$ P, then* NP = P.

The notion is of interest only if NP $\neq$ P, for otherwise every set is NP-hard. Namely, if NP = P, so that every set $L \in$ NP belongs to P, by Homework 7.1, for every set A, if $L \in$ NP, then $L \leq_T^P A$.

Trivially, every NP-complete set is NP-hard. By Homework 7.1, the complement of every NP-complete set is NP-hard, but only one call to the oracle is needed in order to Turing-reduce a set to its complement, so in a sense this example is trivial also. Let us consider the following example.

K^{th} LARGEST SUBSET
> **instance** A finite set A, a positive integer size $s(a)$ for each $a \in A$, and two nonnegative integers $B \leq \sum_{a \in A} s(a)$ and $K \leq 2^{\|A\|}$
> **question** Are there at least K distinct subsets $A' \subseteq A$ that satisfy $s(A') \leq B$, where $s(A') = \sum_{a \in A'} s(a)$?

The size of an instance is $O(\|A\| \log s(A))$, where $s(A) = \sum_{a \in A} s(a)$. This problem does not appear to belong to NP, for the natural way to solve it nondeterministically involves guessing K subsets of A, and there is no way to write down such a guess using only a polynomial number of symbols in the size of an instance. There is no known polynomial-time many-one reduction from any NP-complete problem to K^{th} LARGEST SUBSET. However, we show next that the NP-complete PARTITION problem is $\leq_T^P$-reducible to K^{th} LARGEST SUBSET. This was shown by Johnson and Kashdan [JK76], and our proof follows the exposition of Garey and Johnson [GJ79].

Theorem 7.2   PARTITION $\leq_T^P K^{th}$ LARGEST SUBSET.

Proof. We show that PARTITION can be solved in polynomial time relative to an oracle O for K^{th} LARGEST SUBSET. (Given an instance (A, s, b, K) of Kth LARGEST SUBSET, the oracle O answers "yes," if (A, s, b, K) is a yes-instance and answers "no" otherwise.)

Let A and s be an instance of the PARTITION problem that is given as input to the following reduction procedure:

1. Compute $s(A) = \sum_{a \in A} s(a)$.
2. If $s(A)$ is not divisible by 2, then halt and do not accept; else $b := s(A)/2$.
3. Determine the number n of subsets $A' \subseteq A$ such that $s(A') \leq b$. This is accomplished by the following binary search procedure:

MIN := 0;
MAX := $2^{\|A\|}$; {in binary}
while MAX − MIN > 1 **do**
    begin
    K := [MAX + MIN]/2;
    Query O with instance (A, s, b, K);
    if the answer is "yes"
        then MIN := K
        else MAX := K
    end;
n := MIN

To see that the binary search procedure finds n, observe that there are always at least MIN subsets A' such that $s(A') \leq b$ and there are never at least MAX subsets A' such that $s(A') \leq b$. Initially, this is true because MIN = 0 and $s(A) > b$.

4. Query O with instance $(A, s, b − 1, n)$. If the answer is "yes," then every subset for which $s(A') \leq b$ also satisfies $s(A') \leq b − 1$. Thus, in this case, A cannot be partitioned. If the answer is "no," then there is a subset A' such that $s(A') = b$, so, in this case, we accept.

As step 3 uses $\|A\|$ calls to the oracle, and only one additional call is used in step 4, the reduction procedure is polynomial-time-bounded. □

The procedure we just described uses the adaptiveness of Turing reducibility to full advantage and suggests that many-one reducibility could not properly capture the intended notion of NP-hardness. This intuition is confirmed by the corollary to the following theorem. In order to make comparisons properly, we introduce the following uniform notation. Let $\leq_r^P$ denote a polynomial-time reducibility (such as $\leq_m^P$ or $\leq_T^P$) and let $\mathcal{C}$ denote an arbitrary complexity class (such as NP). Define a set A to be $\leq_r^P$-*hard* for $\mathcal{C}$ if for all $L \in \mathcal{C}$, $L \leq_r^P A$. Define a set A to be $\leq_r^P$-*complete* for $\mathcal{C}$ if $A \in \mathcal{C}$ and A is $\leq_r^P$-hard for $\mathcal{C}$. So, $\leq_T^P$-hard for NP is the same as NP-hard, and $\leq_m^P$-complete for NP is the same as NP-complete. Assuming that P $\neq$ NP, we prove the existence of sets that are NP-hard but not $\leq_m^P$-hard for NP.

Theorem 7.3   ([SG77]) *For each decidable set $A \notin$ P, there is a decidable set B such that $A \leq_T^P B$ but $A \not\leq_m^P B$. In particular, $A \leq_T^P B$ by a reduction procedure that on every input makes* two *queries to the oracle.*

Corollary 7.1   *If* P $\neq$ NP, *then there exists a set that is $\leq_T^P$-hard for* NP *but not $\leq_m^P$-hard for* NP.

Proof of Corollary 7.1. If P $\neq$ NP, then the NP-complete language SAT is not in P. By Theorem 7.3, there is a decidable set B such that SAT $\leq_T^P B$ but SAT $\not\leq_m^P B$. That is, B is $\leq_T^P$-hard for NP but not $\leq_m^P$-hard for NP. □

Now we prove the theorem.

Proof. Let A be a decidable set that is not in P. As in the proof of Theorem 7.1, we will construct B in stages. We will ensure that $A \not\leq^P_m B$ by diagonalization, and we will ensure that $A \leq^P_T B$ by preserving the condition

$$x \in A \Leftrightarrow \text{exactly one of } x0 \text{ and } x1 \text{ belongs to } B. \tag{7.1}$$

Recall that $\{F_i\}_i$ is an effective presentation of the class of polynomial-time-computable functions, and let f_i denote the function computed by F_i. At stage 0, B is completely undefined, and at stage i, $i > 0$, we assume for some n that B is already defined for all words of length less than n and we call this set $B(n)$.

The construction at stage i consists of the following steps:

1. Find the smallest x such that either
    (a) $|f_i(x)| < n$ and $x \in A \Leftrightarrow f_i(x) \notin B(n)$, or
    (b) $|f_i(x)| \geq n$.
    If (a) holds for the x that is found, then go directly to step 3 (in this case f_i clearly does not $\leq^P_m$-reduce A to B), and if (b) holds, then go to step 2.
2. Let $f_i(x) = za$, where $a \in \{0, 1\}$, and let $\bar{a}$ denote the complement of a ($\bar{0} = 1$ and $\bar{1} = 0$). Decide membership of $f_i(x) = za$ in B so that $x \in A \Leftrightarrow f_i(x) \notin B$ (hence, f_i does not $\leq^P_m$-reduce A to B). Then decide membership of $z\bar{a} \in B$ so that if $z \in A$, then exactly one of $z0$ and $z1$ belongs to B, and if $z \notin A$, then either both or none of $z0$ and $z1$ belongs to B (hence, Condition 7.1 is preserved).
3. Let $m = 1 + \max\{n, |f_i(x)|\}$ and extend the definition of B to all words of length less than m in a manner that is consistent with Condition 7.1.

This completes the construction.

Step 1 always finds a string x, for otherwise A is many-one reducible in polynomial time to the finite set $B(n)$, which would imply that $A \in$ P. Steps 2 and 3 can be carried out because membership of a string za is decided if and only membership of $z\bar{a}$ is decided. At each stage B is defined on a larger initial segment of Σ^*, so B is eventually defined for every finite length. B is a decidable set because the inductive definition gives an effective procedure for determining membership in B. The construction ensures that $A \leq^P_T B$ and that $A \not\leq^P_m B$. □

What can we say about sets that are $\leq^P_T$-complete for NP? By Proposition 7.1, $\leq^P_T$-complete sets capture the complexity of NP in the same manner as do $\leq^P_m$-complete sets. That is, the following theorem holds.

Theorem 7.4   *If A is $\leq^P_T$-complete for NP, then $A \in$ P if and only if P $=$ NP.*

The proof follows immediately from Proposition 7.1.

It is not known whether there exist sets that are $\leq^P_T$-complete for NP that are not $\leq^P_m$-complete for NP. Whereas we have provided technical justification to support the use of $\leq_T^P$ in the definition of NP-hard, no such technical justification exists to support the use of $\leq_m^P$ in the definition of NP-complete. It works! Thousands of NP-complete problems have been discovered and they are all $\leq_m^P$-equivalent. Also, whether there exist sets A and B in NP such that $A \leq_T^P B$ but $A \not\leq_m^P B$ is an open question.

7.2 Search Problems

Many of the combinatorial decision problems we have examined arise more naturally as problems that involve computing output values that are more useful than accept or reject. For example, one does not care to know merely whether a graph has a Hamiltonian circuit, but one wants a Hamiltonian circuit to be output, if in fact one exists. A given graph might have no Hamiltonian circuit, or there might be several, or even exponentially many. Thus, it is natural to think of the Hamiltonian Circuit problem as a partial multivalued function. Moreover, this function has an obvious nondeterministic algorithm: Guess a path; if it is a Hamiltonian circuit, then output the path.

The problem of computing a Hamiltonian circuit is one example of the more general question of whether witnesses can be computed for sets in NP. The problem of computing witnesses for a set in NP is called a *search* problem. We formalize this as follows: Recall (Theorem 6.1) that a set L belongs to NP if and only if there are a polynomial-time recognizable relation R_L and a polynomial p_L such that, for all x,

$$x \in L \Leftrightarrow \exists y[|y| \leq p_L(|x|) \text{ and } R_L(x, y)].$$

We say that R_L and p_L *define* L. Given a set L, relation R_L, and polynomial p_L that define L, the *search problem* for L (*search problem* for R_L and p_L) is the problem of finding an algorithm that for each instance x computes a string y such that $|y| \leq p_L(|x|)$ and $R_L(x, y)$ if $x \in L$. Obviously, L can be decided in polynomial time from any oracle for solving the search problem for L. We are interested in the converse question. As an important application of $\leq_T^P$-reducibility, we will prove that the search problem for every $\leq_T^P$-complete set L has an algorithm that is polynomially equivalent to L.

Definition 7.3 *Let $L \in$ NP and let R_L and p_L define L.*

$$\mathrm{Prefix}(R_L, p_L) = \{\langle x, u\rangle \mid u \text{ is a prefix of a witness } y \text{ such that}$$
$$|y| \leq p_L(|x|) \text{ and } R_L(x, y)\}.$$

Proposition 7.2   *1.* $\mathrm{Prefix}(R_L, p_L) \in$ NP.

2. $L \leq_m^P \mathrm{Prefix}(R_L, p_L)$.

3. If L is NP-complete, then $\mathrm{Prefix}(R_L, p_L)$ is NP-complete.

4. If L is $\leq_T^P$-complete for NP, then $\mathrm{Prefix}(R_L, p_L)$ is $\leq_T^P$-complete for NP.

begin
input x in $\{0, 1\}^*$;
$y := \lambda$; {the empty string}
while $|y| \le p_L(|x|)$ and $\neg R_L(x, y)$ and $\langle x, y \rangle \in \text{Prefix}(R_L, p_L)$ **do**
if $\langle x, y1 \rangle \in \text{Prefix}(R_L, p_L)$
      then $y := y1$
      else if $\langle x, y0 \rangle \in \text{Prefix}(R_L, p_L)$
           then $y := y0$;
if $R_L(x, y)$, then accept and output y
end.

FIGURE 7.1. A polynomial time-bounded reduction procedure that reduces the search problem for L to $\text{Prefix}(R_L, p_L)$.

Theorem 7.5   *The search problem for R_L and p_L is Turing-reducible in polynomial time to $\text{Prefix}(R_L, p_L)$.*

     Proof. Fig. 7.1 gives an adaptive reduction procedure that accesses $\text{Prefix}(R_L, p_L)$ as an oracle. It is obvious that the procedure is correct—for each input word x, the procedure outputs a string y if and only if y is a witness for $x \in L$—and it is obvious that the procedure runs in polynomial time. $\square$

     The following corollary follows immediately.

Corollary 7.2   *If $L \equiv_T^P \text{Prefix}(R_L, p_L)$, then the search problem for R_L and p_L is Turing-reducible in polynomial time to L.*

Corollary 7.3   *If L is $\le_T^P$-complete for* NP, *then the search problem for L (i.e., for R_L and p_L) is Turing-reducible in polynomial time to L.*

     Proof. If L is $\le_T^P$-complete for NP, then $L \equiv_T^P \text{Prefix}(R_L, p_L)$ follows from Proposition 7.2. So the result follows from Corollary 7.2. $\square$

     Thus, for every $\le_T^P$-complete set L, it is no harder to compute witnesses for L than it is to decide membership in L. Especially, for any $\le_T^P$-complete set L, the search problem for L is solvable in polynomial time if and only if $L \in$ P if and only if NP $=$ P.

     The following notion of *self-reducibility* is important in many complexity theory studies, but we give the definition at this time only to develop the following homework exercises. Loosely speaking, a set is self-reducible if the membership question for any element can be reduced in polynomial-time to the membership question for a number of shorter elements, and a set is *disjunctively* self-reducible if there is a polynomial-time-computable transducer that for any element computes a number of smaller elements $x_1, \ldots, x_n$ such that $x \in L$ if and only if at least one of the smaller elements $x_1, \ldots, x_n$ belongs to L. The classic example is SAT: SAT is disjunctive self-reducible because a Boolean formula $\phi(x_1, \ldots, x_n)$

is satisfiable if and only if at least one of the "shorter" formulas $\phi(0, x_2, \ldots, x_n)$ or $\phi(1, x_2, \ldots, x_n)$ is satisfiable. The formal definition, due to Meyer and Paterson [MP79], follows.

Definition 7.4   *A polynomial-time-computable partial order $<$ on Σ^* is OK if and only if there exist polynomials p and q such that*

    1. *each strictly decreasing chain is finite and every finite decreasing chain is shorter than p of the length of its maximum element, and*

    2. *for all $x, y \in \Sigma^*$, $x < y$ implies that $|x| \leq q(|y|)$.*

Definition 7.5   *A set L is* self-reducible *if there is an OK partial order $<$ and a deterministic polynomial-time-bounded machine M such that M accepts L with oracle L and, on any input x, M asks its oracle only about words strictly less than x in the partial order. L is* disjunctive *self-reducible if, in addition, on every input word x, the query machine either*

    (i) *computes a set of queries $x_1, \ldots, x_n$ in polynomial time so that*

$$x \in L \Leftrightarrow \{x_1, \ldots, x_n\} \cap L \neq \emptyset$$

    or

    (ii) *decides membership of x in L in polynomial time without queries to the oracle.*

Homework 7.4   1. *If L is self-reducible, then $L \in$ PSPACE.*

    2. *If L is disjunctive self-reducible, then $L \in$ NP. ([Ko83])*

    3. *For every polynomial-time recognizable relation R and polynomial p, Prefix(R, p) is disjunctive self-reducible. ([Sel88])*

    4. *If L is disjunctive self-reducible, then there are a relation R_L and polynomial p_L that define L such that $L \equiv_T^P \text{Prefix}(R_L, p_L)$. ([Sel88])*

7.3   The Structure of NP

In this section we will continue to look more closely at the complexity class NP. Thus far, we know that P is a subset of NP and that all complete sets (either $\leq_m^P$-complete or $\leq_T^P$-complete) belong to NP and, by Theorem 7.4, capture the complexity of NP. We want to discover whether there are problems in NP whose complexity lies strictly between P and the complete sets.

Recall that the $\leq_T^P$-degree of a set A consists of all sets B that are $\leq_T^P$-equivalent to A. If $A \in$ NP, then we will say that the $\leq_T^P$-degree of A is "contained in" NP. This does not imply that every set in the $\leq_T^P$-degree of A belongs to NP. For example, suppose that A is an NP-complete set. Then $\overline{A}$ belongs to the $\leq_T^P$-degree of A, but, since we do not expect that co-NP $=$ NP, by Homework 6.11, we do not expect that $\overline{A}$ belongs to NP.

At this point in the course, three logical possibilities may occur:

1. $P = NP$, in which case all sets in NP are $\leq_T^P$-complete for NP, and therefore, NP contains exactly one $\leq_T^P$-degree. (Indeed, in this case, with the exception of $\emptyset$ and Σ^*, all sets in NP would be $\leq_m^P$-complete. However, we choose to carry out this exercise for $\leq_T^P$-reducibility.)

2. $P \neq NP$, and NP contains exactly two different $\leq_T^P$-degrees; one of them is P and the other is the collection of all $\leq_T^P$-complete sets.

3. $P \neq NP$, and there exists a set in NP $-$ P that is not $\leq_T^P$-complete.

We will prove that case 2 cannot occur. Thus, if $P \neq NP$, then there exist sets in NP that are neither in P nor $\leq_T^P$-complete. The theorem is due to Ladner [Lad75], but we will see the result as a corollary to a more general theorem that was proved by Schöning [Sch82].

Definition 7.6 *Two sets A and B are* equal almost everywhere *($A = B$ a.e.) if the symmetric difference of A and B, $A \triangle B$, is a finite set. A class of sets $\mathcal{C}$ is* closed under *finite* variations *if $A \in \mathcal{C}$ and $A = B$ a.e. implies $B \in \mathcal{C}$.*

Since every Turing machine can be made to change its acceptance behavior on a finite set by storing a finite table in its control, without changing its use of computational resources, the complexity classes P and NP are closed under finite variation.

Given a deterministic Turing machine M that halts on every input, let T_M denote the running time of M. We will be interested in certain total computable functions and their Turing-machine computations. Define a function $f : N \rightarrow N$ to be *fast* if the following two properties hold:

1. for all $n \in N$, $f(n) > n$, and

2. there is a Turing machine M that computes f in unary notation such that M writes a symbol on its output tape every move of its computation. In particular, for every n, $f(n) = T_M(n)$.

Proposition 7.3 *For every total computable function f, there is a fast function f' such that, for all n, $f'(n) > f(n)$.*

Proof. Since f is computable, there is a Turing machine M that on input 1^n halts after a finite number of steps with $1^{f(n)}$ written on its output tape. Modify M to M' such that M' has one additional tape, which will be M''s write-only output tape, and such that M', on any input of the form 1^n, behaves like M on input 1^n and, in addition, writes the symbol 1 on its output tape every time it moves. When M' completes its simulation of M, then M' makes one additional move, writing one additional symbol on its output tape. Then M' computes a fast function f', and since on every input M' is simulating M, $f'(n) > f(n)$ must hold for all n.

$\square$

For any function f, define $f^n(x)$ to be the n-fold iteration of f on x ($f^0(x) = x$, $f^1(x) = f(x)$, and $f^{n+1}(x) = f(f^n(x))$). For any function f defined on the set of natural numbers, define

$$G[f] = \{x \in \Sigma^* \mid f^n(0) \le |x| < f^{n+1}(0), \text{ for even } n\}.$$

Lemma 7.1   *If f is fast, then $G[f] \in \mathrm{P}$.*

Proof. On input x, compute 0, $f(0)$, $f(f(0))$, ..., in unary notation, until a word of length at least $|x|$ is obtained, and determine whether the number of f-applications is even or odd. Clearly, at most $|x|$ iterations are needed. The running time is calculated as follows: It takes $f(0)$ steps to compute $f(0)$; it takes $f(f(0))$ steps to compute $f(f(0))$; and so on. As long each of these values is $\le |x|$, so is the running time to compute each value. We would use more than $|x|$ steps only when trying to compute $f^{n+1}(0)$ such that $|x| < f^{n+1}(0)$, but there is no need to complete a computation of $f^{n+1}(0)$. Instead, permit at most $|x| + 1$ steps on the computation of each value. If some computation uses $|x| + 1$ steps, then stop the iteration. There are at most $|x|$ values and each uses at most $|x| + 1$ steps, so the total running time is $O(|x|^2)$. $\square$

Theorem 7.6   *Let A and B be decidable sets and let $\mathcal{C}_1$ and $\mathcal{C}_2$ be classes of decidable sets with the following properties:*

1. *$A \notin \mathcal{C}_1$ and $B \notin \mathcal{C}_2$;*
2. *$\mathcal{C}_1$ and $\mathcal{C}_2$ are effectively presentable; and*
3. *$\mathcal{C}_1$ and $\mathcal{C}_2$ are closed under finite variations.*

Then there exists a decidable set C such that

1. *$C \notin \mathcal{C}_1$ and $C \notin \mathcal{C}_2$, and*
2. *if $A \in \mathrm{P}$ and $B \ne \emptyset$ and $B \ne \Sigma^*$, then $C \le_m^{\mathrm{P}} B$.*

First we show how to obtain from Theorem 7.6 the result in which we are interested. In order to apply the theorem, we need to show that the class of $\le_T^{\mathrm{P}}$-complete sets for NP is effectively presentable. The demonstration of this is significantly more sophisticated than simply attaching polynomial-time Turing-machine clocks, as has worked thus far.

Lemma 7.2   *The class of all $\le_T^{\mathrm{P}}$-complete sets for NP is effectively presentable.*

Proof. Let $\{NP_i\}_i$ be the effective presentation of NP. Let $\{M_i\}_i$ be an effective enumeration of oracle Turing machines such that machine M_i runs in time

$p_i(n) = n^i + i$ and such that every polynomial-time-bounded reduction procedure can be implemented by some M_i. (Simply attach a polynomial clock to each oracle Turing machine, as in Section 3.2.) To construct an effective presentation $\{Q_i\}_i$ of the $\leq_T^P$-complete sets for NP, define Q_n, $n = \langle i, j \rangle$, to be the machine that behaves as follows: On input x, for each string y such that $|y| < |x|$, test whether

$$y \in \text{SAT} \Leftrightarrow y \in L(M_j, L(NP_i)),$$

that is, test whether M_j is correctly reducing SAT to $L(NP_i)$. If this test is true for all such y, then Q_n is to accept x if and only if NP_i accepts x. Otherwise, Q_n is to accept x if and only if $x \in \text{SAT}$.

Suppose X is a $\leq_T^P$-complete set for NP. Then, for some i, $X = L(NP_i)$ and for some j, $\text{SAT} = L(M_j, X)$. Thus, the test will always be true, from which it follows that $L(Q_{\langle i,j \rangle}) = L(NP_i) = X$. Now we need to show for each n that $L(Q_n)$ is $\leq_T^P$-complete for NP. If the test is true for each input x, then $L(Q_n) = L(NP_i)$ is $\leq_T^P$-complete because SAT $\leq_T^P$-reduces to it. However, if for some input x the test fails, then it fails for all strings z such that $|x| \leq |z|$. In this case $L(Q_n) = \text{SAT}$ a.e. Thus, in either case $L(Q_n)$ is $\leq_T^P$-complete for NP. Thus, $\{Q_i\}_i$ is an effective presentation of the $\leq_T^P$-complete sets for NP. □

Homework 7.5 *Let $B \in$ NP. Show that $\{C \in$ NP $\mid B \leq_T^P C\}$ is effectively presentable.*

Corollary 7.4 *If $P \neq$ NP, then there exists a set C in NP $-$ P that is not $\leq_T^P$-complete for NP.*

Proof. Let $A = \emptyset$ and $B = \text{SAT}$, and let $\mathcal{C}_1$ be the collection of all $\leq_T^P$-complete sets for NP, and $\mathcal{C}_2 = $ P. If $P \neq$ NP, then A is not $\leq_T^P$-complete and $B \notin$ P. The complexity class P is effectively presentable, and by Lemma 7.2 the class of all $\leq_T^P$-complete sets for NP is effectively presentable. Thus, Theorem 7.6 is applicable, so there is a decidable set C that satisfies both consequences. The first consequence yields $C \notin$ P and C is not $\leq_T^P$-complete for NP. By the second consequence of Theorem 7.6, $C \leq_m^P$ SAT, from which it follows that $C \in$ NP. Thus, C has all the desired properties. □

Now we will turn to the proof of Theorem 7.6. If R is a unary relation on Σ^*, then $\min\{z \mid R(z)\}$ denotes the lexicographically smallest string z such that $R(z)$, if such a z exists, and is undefined otherwise.

Proof of Theorem 7.6. Let $\{M_i\}_i$ and $\{N_i\}_i$ be effective presentations of $\mathcal{C}_1$ and $\mathcal{C}_2$, respectively. Define functions

$$f_1(n) = \max\{|\min\{z \mid |z| \geq n \text{ and } z \in L(M_i) \triangle A\}| \mid i \leq n\} + 1, \text{ and}$$
$$f_2(n) = \max\{|\min\{z \mid |z| \geq n \text{ and } z \in L(N_i) \triangle B\}| \mid i \leq n\} + 1.$$

We prove that f_1 and f_2 are total computable functions. Since $A \notin \mathcal{C}_1$, for all i, $A \neq L(M_i)$. As $\mathcal{C}_1$ is closed under finite variations, for all i, $L(M_i) \triangle A$ is an infinite set. Thus, for all i, and for all $n \geq i$, there is a string z such that $|z| \geq n$

and $z \in L(M_i) \triangle A$. Observe that the relation defined by "$z \in L(M_i) \triangle A$" is decidable, because A is decidable and M_i halts on all inputs. Min is a computable operator and taking the maximum over a finite sets is a computable operator, so f_1 is computable. The same argument applies to f_2.

Since $\max(f_1, f_2)$ is a total computable function, by Proposition 7.3 there exists a fast function f such that for all n, $f(n) \geq \max(f_1(n), f_2(n))$, and, by Lemma 7.1, $G[f] \in$ P. We prove that the set $C = (G[f] \cap A) \cup (\overline{G[f]} \cap B)$ has the desired properties. (The intuition is this: In order to have $C \not\subseteq C_1$, make C look like A for all strings in $G[f]$. In order to have $C \not\subseteq C_2$, make C look like B for all strings that are not in $G[f]$.)

The definition of f_1 implies the following:

$$j \leq n \Rightarrow \exists z(n \leq |z| < f_1(n) \text{ and } z \in L(M_j) \triangle A). \tag{7.2}$$

Suppose that $C \in C_1$. Then, there is an index j such that $C = L(M_j)$. Select n to be an even positive integer such that $f^n(0) \geq j$. Substituting $f^n(0)$ for n in Equation 7.2, there is a string z such that $f^n(0) \leq |z| < f_1(f^n(0)) < f^{n+1}(0)$ and $z \in L(M_j) \triangle A$. Thus, $z \in G[f]$ and $z \in L(M_j) \triangle A$, which implies, using the definition of C, that $z \in L(M_j) \triangle C$. This is a contradiction. We conclude that $C \not\subseteq C_1$. A similar argument shows that $C \not\subseteq C_2$.

Now we show that the second consequence holds. Suppose that $A \in$ P and $B \neq \emptyset$ and $B \neq \Sigma^*$. Let u and v be fixed words that belong to B and $\overline{B}$, respectively. Then $C \leq_m^P B$ via the following polynomial-time-computable function g:

$$g(x) = \begin{cases} x & \text{if } x \in \overline{G[f]}, \\ u & \text{if } x \in G[f] \text{ and } x \in A, \\ v & \text{if } x \in G[f] \text{ and } x \notin A. \end{cases}$$

This completes the proof. $\qquad\square$

Homework 7.6   (i) *Give the argument to show that $C \not\subseteq C_2$.*

(ii) *Show that $x \in C \Leftrightarrow g(x) \in B$.*

Homework 7.7   *Let $C_0 = (G[f] \cap A) \cup (\overline{G[f]} \cap B)$ be the set constructed in the proof of Theorem 7.6, and let $C_1 = (\overline{G[f]} \cap A) \cup (G[f] \cap B)$. Show that C_1 satisfies all the consequences of Theorem 7.6 as well.*

Consider the proof of Theorem 7.6 as specialized to the proof of Corollary 7.4. Since $A = \emptyset$ in the proof of Corollary 7.4, $C = \overline{G[f]} \cap$ SAT. Also, recall that $\overline{G[f]}$ belongs to P. We see that C is the intersection of SAT with a set that can be recognized in polynomial time. Thus, if P $\neq$ NP, there is a set of formulas of propositional logic that can be recognized in polynomial time, but the restriction of the satisfiability problem to this set of formulas is a set in NP $-$ P that is not $\leq_T^P$-complete for NP.

For any set X and Y, define

$$X \oplus Y = \{0x \mid x \in X\} \cup \{1x \mid x \in Y\}.$$

Homework 7.8   *Prove the following:*

(i) $X \leq_T^P X \oplus Y$ and $Y \leq_T^P X \oplus Y$;

(ii) $X \leq_T^P Z$ and $Y \leq_T^P Z$ implies $X \oplus Y \leq_T^P Z$;

(iii) $X \leq_T^P Y$ and $Z \leq_T^P X \oplus Y$ implies $Z \leq_T^P Y$.

Corollary 7.5   *If* $P \neq NP$, *then there exist* $\leq_T^P$-*incomparable members of* NP. *That is, there exist sets* C_0 *and* C_1 *in* NP *such that* $C_0 \not\leq_T^P C_1$ *and* $C_1 \not\leq_T^P C_0$.

Proof. As in the proof of Corollary 7.4, let $A = \emptyset$ and $B = $ SAT, and let $\mathcal{C}_1$ be the collection of all $\leq_T^P$-complete sets for NP, and $\mathcal{C}_2 = $ P. From the proof of Theorem 7.6, and by Homework 7.7, $C_0 = \overline{G[f]} \cap$ SAT and $C_1 = G[f] \cap$ SAT belong to $NP - P$ and neither C_0 nor C_1 is $\leq_T^P$-complete for NP. Thus, SAT $\not\leq_T^P C_0$ and SAT $\not\leq_T^P C_1$. It is straightforward that SAT $\leq_T^P C_0 \oplus C_1$. So it follows from Homework 7.8, item (iii), that $C_0 \not\leq_T^P C_1$ and $C_1 \not\leq_T^P C_0$. □

Corollary 7.6   *If* $P \neq NP$, *then for every set* $B \in NP - P$, *there is a set* $C \in NP - P$ *such that* $C \leq_T^P B$ *and* $B \not\leq_T^P C$.

By repeated application of Corollary 7.6, if $P \neq NP$, then NP contains countably many distinct $\leq_T^P$-degrees that form an infinite descending hierarchy.

Proof. Let $A = \emptyset$ and $B = $ SAT. Let $\mathcal{C}_1 = \{C \in NP \mid B \leq_T^P C\}$ and $\mathcal{C}_2 = $ P. By Homework 7.5, we may apply Theorem 7.6, and the result is a set C that satisfies the asserted conditions. □

It is instructive to know that there are reasonable classes of sets that are not effectively presentable. We demonstrate this in the next corollary.

Corollary 7.7   *If* $P \neq NP$, *then* $NP - P$ *is not effectively presentable.*

Proof. Suppose that $P \neq NP$ and $NP - P$ is effectively presentable. Then $A = \emptyset$, $B = $ SAT, $\mathcal{C}_1 = NP - P$, and $\mathcal{C}_2 = $ P satisfy the hypotheses of Theorem 7.6. It follows that there is a set C that is not in $\mathcal{C}_1$ and not in $\mathcal{C}_2$, hence not in NP, but $\leq_m^P$-reducible to SAT, hence in NP, a contradiction. □

Homework 7.9   *Show the following: If* $P \neq NP$, *then* $NP - \{\leq_T^P$-*complete sets for NP*$\}$ *is not effectively presentable.*

7.3.1   Composite Number and Graph Isomorphism

The two most famous combinatorial problems that are believed to be intermediate problems in $NP - P$ (with greater or lesser conviction) are the following COMPOSITE NUMBER and GRAPH ISOMORPHISM problems.

GRAPH ISOMORPHISM
      instance Two graphs $G_1 = (V_1, E_1)$ and $G_2 = (V_2, E_2)$
      question Are G_1 and G_2 isomorphic? That is, is there a one-to-one onto function $f : V_1 \mapsto V_2$ such that $\{u, v\} \in E_1 \Leftrightarrow \{f(u), f(v)\} \in E_2$?

COMPOSITE NUMBER

> **instance** A positive integer n, given in binary
> **question** Are there positive integers $j, k > 1$ such that $n = j \cdot k$?

It is obvious that both problems belong to NP. The complement of the COMPOSITE NUMBER problem is the PRIMALITY problem: Given a positive integer n, is n a prime number? In 1975, Pratt [Pra75] demonstrated that PRIMALITY belongs to NP. Thus, if n is a prime number, there exists a short proof of this that can be verified in polynomial time. Pratt's result implies that the COMPOSITE NUMBER problem belongs to NP ∩ co-NP, so COMPOSITE NUMBER cannot be NP-complete unless NP is closed under complements. This is fairly strong evidence that COMPOSITE NUMBER is not NP-complete. In a sense, the only evidence that the COMPOSITE NUMBER problem does not belong to P is the test of time—one is tempted to say that the study of the complexity of the PRIMALITY problems originates with Eratosthenes in the third century B.C. In 1976 Miller [Mil76] proved that testing whether a positive integer is composite or prime can be done deterministically in polynomial time if the "extended Riemann hypothesis" of number theory is true. Also, there exist very good probabilistic algorithms for primality that operate in polynomial time. (This is merely an allusion to an important topic that we will take up in Part II.)

No polynomial-time algorithm for the GRAPH ISOMORPHISM problem is known, but polynomial-time algorithms are known when this problem is restricted to important classes of graphs. Schöning [Sch88] has shown that the GRAPH ISOMORPHISM problem is "nearly" in NP ∩ co-NP. The technical result provides strong evidence that GRAPH ISOMORPHISM is not NP-complete, but we are lacking the technical background to present the result here.

Now we will prove the result of Pratt [Pra75]. We begin with the following theorems of number theory. Recall from Definition 1.15 that for any positive integer n, if $1 < x < n$, the *order* of x (mod n), which we will denote $\mathrm{ord}_n(x)$, is the least positive integer j such that $x^j \equiv 1$ (mod n).

Theorem 7.7   *A positive integer $n > 2$ is prime if and only if there is an integer x, $1 < x < n$, of order $n - 1$ (mod n).*

Proof. Assume n is prime. By Corollary 1.3, Fermat's theorem, $x^{n-1} \equiv 1$ (mod n) for all $x < n$. By Theorem 1.17 and Corollary 1.17, since n is prime, Z_n, the set of integers modulo n, is a finite field and the multiplicative group of nonzero elements is cyclic. Thus, the multiplicative group of noup of nonzero elements has a generator x. By definition, x is an element of order $n - 1$.

If n is not prime, then $(Z_n, \cdot_n)$ is not a group, from which it follows that no element of Z_n can have order $n - 1$ (mod n). $\qquad\square$

Theorem 7.8 $x^s \equiv 1$ (mod n) *if and only if s is a multiple of* $\mathrm{ord}_n(x)$.

Proof. If s is a multiple of $\mathrm{ord}_n(x)$, then trivially, for some k, $x^s \equiv x^{k(\mathrm{ord}_n(x))} \equiv 1^k \equiv 1$ (mod n).

Assume s is not a multiple of $\text{ord}_n(x)$ and $x^s \equiv 1 \pmod{n}$. Without loss of generality, we may assume that $\text{ord}_n(x) < s < 2(\text{ord}_n(x))$. For, if $s \geq 2(\text{ord}_n(x))$, then we can reduce s by $\text{ord}_n(x)$ and still have $x^s \equiv 1 \pmod{n}$. (That is, $x^{s-\text{ord}_n(x)} \equiv x^s x^{-\text{ord}_n(x)} \equiv x^s 1 \equiv 1 \pmod{n}$.) With this assumption, $x^s \equiv 1 \equiv x^{\text{ord}_n(x)} \pmod{n}$. Thus, $x^{s-\text{ord}_n(x)} \equiv 1 \pmod{n}$. But $s - \text{ord}_n(x) < \text{ord}_n(x)$, which, by definition of $\text{ord}_n(x)$, is a contradiction. $\qquad \square$

Lemma 7.3   *Let x and y be integers such that $0 \leq x, y < n$. Then*

> *(i) $x + y \pmod{n}$ can be computed in time $O(\log n)$;*
> *(ii) $x \cdot y \pmod{n}$ can be computed in time $O(\log^2 n)$;*
> *(iii) $x^y \pmod{n}$ can be computed in time $O(\log^3 n)$.*

Proof. Remember that n and all other arithmetic values are written in binary and that $|n| = O(\log n)$. Thus, (i) and (ii) are obvious. The following algorithm computes $x^y \pmod{n}$ by the method of successive squares: Let $a_m \ldots a_1$ be the binary representation of $y \pmod{n}$.

> $A := 1;$
> $w := x;$
> **for** $i := 1$ **to** m **do**
> > **begin**
> > > if $a_i = 1$ **then** $A := A \cdot w \pmod{n}$
> > > $w := w^2 \pmod{n}$
> > **end**
> $\{A = x^y \pmod{n}\}$

This algorithm executes $O(\log n)$ operations that can be computed in $O(\log^2 n)$ steps. Thus, $x^y \pmod{n}$ can be computed in time $O(\log^3 n)$. $\qquad \square$

Theorem 7.9   PRIMALITY *belongs to* NP.

Proof. Fig. 7.2 contains a nondeterministic, recursive algorithm for testing whether an integer is prime. First we show that the algorithm is correct. Suppose the algorithm accepts n. After the first three steps, we know by Theorem 7.8 that $\text{ord}_n(x)$ divides $n - 1$. After step 5 we know that $p_1 \cdots p_k = n - 1$ is a prime factorization of $n - 1$, and after step 6 we know that $\text{ord}_n(x)$ does not divide any factor of $n - 1$. Thus, $\text{ord}_n(x) = n - 1$, so by Theorem 7.7 n is prime. Conversely, if n is prime, then there is an x such that $\text{ord}_n(x) = n - 1$, so there is a computation path that passes each test.

We need to show that the algorithm in Fig. 7.2 can be implemented by a nondeterministic Turing machine in polynomial time. By Lemma 7.3, step 3 can be done in $O(\log^3 n)$ steps. Since the maximum number of prime factors of $n - 1$ occurs in the case where $n - 1$ is a power of 2, the number of prime factors of $n - 1$ is at most $O(\log n)$. Hence, the value of k in step 4 is at most $\log n$, and by Lemma 7.3 step 4 requires at most $O(\log^3 n)$ steps. Each calculation of the

1. Input $n > 2$.
2. Nondeterministically guess x, where $1 < x < n$.
3. Verify that $x^{n-1} \equiv 1 \pmod{n}$. If not, then halt without accepting.
4. Nondeterministically guess a multiset of positive integers $p_1, p_2, \ldots, p_k$ and verify that $p_1 \cdots p_k = n - 1$. If not, then halt without accepting.
5. Recursively, verify that each p_i, $1 \leq i \leq k$, is a prime number. If not all are prime, then halt without accepting.
6. For each $1 \leq i \leq k$, verify that $x^{(n-1)/p_i} \not\equiv 1 \pmod{n}$. If not, then halt without accepting.
7. Accept.

FIGURE 7.2. A recursive, nondeterministic algorithm for PRIMALITY.

form $x^{(n-1)/p_i} \pmod{n}$ can be done be done in $O(\log^3 n)$ steps. Step 6 contains at most $O(\log n)$ such calculations, so step 6 can be done in $O(\log^4 n)$ steps. To complete the analysis, we need to add the time taken for step 5. We calculate this by induction. More exactly, we prove by induction that the number of steps to recognize that n is prime is bounded by $O(\log^5 n)$. We assume as induction hypothesis that each recursive call can be executed in $O(\log^5 n)$ steps. So step 5 takes at most

$$\sum_{i=1}^{k} O(\log^5 p_i) \leq O(\log^5 n)$$

steps. (To verify the inequality, observe that $\log^5 a + \log^5 b \leq \log^5 ab$, and $\prod_{i=1}^{k} p_i$ is less than n.) Thus, the number of steps for an incarnation is

$$O(\log^3 n) + O(\log^3 n) + \sum_{i=1}^{k} O(\log^5 p_i) + O(\log^4 n) = O(\log^5 n),$$

and this completes the proof. $\qquad\qquad\square$

7.3.2 Reflection

Before continuing with our technical development, let's pause to reflect on the question of whether P = NP. As we have seen in our discussion of NP-complete and NP-hard problems, this question has great consequence for numerous areas of computer science and for computational problems in other sciences. The general belief among those who have thoughtfully considered the question is that P is not equal to NP. There is no compelling scientific basis for this belief, only the intuition developed over time by those working in this field.

Regardless of what might be proved in the future, technology needs to live with the current situation. That is, there is no known efficient method to solve

NP-complete or NP-hard problems. For this reason many techniques for dealing with intractability have been developed. One of the triumphs of the theory of computing has been the creation of approximation algorithms for NP-complete problems. These are practical algorithms with provable performance guarantees that offer close to optimal solutions [Hoc96].

Intractability is by no means wholly a bad thing. Although we are not studying the relationship between complexity theory and cryptography in this text, let us mention that if P = NP, then modern cryptography would not exist and neither would much of the security of computer systems and digital transactions [Sel89]. As well, the beautiful and intricate theory that we have been studying, based on the underlying assumption that P differs from NP, would be nullified. This comment is true of the topic that we take up next.

7.4   The Polynomial Hierarchy

The polynomial hierarchy was defined by Stockmeyer [MS72, Sto76] and is a polynomial-time analog of the arithmetical hierarchy (Definition 3.11). In addition to Stockmeyer, several important properties were proved by Wrathall [Wra76]. The polynomial hierarchy adds a potential infinity of complexity classes between P and PSPACE and is another useful tool for the classification of combinatorial problems.

The oracle Turing machines we have considered so far are all deterministic, but now let us define a set A to be *nondeterministic Turing-reducible to B* in polynomial time ($A \leq_T^{NP} B$) if there is a nondeterministic polynomial-time-bounded oracle Turing machine M such that $A = L(M, B)$. For any set A, let $P^A = \{B \mid B \leq_T^P A\}$ and let $NP^A = \{B \mid B \leq_T^{NP} A\}$. So P^A (NP^A) is the class of sets accepted deterministically (nondeterministically, respectively) in polynomial time relative to the set A. For a class of sets $\mathcal{C}$, let $P^{\mathcal{C}} = \bigcup\{P^A \mid A \in \mathcal{C}\}$ and $NP^{\mathcal{C}} = \bigcup\{NP^A \mid A \in \mathcal{C}\}$. Then the *polynomial hierarchy* is the collection of all classes $\{\Sigma_k^P, \Pi_k^P, \Delta_k^P\}_{k \geq 0}$, where these classes are defined inductively as follows:

$$\Sigma_0^P = \Pi_0^P = \Delta_0^P = P,$$

and, for $k \geq 0$,

$$\Sigma_{k+1}^P = NP^{\Sigma_k^P},$$
$$\Pi_{k+1}^P = \text{co-}\Sigma_{k+1}^P, \text{ and}$$
$$\Delta_{k+1}^P = P^{\Sigma_k^P}.$$

Example 7.1   *1.* $\Sigma_1^P = NP^{\Sigma_0^P} = NP^P = NP$.

    2. $\Pi_1^P = \text{co-NP}$.

    3. $\Delta_1^P = P^P = P$.

4. $\Delta_2^P = P^{NP}$.

5. $\Sigma_2^P = NP^{NP}$.

We see from these examples that the polynomial hierarchy extends the classes P and NP. It is not known whether any of the classes are distinct or whether there are infinitely many classes. We will begin by establishing several basic properties.

Proposition 7.4   *For all* $k \geq 0$, $\Sigma_k^P \bigcup \Pi_k^P \subseteq \Delta_{k+1}^P \subseteq \Sigma_{k+1}^P \cap \Pi_{k+1}^P$.

For the proof, observe that $A \in \Sigma_k^P$ implies $\overline{A} \in P^{\Sigma_k^P} = \Delta_{k+1}^P$. Define

$$PH = \bigcup \{\Sigma_k^P \mid k \geq 0\}.$$

Proposition 7.5   PH $\subseteq$ PSPACE.

Proof. The proof is by induction, and cases $k = 0$ and $k = 1$ are already known. Assume $\Sigma_k^P \subseteq$ PSPACE. Then $\Sigma_{k+1}^P = NP^{\Sigma_k^P} \subseteq NP^{PSPACE} =$ PSPACE, by Corollary 5.7.   □

It is not known whether $\Sigma_1^P \subset \Sigma_2^P$ or whether $\Sigma_k^P \subset \Sigma_{k+1}^P$ for any $k \geq 0$. After all,

$$P \subseteq NP = \Sigma_1^P \subseteq \Sigma_2^P \subseteq \cdots \subseteq PH \subseteq PSPACE,$$

and it is not known whether any of these classes separate.

Proposition 7.6   *The following are equivalent for all* $k \geq 1$:

(i) $\Sigma_k^P = \Sigma_{k+1}^P$;

(ii) $\Pi_k^P = \Pi_{k+1}^P$;

(iii) $\Sigma_k^P = \Pi_k^P$;

(iv) $\Sigma_k^P = \Pi_{k+1}^P$;

(v) $\Pi_k^P = \Sigma_{k+1}^P$.

Proof. Assertions (i) and (ii) are equivalent by definition. Only the proof that (iii) implies (i) is interesting. We leave all other directions as a homework exercise.

Assume $\Sigma_k^P = \Pi_k^P$ and let $L \in \Sigma_{k+1}^P$. There is a set $L' \in \Sigma_k^P$ such that $L \in NP^{L'}$. Then there are sets L_1 and L_2, both belonging to Σ_{k-1}^P, so that $L' \in NP^{L_1}$ and $\overline{L'} \in NP^{L_2}$. The latter is true because, by hypothesis, $\overline{L'} \in \Sigma_k^P$. Let M', M_1, and M_2 be machines that witness the oracle procedures $L \in NP^{L'}$, $L' \in NP^{L_1}$, and $\overline{L'} \in NP^{L_2}$, respectively. Observe that the set $L_1 \oplus L_2$ belongs to Σ_{k-1}^P. Design a nondeterministic oracle Turing machine M to accept L with oracle $L_1 \oplus L_2$ as follows, thereby demonstrating that $L \in \Sigma_k^P$: The machine M simulates M' except that M replaces queries q to L' by simultaneous simulations of M_1 and M_2 on input q to the oracle $L_1 \oplus L_2$. Specifically, M, when simulating M_1, replaces queries w to M_1's oracle with queries $0w$, and, when simulating M_2, replaces

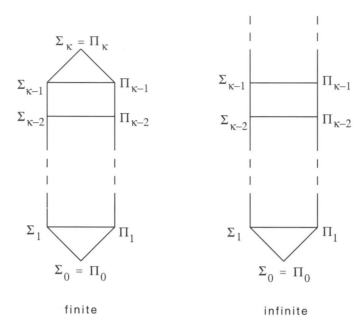

$$\Sigma_\kappa = \Pi_\kappa$$

$\Sigma_{\kappa-1}$ $\Pi_{\kappa-1}$

$\Sigma_{\kappa-2}$ $\Pi_{\kappa-2}$

Σ_1 Π_1

$$\Sigma_0 = \Pi_0$$

finite

$\Sigma_{\kappa-1}$ $\Pi_{\kappa-1}$

$\Sigma_{\kappa-2}$ $\Pi_{\kappa-2}$

Σ_1 Π_1

$$\Sigma_0 = \Pi_0$$

infinite

FIGURE 7.3. The polynomial hierarchy.

queries w with queries $1w$. Then M continues its simulation of M' in the "yes" state if M_1 accepts q, M continues its simulation of M' in the "no" state if M_2 accepts q, and M halts without accepting if neither M_1 nor M_2 accepts. It is easy to see that M behaves as we claimed. Thus, $\Sigma_{k+1}^P \subseteq \Sigma_k^P$ follows.   □

Homework 7.10 *Complete the proof of Proposition 7.6.*

In particular, NP $=$ co-NP $\Leftrightarrow$ $\Sigma_1^P = \Sigma_2^P$. The following result shows that if for some $k \geq 1$, $\Sigma_k^P = \Pi_k^P$, then for all $j \geq k$, $\Sigma_j^P = \Pi_j^P = \Sigma_k^P$. Thus, the polynomial hierarchy must be of one of the forms given in Fig. 7.3. No two "points" among Σ_k^P, Π_k^P, $k \geq 1$, may be equal to any of the rest without the entire hierarchy collapsing from that point upward. Conversely, if any two points can be shown to be distinct, the entire "ladder" must exist at distinct points from that level down. In particular, NP $=$ P if and only if PH $=$ P.

Theorem 7.10 *If for some $k \geq 1$, $\Sigma_k^P = \Pi_k^P$, then for all $j \geq k$, $\Sigma_j^P = \Pi_j^P = \Sigma_k^P$.*

Proof. The proof is by induction on j. The base case $j = k$ is immediate. Assume as induction hypothesis that $\Sigma_{j-1}^P = \Pi_{j-1}^P \subseteq \Sigma_k^P$ for some $j > k$. Then, by Proposition 7.6, $\Sigma_j^P = \Sigma_{j-1}^P \subseteq \Sigma_k^P$ and $\Pi_j^P = \Sigma_{j-1}^P \subseteq \Sigma_k^P$. The conclusion immediately follows.   □

The following theorem generalizes Theorem 6.1.

Theorem 7.11   *For all $k \geq 1$, $L \in \Sigma_k^P$ if and only if there are a polynomial $q(n)$ and a relation $R(x, y_1, \ldots, y_k)$ in P such that*

$$x \in L \Leftrightarrow \exists y_1 \forall y_2 \ldots Q_k y_k R(x, y_1, \ldots, y_k), \qquad (7.3)$$

where the quantifiers alternate ($Q_k = \forall$ if k is even, and $Q_k = \exists$ if k is odd) and $y_1, \ldots, y_k$ range over words of length $\leq q(|x|)$. Dually, $L \in \Pi_k^P$ if and only if

$$x \in L \Leftrightarrow \forall y_1 \exists y_2 \ldots Q_k' y_k R'(x, y_1, \ldots, y_k), \qquad (7.4)$$

Proof. For each k, let $\mathcal{E}_k$ ($\mathcal{A}_k$) denote the set of all languages L that satisfy Equation 7.3 (Equation 7.4, respectively). We want to prove for all $k \geq 1$ that $\mathcal{E}_k = \Sigma_k^P$ and $\mathcal{A}_k = \Pi_k^P$. Note for all k that $\mathcal{A}_k = co - \mathcal{E}_k$, so if $\mathcal{E}_k = \Sigma_k^P$, then $\mathcal{A}_k = \Pi_k^P$ follows.

Theorem 6.1 gives the base case, $k = 1$. Let $k \geq 1$, and assume as induction hypothesis that the assertions hold for k. Let $L \in \mathcal{E}_{k+1}$ satisfy the conditions of Equation 7.3. Define $L' = \{\langle x, y_1 \rangle \mid \forall y_2 \ldots Q_{k+1} y_{k+1} R(x, y_1, \ldots, y_{k+1})\}$. By the induction hypothesis, $L' \in \Pi_k^P$. L is accepted by a nondeterministic polynomial-time-bounded oracle Turing machine that, on input x, guesses $y_1 \leq q(|x|)$ and accepts if and only if the pair $\langle x, y_1 \rangle$ belongs to L'. Thus, $L \in \mathrm{NP}^{\Pi_k^P}$. But $\mathrm{NP}^{\Pi_k^P} = \mathrm{NP}^{\Sigma_k^P} = \Sigma_{k+1}^P$, so $L \in \Sigma_{k+1}^P$. Thus, $\mathcal{E}_{k+1} \subseteq \Sigma_{k+1}^P$.

The converse is more complicated. Let $L \in \Sigma_{k+1}^P$. Let $L' \in \Sigma_k^P$ such that $L \in \mathrm{NP}^{L'}$ and let M be a nondeterministic polynomial-time-bounded oracle Turing machine that accepts L with oracle L'. Define L_1 to be the set of all tuples $\langle x, y, u, v \rangle$ such that y is a computation of M on x that causes M to query its oracle about the strings in $u = \langle u_1, \ldots, u_m \rangle$ and $v = \langle v_1, \ldots, v_n \rangle$ and that causes M to accept x if the answers are "yes" to the strings in u and "no" to the strings in v. Observe that $L_1 \in \mathrm{P}$ and $|y|$, $|u|$, and $|v|$ are bounded by a polynomial in $|x|$. The following property is satisfied:

$$x \in L \Leftrightarrow \exists y \exists u \exists v [\langle x, y, u, v \rangle \in L_1 \wedge u = \langle u_1, \ldots, u_m \rangle \wedge v = \langle v_1, \ldots, v_n \rangle$$
$$\wedge u_1 \in L' \wedge \cdots \wedge u_m \in L' \wedge v_1 \in \overline{L'} \wedge \cdots \wedge v_n \in \overline{L'}]. \qquad (7.5)$$

By induction hypothesis, $L' \in \mathcal{E}_k$ and $\overline{L'} \in \mathcal{A}_k$. For each assertion $u_i \in L'$ and $v_j \in \overline{L'}$ that occurs in Equation 7.5, substitute the corresponding alternating quantifier expression. Then move all quantifiers forward into prenex normal form in the usual way. The result is an expression with $k + 1$ blocks of alternating quantifiers such that the first quantifier is existential, all are bounded by a polynomial in the length of x, and the matrix is a relation in P. To complete the proof, we observe that a block of quantifiers of the same kind can be replaced by a single quantifier with the help of pairing functions: Recall that if $z = \langle x, y \rangle$, then $\tau_1(z) = x$, $\tau_2(z) = y$, and these functions are computable in polynomial time. The extension to arbitrary n-tuples appears in Section 3.3. Any formula $\exists z_1 \exists z_2 S(x, z_1, z_2)$ can be replaced by the equivalent formula $\exists z[S(x, \tau_1(z), \tau_2(z))]$, and $\forall z_1 \forall z_2 S(x, z_1, z_2)$ can be replaced by $\forall z[S(x, \tau_1(z), \tau_2(z))]$. Thus, the expression in Equation 7.5 can be converted into an expression with $k + 1$ alternating quantifiers, thereby demonstrating that $L \in \mathcal{E}_{k+1}$. Therefore, $\mathcal{E}_{k+1} = \Sigma_{k+1}^{P}$ and $\mathcal{A}_{k+1} = \Pi_{k+1}^{P}$. $\square$

The following example elucidates the proof techniques that we just described.

Example 7.2 *Let $L \in \Sigma_3^{P}$ be given by $L \in NP^{L'}$, where $L' \in \Pi_2^{P}$. Assume*

$$x \in L' \Leftrightarrow \forall z_1 \exists z_2 R(x, z_1, z_2). \tag{7.6}$$

Suppose L_1 is defined as in the proof of Theorem 7.11 and suppose that

$$x \in L \Leftrightarrow \exists y \exists u \exists v [\langle x, y, u, v \rangle \in L_1 \wedge u = \langle u_1, u_2 \rangle \wedge v = \langle v_1 \rangle$$
$$\wedge u_1 \in L' \wedge u_2 \in L' \wedge v_1 \in \overline{L'}]. \tag{7.7}$$

We use Equation 7.6 to substitute into Equation 7.7 in order to get the following equivalence:

$$x \in L \Leftrightarrow \exists y \exists u \exists v [\langle x, y, u, v \rangle \in L_1 \wedge u = \langle u_1, u_2 \rangle \wedge v = \langle v_1 \rangle \wedge$$
$$\forall z_1 \exists z_2 R(u_1, z_1, z_2) \wedge \forall s_1 \exists s_2 R(u_2, s_1, s_2) \wedge \exists t_1 \forall t_2 \neg R(v_1, t_1, t_2)] \tag{7.8}$$

$$\Leftrightarrow \exists y \exists u \exists v \exists t_1 \forall z_1 \forall s_1 \forall t_2 \exists z_2 \exists s_2 [\langle x, y, u, v \rangle \in L_1 \wedge u = \langle u_1, u_2 \rangle$$
$$\wedge v = \langle v_1 \rangle \wedge R(u_1, z_1, z_2) \wedge R(u_2, s_1, s_2) \wedge \neg R(v_1, t_1, t_2)]. \tag{7.9}$$

Let $M(x, y, u, v, t_1, z_1, s_1, t_2, z_2, s_2)$ denote the matrix of the expression in line 7.9. Observe that the relation M belongs to P. Finally, writing $y_1 = \langle y, u, v, t_1 \rangle$, $y_2 = \langle z_1, s_1, t_2 \rangle$, and $y_3 = \langle z_2, s_2 \rangle$, we collapse like quantifiers to get the following:

$$x \in L \Leftrightarrow \exists y_1 \forall y_2 \exists y_3 M(x, \tau_{41}(y_1), \tau_{42}(y_1), \tau_{43}(y_1), \tau_{44}(y_1), \tau_{31}(y_2),$$
$$\tau_{32}(y_2), \tau_{33}(y_2), \tau_1(y_3), \tau_2(y_3)).$$

This is the three-alternating-quantifier expression that defines L.

Corollary 7.8 *$A \leq_m^{P} B$ and $B \in \Sigma_n^{P}$ implies $A \in \Sigma_n^{P}$.*

Corollary 7.9 *Let $L \in \Sigma_k^{P}$, $k \geq 1$. There are a binary relation $R \in \Pi_{k-1}^{P}$ and a polynomial q such that*

$$x \in L \Leftrightarrow \exists y[|y| \leq q(|x|) \text{ and } R(x, y)].$$

Given an oracle Turing machine M, we sometimes let $M^{()}$ denote M and let M^A denote M operating with A as the oracle. Much of the theory about NP that we developed in Chapter 4 carries over with only minimal alteration of proofs to NP^A, for any oracle set A, and we may apply this fact with dispatch to obtain results about the polynomial hierarchy. For example, we attach polynomial-time clocks to nondeterministic polynomial-time-bounded oracle Turing machines to construct an effective enumeration $\{NP_i^{(\,)}\}_{i \geq 1}$ of nondeterministic polynomial-time-bounded oracle Turing machines such that for every oracle A, $\{NP_i^A\}_{i \geq 1}$ is an effective presentation of NP^A. We define $\mathcal{U}^A$ and K^A as follows:

$$\mathcal{U}^A = \{\langle i, x, 0^n \rangle | \text{ some computation of } NP_i^A \text{ accepts } x \text{ in fewer than } n \text{ steps}\}$$

and

$$K^A = \{i \mid NP_i^A \text{ accepts } i \text{ within } |i| \text{ steps}\}.$$

Theorem 7.12 *For any oracle A, $\mathcal{U}^A$ and K^A are $\leq_m^P$-complete for NP^A.*

The proofs are given in the proofs of Theorems 6.6 and 6.9. The only change is that i is the index of NP_i^A rather than NP_i. Now we will use this result to obtain complete sets for each level of the polynomial hierarchy. The discussion can be carried out with $\mathcal{U}^A$ as the starting point, but it is somewhat more traditional to use K^A. First, let us single out the following two consequences of Theorem 7.12.

Corollary 7.10 $NP^A \neq P^A$ *implies* $K^A \not\leq_T^P A$.

Corollary 7.11 $B \in NP^A$ *if and only if* $B \leq_m^P K^A$.

Define $K^{(1)} = K$, and for $n \geq 1$, $K^{(n+1)} = K^{K^{(n)}}$. Thus, $K^{(2)} = K^K$.

Theorem 7.13 *For all $n \geq 1$, $K^{(n)}$ is $\leq_m^P$-complete for Σ_n^P.*

Proof. The proof is by induction on n. The base $n = 1$ is given by Theorem 6.9. As induction hypothesis, suppose the assertion is true for some $n \geq 1$. By definition $K^{(n+1)} = K^{K^{(n)}}$, and by induction hypothesis $K^{(n)} \in \Sigma_n^P$. So $K^{(n+1)} \in NP^{\Sigma_n^P} = \Sigma_{n+1}^P$.

Let $B \in \Sigma_{n+1}^P$. For some $A \in \Sigma_n^P$, $B \in NP^A$, and by the induction hypothesis, $A \leq_m^P K^{(n)}$. It is easy to see that $B \in NP^{K^{(n)}}$: Let M be a nondeterministic polynomial-time-bounded Turing machine such that $B = L(M, A)$ and let f be a many-one polynomial-time reduction from A to $K^{(n)}$. Define M_1 to be an oracle Turing machine that simulates M except that whenever M enters a query state with a word w on its query tape, M_1 should write $f(w)$ on its query tape and then M_1 should query the oracle $K^{(n)}$. Obviously, $B = L(M_1, K^{(n)})$, so $B \in NP^{K^{(n)}}$.

Using Corollary 7.11, we have $B \leq_m^P K^{K^{(n)}} = K^{(n+1)}$. Thus, $K^{(n+1)}$ is $\leq_m^P$-complete for Σ_{n+1}^P. $\square$

Definition 7.7 *For each $k \geq 0$, define*

$$A_k = \{\langle k, i, x, 0^m, 0^n \rangle \mid (\exists y_1, |y_1| \leq m) \cdots (Q_k y_k, |y_k| \leq m)$$
$$[P_i \text{ accepts } \langle x, y_1, \cdots, y_k \rangle \text{ in } \leq n \text{ steps}]\}.$$

Homework 7.11 *Use Theorem 7.11 to show for each $k \geq 0$ that A_k is $\leq_m^P$-complete for Σ_k^P.*

The first and most well-known collection of problems shown to be $\leq_m^P$-complete for Σ_k^P, $k \geq 1$, are extensions of the satisfiability problem that are formed by quantifying Boolean formulas with k alternating quantifiers. We define these now.

For $i = 1, \ldots, k$, let X^i be a sequence of Boolean variables $\{x[i, j] \mid 1 \le j \le n_i\}$, where $n_i \ge 1$. Consider a Boolean formula $F(X^1, \ldots, X^k)$ in which the occurrence of X^i denotes occurrences of $x[i, 1], \ldots, x[i, n_i]$, the variables in $X^1, \ldots, X^k$ occur in F, and no other variables occur in F. Let $\exists X^i$ denote $\exists x[i, 1] \ldots \exists x[i, n_i]$, and let $\forall X^i$ denote $\forall x[i, 1] \ldots \forall x[i, n_i]$.

Definition 7.8   *For each $k \ge 1$, B_k is the set of all Boolean formulas $F(X^1, \ldots, X^k)$ such that*

$$\exists X^1 \forall X^2 \cdots Q X^k [F(X^1, \ldots, X^k) \text{ is true}].$$

Observe that B_1 is the set of all satisfiable formulas.

Example 7.3   *Let $F = (x[1, 1] \wedge x[1, 2]) \vee x[2, 1]$. Then $F \in B_2$.*

We will prove, for all $k \ge 1$, that B_k is $\le_m^P$-complete for Σ_k^P. By Theorem 7.11, for each $k \ge 1$, $B_k \in \Sigma_k^P$. Clearly, case $k = 1$ is a restatement of the important corollary to the Cook–Levin theorem, Corollary 6.2, so it is natural to give a proof by induction that uses the characterization given in Theorem 7.11. First we need to develop some technical apparatus. Consider functions ρ that map positive integers into Boolean formulas and have the following property: There exist $k \ge 1$, $v \ge 2$, and polynomials $p_1, \ldots, p_k$ such that for all $n \ge 1$, the variables in $\rho(n)$ are

$$X^m = \{x[m, j] \mid 1 \le j \le p_m(n)\}, 1 \le m \le k,$$
$$I = \{x[k + i, j] \mid 1 \le i \le n, 0 \le j \le v\}.$$

For a word $w = s_{k_1} \ldots s_{k_n}$ of length n over the finite alphabet $\{s_0, s_1, \ldots, s_v\}$, $\rho(n, w)$ denotes the formula resulting from $\rho(n)$ by the following assignment to the variables in the set I: $x[k + i, j] = 1$ if and only if the ith symbol of w is s_j. The only variables in $\rho(n, w)$ are the variables in $X^1, \ldots, X^k$.

Theorem 7.14   *For $k \ge 1$, for each language L in Σ_k^P or Π_k^P, there is a function ρ_L (as described in the previous paragraph) such that the function $(\lambda w)\rho_L(|w|, w)$ is computable in polynomial time and the following properties hold: If $L \in \Sigma_k^P$, then*

$$w \in L \Leftrightarrow \exists X^1 \forall X^2 \cdots Q X^k [\rho_L(|w|, w) \text{ is true}] \quad .$$
$$\Leftrightarrow \rho_L(|w|, w) \in B_k;$$

and, if $L \in \Pi_k^P$, then

$$w \in L \Leftrightarrow \forall X^1 \exists X^2 \cdots Q' X^k [\rho_L(|w|, w) \text{ is true}].$$

Proof.   The proof is by induction, and we consider the base case $k = 1$. Assume L belongs to NP and let M be a single-tape nondeterministic polynomial-time-bounded Turing machine that accepts L in the manner described in Section 5.3.

Recall the construction in the proof of Theorem 6.8 and recall that the formula constructed there may contain Boolean variables $S[i, j, m]$, for each $0 \leq i \leq p(n)$, $1 \leq j \leq p(n) + 1$, and $0 \leq m \leq v$, with the intended meaning that $S[i, j, m]$ should evaluate to True if at time i the jth tape square contains the symbol s_m. In particular, given an input word $w = s_{k_1} \ldots s_{k_n}$, formula G_4 contains the conjunction

$$S[0, 1, k_1] \wedge S[0, 2, k_2] \wedge \cdots \wedge S[0, n, k_n] \tag{7.10}$$

that binds the input to the first n squares of the tape before computation begins. Define $\rho_L(n)$ to be the formula constructed in Theorem 6.8 with the following exception: Replace the conjunction listed in 7.10 that binds the input word to the tape with the cnf formula

$$(\bigvee_{1 \leq m \leq v} S[0, 1, m]) \wedge (\bigvee_{1 \leq m \leq v} S[0, 2, m]) \wedge \cdots \wedge (\bigvee_{1 \leq m \leq v} S[0, n, m]),$$

which stipulates that each of the first n tape squares contains a nonblank symbol but otherwise leaves the input word unspecified. Let X^1 be the set of all other variables. For each word $w = s_{k_1} \ldots s_{k_n}$ of length n, define $\rho_L(|w|, w)$ to be the formula that results by assigning

$$S[0, 1, k_1] = \cdots = S[0, n, k_n] = 1$$

and all other variables in I to 0. Then, it follows from Theorem 6.8 that $(\lambda w)\rho_L(|w|, w)$ is polynomial-time-computable and that

$$w \in L \Leftrightarrow \rho_L(|w|, w) \text{ is satisfiable}$$
$$\Leftrightarrow \exists X_1[\rho_L(|w|, w) \text{ is true}]$$
$$\Leftrightarrow \rho_L(|w|, w) \in B_1.$$

The assertion for $L \in \Pi_1^P$ follows immediately.

Let $k \geq 1$ and assume as induction hypothesis that the theorem holds for k. Let $L \in \Sigma_{k+1}^P$. By Corollary 7.9, there are a relation $R \in \Pi_k^P$ and a polynomial q such that

$$x \in B \Leftrightarrow \exists y[|y| \leq q(|x|) \text{ and } R(x, y)].$$

Let # be a symbol not in the alphabet of L, and let $L_1 = \{x\#y \mid R(x, y)\}$. $L_1 \in \Pi_k^P$, so by induction hypothesis there is a function ρ_{L_1} such that

$$x\#y \in L_1 \Leftrightarrow \forall X^1 \exists X^2 \cdots Q' X^k [\rho_{L_1}(|x\#y|, x\#y) \text{ is true}].$$

The input variables in $\rho_{L_1}(n + 1 + q(n))$ are

$$I_1 = \{x[k + i, j] \mid 1 \leq i \leq n, 0 \leq j \leq v\}$$

for an initial substring of length n of the input, all variables $x[k + n + 1, j]$, $0 \leq j \leq v$, and

$$I_2 = \{x[k+i, j] \mid n+2 \le i \le q(n), 0 \le j \le v\}$$

for the remainder of the string.

We construct $\rho_L(n)$ from $\rho_{L_1}(n+1+q(n))$ as follows: Retain I_1 as the input variables I and set the variable $x[k+n+1, 0] = 1$, assuming that $s_0 = \#$, and set $x[k+n+1, j] = 0$ for $j \ge 1$. Change X^k to X^{k+1}, X^{k-1} to X^k, ..., and X^1 to X^2. Then convert the variables that remain in I_2 to $X^1 = \{x[1, j] \mid 1 \le j \le (q(n) - (n+1))v\}$. $(\lambda w)\rho(|w|, w)$ is computable in polynomial time by the induction hypothesis. For any string w of length n, $w \in L$ if and only if there is an assignment I_2 in $\rho_{L_1}(n+1+q(n))$ such that if the variables in I_1 are assigned to describe w, then

$$\forall X^2 \exists X^3 \cdots Q' X^{k+1}[\rho_{L_1}(n+1+q(n)) \text{ with these assignments is true}].$$

Thus,

$$w \in L \Leftrightarrow \exists X_1 \forall X_2 \cdots Q X_k[\rho_L(|w|, w) = T].$$

This is what we needed to prove. The case for $L \in \Pi^P_{k+1}$ follows immediately. $\square$

Corollary 7.12   *For all $k \ge 1$, B_k is $\le^P_m$-complete for Σ^P_k.*

Proof. Clearly, each B_k is in Σ^P_k. For each $k \ge 1$, and $L \in \Sigma^P_k$, $(\lambda w)\rho_L(|w|, w)$ is an $\le^P_m$-reduction from L to B_k. $\square$

Although the polynomial hierarchy was first defined and studied by Stockmeyer [Sto76], it was anticipated by Karp [Kar72]. Our proof that K^n is $\le^P_m$-complete for Σ^P_n is a straightforward application of techniques that are standard in computability theory and that we hinted at in Section 3.9; their first use in complexity theory may be due to Heller [Hel81]. Theorem 7.11 is due to Wrathall [Wra76]. Stockmeyer [Sto76] discovered that B^n is $\le^P_m$-complete for Σ^P_n. Our proof is adapted from Wrathall's [Wra76]. Natural complete problems are known for Δ^P_2 [Kre88, Pap84] and for Σ^P_2 [Sto76]. Natural complete problems are not known for higher levels of the polynomial hierarchy. Then again, in what sense would a problem that required at least three alternating quantifiers to describe be natural?

7.5   Complete Problems for Other Complexity Classes

Complete problems are not known for POLYLOGSPACE, but for all other complexity classes in our list of standard classes (Section 4.1), it is possible to define appropriate reducibilities and to find complete problems in the class with respect to those reducibilities. We will examine the more interesting cases here.

7.5.1   PSPACE

We give several approaches to showing the existence of $\le^P_m$-complete problems for PSPACE.

Proposition 7.7   PSPACE *is effectively presentable.*

Letting DM_i be the ith deterministic Turing machine (Section 6.3) and M_j be a deterministic Turing machine that fully space-constructs $p_j(n) = n^j + j$, define PS_k, where $k = \langle i, j \rangle$, to be a single-tape deterministic Turing machine that behaves as follows: On an input word x of length n, PS_k first simulates M_j in order to mark $p_j(n)$ cells on the work tape. Then, PS_k begins a multitrack one-tape simulation of DM_i. If DM_i ever attempts to leave the marked region, then PS_k halts and rejects its input. If DM_i reaches an accepting state without leaving the marked region, then PS_k halts and accepts.

Homework 7.12   *Prove Proposition 7.7 by showing that* $\{PS_i\}_{i \geq 1}$ *effectively presents* PSPACE.

Also, PSPACE is obviously closed under $\leq_m^P$-reductions.

Proposition 7.8 $A \leq_m^P B$ *and* $B \in$ PSPACE *implies* $A \in$ PSPACE.

In analogy with the set $\mathcal{U}$, which we easily showed to be NP-complete (Theorem 6.6), let us define

$$\mathcal{U}_{\text{PS}} = \{\langle i, x, 0^l \rangle \mid PS_i \text{ accepts } x \text{ in space } \leq l\}.$$

Homework 7.13   *Show that* $\mathcal{U}_{\text{PS}}$ *is* $\leq_m^P$-*complete for* PSPACE.

Theorem 7.15   *If for all* $k \geq 0$, $\Sigma_k^P \subset \Sigma_{k+1}^P$, *then* PH $\subset$ PSPACE.

Proof. We prove the contrapositive. If PSPACE $\subseteq$ PH, then for some $k \geq 0$, $\mathcal{U}_{\text{PS}} \in \Sigma_k^P$. Let $A \in$ PSPACE. Since $\mathcal{U}_{\text{PS}}$ is $\leq_m^P$-complete for PSPACE, $A \leq_m^P \mathcal{U}_{\text{PS}}$. However, by Corollary 7.8, $A \in \Sigma_k^P$. Thus, PSPACE $\subseteq \Sigma_k^P$, from which $\Sigma_{k+1}^P \subseteq \Sigma_k^P$ follows. $\qquad\square$

Homework 7.14   *Show that the set of all* $\leq_T^P$-*complete sets for* PSPACE *is effectively presentable.* *(Hint: Study the proof of Lemma 7.2.)*

Theorem 7.16   *If* PH $\subset$ PSPACE, *then there exist sets in* PSPACE *that are not* $\leq_T^P$-*complete for* PSPACE *and that are not in the polynomial hierarchy.*

Proof. We use Theorem 7.6. If PH $\subset$ PSPACE, then $\mathcal{U}_{\text{PS}}$ is not in PH, as we have just shown. Thus, $A = \emptyset$, $B = \mathcal{U}_{\text{PS}}$, $\mathcal{C}_1 = \{\leq_T^P$-complete sets for PSPACE$\}$, and $\mathcal{C}_2 = $ PH satisfy the hypotheses of Theorem 7.6. $\qquad\square$

If PH $\subset$ PSPACE, then the collection of problems that lie between PSPACE and PH turns out to be rich and have a complex structure [AS89]. Our next goal is to show that $A_\omega = \bigcup_{k \geq 1} A_k$ is $\leq_m^P$-complete for PSPACE, where A_k is defined in Definition 7.7.

Homework 7.15   *Show that* $A_\omega \in$ DLBA.

Theorem 7.17 A_ω *is* $\leq_m^P$-*complete for* PSPACE.

Proof. We need to show for all $L \in$ PSPACE that $L \leq_m^P A_\omega$. Let M be a single-tape, deterministic, polynomial-space-bounded Turing machine that accepts L. For some $c > 0$ and polynomial p, M makes no more than $c^{p(n)}$ moves on any input of length n. Also, we assume that $p(n)$ is the length of every configuration of M on an input of length n. We let I_0^x denote the initial configuration of M on input x, and we define relations $INITIAL_M$ and $ACCEPT_M$ such that $INITIAL_M(I)$ if and only if I is an initial configuration and $ACCEPT_M(I)$ if and only if I is an accepting configuration of M. Observe that $INITIAL_M$ and $ACCEPT_M$ belong to P; i.e.; whether $INITIAL_M(I)$ or $ACCEPT_M(I)$ is true can be decided deterministically in polynomial time.

Next, for every $j \geq 1$, we effectively define a formula $F_j(I_1, I_2)$ such that $F_j(I_1, I_2)$ is true if and only if $I_1 \vdash_M^* I_2$ by a sequence of at most 2^j moves. With this accomplished, for every input word x, $x \in L$ if and only if

$$Q_x = \exists I_f [F_{p(n) \log c}(I_0^x, I_f) \wedge INITIAL_M(I_0^x) \wedge ACCEPT_M(I_f)]$$

is true.

The basis step, $j = 0$, is given by

$$F_0(I_1, I_2) = (I_1 = I_2) \vee (I_1 \vdash_M I_2).$$

The obvious approach to the induction step would be to write

$$F_j(I_1, I_2) = \exists I [F_{j-1}(I_1, I) \wedge F_{j-1}(I, I_2)].$$

However, were we to do this, F_j would have double the length of F_{j-1}, so the length of $F_{p(n) \log c}(I_0^x, I_f)$ would be at least $c^{p(n)}$ and therefore could not be written in polynomial time.

Instead, let us define

$$F_j(I_1, I_2) = \exists I \forall J \forall K [[(J = I_1 \wedge K = I) \vee (J = I \wedge K = I_2)]$$
$$\rightarrow F_{j-1}(J, K)].$$

The advantage is that here F_j contains only one copy of F_{j-1}.

Since $p(n)$ is the length of each configuration, the length of F_j is a polynomial in the length of n plus the length of F_{j-1}. Thus, the length of F_j is $O(jp(n))$, and the length of $F_{p(n) \log c}$ is $O(p(n)^2)$. In particular, $F_{p(n) \log c}$ can be constructed in polynomial time in the length of the input word. Let Q_x' be the result of transforming Q_x into prenex normal form and collapsing blocks of like quantifiers. The prefix of Q_x' is a block of at most a polynomial number of alternating quantifiers such that the first quantifier is existential, say $\exists y_1 \ldots Q y_k$, where $k = q(|x|)$ and q is a polynomial such that $q(|x|) = O(p(n)^2)$. The matrix of Q_x' is a Boolean combination of expressions of the form $INITIAL_M(I)$, $ACCEPT_M(I)$, and $I = J$. These relations are decidable in polynomial time. Thus, there is a deterministic, polynomial-time-bounded Turing machine P_i that decides the matrix of Q_x'. Furthermore, for each $j \leq k$, $|y_j| \leq p(|x|)$. Thus, there is a polynomial r such that

P_i decides membership of $\langle x, y_1, \ldots, y_k \rangle$ within $r(|x|)$ steps. To summarize, the following equivalences hold:

$$x \in L \Leftrightarrow Q_x \text{ is true}$$
$$\Leftrightarrow Q'_x \text{ is true}$$
$$\Leftrightarrow (\exists y_1, |y_1| \le p(|x|)) \cdots (Q_k y_k, |y_k| \le p(|x|))$$
$$[\ P_i \text{ accepts } \langle x, y_1, \cdots, y_k \rangle \text{ in } \le r(|x|) \text{ steps }].$$
$$\Leftrightarrow \langle k, i, x, 0^{p(|x|)}, 0^{r(|x|)} \rangle \in A_\omega.$$

Let $f(x) = \langle k, i, x, 0^{p(|x|)}, 0^{r(|x|)} \rangle$, for all x. It is clear that f is a polynomial-time many-one reduction from L to A_ω.

$\square$

Homework 7.16 *Show that True Quantified Boolean Formulas, $TQBF = B_\omega = \bigcup_{k \ge 1} B_k$, are $\le_m^P$-complete for PSPACE. Hint: The proof is an analog of the Cook–Levin theorem, Theorem 6.8, in which a polynomial-space-bounded computation is simulated instead of a polynomial-time-bounded computation. The fact that the number of steps in the computation is $c^{p(n)}$ is handled exactly as in the proof of the previous theorem.*

PSPACE seems to capture the computational complexity of various games. Even and Tarjan [ET76], for example, have shown that a version of HEX is $\le_m^P$-complete for PSPACE. We note in passing that complete languages for PSPACE are frequently complete for smaller space-bounded classes as well. For example, we have seen that A_ω belongs to DLBA. Thus, A_ω is $\le_m^P$-complete for DLBA and LBA as well.

The results in this section should not suggest that forming the infinite union of complete sets for each Σ_n^P always produces a complete set for PSPACE. For example, it is not known whether $\bigcup_{n \ge 1} K^{(n)}$ is complete for PSPACE.

Oracles for the P =?NP Question

The next result demonstrates that the hypothesis of Corollary 7.10 does not always hold.

Theorem 7.18 *If A is a $\le_m^P$-complete language for PSPACE, then $NP^A = P^A$.*

Proof. $NP^A \subseteq NP^{PSPACE} \subseteq PSPACE$, and, since A is complete for PSPACE, $PSPACE \subseteq P^A$. Thus, $NP^A \subseteq P^A$.

$\square$

In contrast, there exists an oracle B such that $NP^B \ne P^B$ [BGS75].

Theorem 7.19 *There exists a decidable set B such that $NP^B \ne P^B$.*

Proof. Following our discussion that led to Theorem 7.12, let $\{P_i^{(\ )}\}_{i \ge 1}$ be an effective enumeration of deterministic polynomial-time-bounded oracle Turing

machines such that for every oracle A, $\{P_i^{(A)}\}_{i \geq 1}$ is an effective presentation of P^A. For each $i \geq 1$, p_i is an upper-bound on the running time of P_i.
Define

$$L(A) = \{x \mid \exists y[|y| = |x| \text{ and } y \in A]\}.$$

For any set A, $L(A) \in NP^A$. Our task is to define A such that for every $i \geq 1$,

$$L(A) \neq L(P_i^A).$$

We define A in stages. At each stage $i > 0$, A is already defined for all words of length less than some length n_i, and we call this set $A(n_i)$. At stage 0, $i_0 = 0$, and $A(0) = \emptyset$.

We do the following at stage i: Select the smallest positive integer n such that $n_i \leq n$ and $p_i(n) < 2^n$. Simulate $P_i^{A(n_i)}$ on input 0^n. This computation can query at most $p_i(n)$ strings, and the length of every query can be at most $p_i(n)$. By the first of these assertions, there must be some string of length n that this computation does not query. Let z be the lexicographically smallest such string.

If $P_i^{A(n_i)}$ rejects 0^n, then we put z into A as follows: Define $n_{i+1} = 2^n$ and define $A(n_{i+1}) = A(n_i) \cup \{z\}$. In this case, the construction guarantees the following claims:

1. $P_i^{A(n_{i+1})}$ rejects 0^n, and, since A will be an extension of $A(n_{i+1})$, P_i^A rejects 0^n;

2. $0^n \in L(A)$.

If $P_i^{A(n_i)}$ accepts 0^n, then we ensure that A contains no strings of length n as follows: Define $n_{i+1} = 2^n$ and define $A(n_{i+1}) = A(n_i)$. Then, $P_i^{A(n_{i+1})}$ accepts 0^n as well. Therefore, P_i^A accepts 0^n. However, $0^n \notin L(A)$.

This completes the construction of A. It should be clear that A is decidable and that, for each $i \geq 1$, $L(A) \neq L(P_i^A)$.   □

We are informed by these results that regardless of whether $P = NP$ or $P \neq NP$, an eventual proof will have to use techniques that do not generalize to all oracles. Many oracle results of this kind are known for other open questions about complexity classes. The deepest of these, due to Yao [Yao85] and Håstad [Hås89], asserts the existence of an oracle relative to which all classes of the polynomial hierarchy are distinct.

7.5.2   Exponential Time

As before, let $\{DM_i\}_{i \geq 1}$ be a standard enumeration of all deterministic Turing machines and $\{M_i\}_{i \geq 1}$ a standard enumeration of all Turing machines. Define

$$U_{\text{EXP}} = \{\langle i, x, l \rangle \mid DM_i \text{ accepts } x \text{ in } \leq l \text{ steps}\}$$

and

$$U_{\text{NEXP}} = \{\langle i, x, l \rangle \mid M_i \text{ accepts } x \text{ in } \leq l \text{ steps}\},$$

where in both cases l is written in binary.

Homework 7.17 *Show that $U_{\text{EXP}} \in$ E and $U_{\text{NEXP}} \in$ NE.*

Theorem 7.20 *U_{EXP} is $\leq_m^{\text{P}}$-complete for EXP and U_{NEXP} is $\leq_m^{\text{P}}$-complete for NEXP.*

Proof. Homework 7.17 provides part of the proof, and the other part is straight-forward. Namely, if $L \in$ EXP, then there exists i such that DM_i is 2^{n^c} time-bounded and DM_i accepts L. Thus, $x \in L \Leftrightarrow \langle i, x, 2^{n^c} \rangle \in U_{\text{EXP}}$. Since 2^{n^c} is written in binary, the function f defined by $f(x) = \langle i, x, 2^{n^c} \rangle$ is computable in polynomial time. Thus, U_{EXP} is $\leq_m^{\text{P}}$-complete for EXP. The proof for U_{NEXP} is similar. $\square$

Since U_{EXP} belongs to E and is $\leq_m^{\text{P}}$-complete for EXP, it follows that U_{EXP} is $\leq_m^{\text{P}}$-complete for E also. Similarly, U_{NEXP} is $\leq_m^{\text{P}}$-complete for NE.

7.5.3   Polynomial Time and Logarithmic Space

We know that L $\subseteq$ NL $\subseteq$ P, but we do not know whether these classes are equal; computational experience suggests that they differ. We will see examples of complete languages L_1 for P such that L_1 belongs to L (NL) if and only if P $\subseteq$ L (P $\subseteq$ NL, respectively). Furthermore, remember that even though POLYLOGSPACE is not equal to P, there is no proof that P is not a subset of POLYLOGSPACE. Complete languages L_1 for P will have the property that $L_1 \in$ POLYLOGSPACE if and only if P $\subseteq$ POLYLOGSPACE. We will see complete languages L_2 for NL; they will have the property that $L_2 \in$ L if and only if NL $\subseteq$ L.

Completeness results for these classes do not suggest intractability as is the case for NP-complete problems or problems that are complete for PSPACE. But they help to show that completeness is a general phenomenon and they reinforce that differing resources are required even among problems that are relatively easy to compute.

We need a new kind of reducibility in order to define completeness for P in a meaningful way, because every set in P other than the emptyset and Σ^* is $\leq_m^{\text{P}}$-complete for P. We consider the logspace transducer. A *logspace transducer* is a $\log n$ space-bounded transducer, as defined in Section 4.1.1. A function f is *logspace computable* if there is a logspace transducer T that computes f.

Definition 7.9 *A set A is* logspace-reducible *to a set B ($A \leq_m^{\log} B$) if there is a logspace-computable function f so that $x \in A \Leftrightarrow f(x) \in B$.*

Proposition 7.9 *$A \leq_m^{\log} B$ implies $A \leq_m^{\text{P}} B$.*

Proof. Since a logspace transducer halts on every input, no configuration can appear in a computation more than once. By Lemma 5.1, there are at most n^c configurations for some constant $c > 0$. Thus, every logspace computation is polynomial-time-bounded. □

In particular, if f is logspace-computable, then, for all x, $|f(x)| \leq |x|^c$ and $\log |f(x)| \leq c \cdot \log |x|$ for some constant $c > 0$.

Theorem 7.21   *The relation $\leq_m^{\log}$ is transitive.*

Next we prove transitivity of logspace reducibility. The proof is not at all obvious. Suppose that T_1 and T_2 are logspace transducers, that T_1 and T_2 compute f_1 and f_2, and that f_1 and f_2 reduce A to B and B to C, respectively. To prove $A \leq_m^{\log} C$, we want to show that the composition $f_2 \circ f_1$ is logspace-computable. The obvious approach would be to simulate T_1 on input x, store the output value $f_1(x)$ on a tape, and simulate T_2 on $f_1(x)$. However, the length of $f_1(x)$ may be larger than $\log |x|$, so it cannot be stored without exceeding the bound of a logspace transducer. Instead, we use a different technique to compute the composition of two functions. The idea is to simulate the entire computation of T_1 on input x each time the simulation of T_2 needs a new input symbol.

Proof. Let T_1 and T_2 be logspace transducers such that T_1 computes f_1 and T_2 computes f_2. Assume that f_1 logspace-reduces A to B, and f_2 logspace-reduces B to C. Clearly, $x \in A \Leftrightarrow f_2(f_1(x)) \in C$. We need to show that $f_2 \circ f_1$ is logspace-computable. Let c be a constant such that on any input x of length n, the length of the output word of T_1 on x cannot exceed n^c. We construct T_3 to logspace-compute $f_2 \circ f_1$ as follows: One storage tape of T_3 holds the input position of T_2 in base 2^c. Since the input position cannot exceed n^c, this number can be stored in $\log n$ space. The other storage tapes of T_3 simulate the storage tapes of T_1 and T_2. If at some time T_2's input head is at position i and T_2 makes a move left or right, T_3 adjusts the state and storage tapes of T_2 accordingly. Then T_3 restarts a simulation of T_1 on x from the beginning and waits until T_1 outputs $i - 1$ or $i + 1$ symbols, depending on whether T_2 moves left or right, respectively. The last symbol scanned is the new symbol scanned by T_2's input head (T_3 does not store the earlier symbols that are output), so T_3 continues its simulation of T_2. There are two special cases: If $i = 1$ and T_2 moves left, we assume that T_2 next scans its left endmarker, and if T_1 halts before producing $i + 1$ output symbols on a right move of T_2, we assume that T_2 next scans its right endmarker. T_3 accepts its input when T_2 accepts its simulated input, and $f_2(f_1(x))$ is the final output value. □

The identity function is logspace-computable, so logspace reducibility is reflexive as well.

Theorem 7.22   *If $A \leq_m^{\log} B$, then*

(i) $B \in$ P *implies* $A \in$ P,

(ii) $B \in$ DSPACE($\log^k n$) *implies* $A \in$ DSPACE($\log^k n$)*, and*

(iii) $B \in$ NSPACE($\log^k n$) *implies* $A \in$ NSPACE($\log^k n$)*.*

Proof. Assertion (i) follows from Proposition 7.9. The second assertion is proved by an adaptation of the previous argument, where T_1 logspace-reduces A to B and T_2 is a $\log^k n$ space bounded Turing machine that accepts B. Assertion 3 is proved similarly. □

Theorem 7.23

1. If $A \in$ DSPACE($\log^k n$) is logspace-complete for P, then

$$P \subseteq DSPACE(\log^k n).$$

2. If $A \in$ NSPACE($\log^k n$) is logspace-complete for P, then

$$P \subseteq NSPACE(\log^k n).$$

3. If $A \in$ L is logspace-complete for NL, then NL $\subseteq$ L.

Proof. Let $A \in$ DSPACE($\log^k n$) be logspace-complete for P. Let $B \in$ P. Then $B \leq_m^{\log} A$, so by Theorem 7.22, $B \in$ DSPACE($\log^k n$). Thus, P $\subseteq$ DSPACE($\log^k n$). The other assertions are proved similarly. □

As has been our customary practice, the quickest way to show existence of a complete set for a complexity class is to show that the class has a universal language and that the universal language is complete. We do this now for P.

Theorem 7.24 *Define*

$$\mathcal{U}_P = \{i\#x\#0^l \mid P_i \text{ accepts } x \text{ within } l \text{ steps}\}, \text{ where } \# \notin \Sigma = \{0, 1\}.$$

$\mathcal{U}_P$ *is logspace-complete for* P.

Proof. It should be clear that $\mathcal{U}_P$ belongs to P. Let $A \in$ P, where $A = L(P_i)$ and $p_i(n) = n^c$. It is obvious that the function f, defined by $f(x) = i\#x\#0^{|x|^c}$, many-one reduces A to $\mathcal{U}_P$. Thus, it suffices to show that f is logspace-computable. Design a transducer T so that, on input x, T writes $i\#x\#$ on the output tape. After this, T marks $\log |x|$ cells on a tape and uses these cells to count to $|x|^c$ in base 2^c, writing the symbol 0 every time it increments its counter. Clearly, T is a logspace transducer and T computes f. □

Theorems 7.21, 7.22, and 7.23 are proved by Jones [Jon75]. Jones [Jon75] and independently Stockmeyer and Meyer [SM73] realized that the reductions in [Coo71b] and [Kar72] are all logspace reductions. Indeed, all of the complete problems in this text are logspace-complete. (In certain instances we must replace use of a polynomial-time-computable pairing function with a simpler encoding scheme as in the definition of $\mathcal{U}_P$.) The reason is that the need for memory in most of these reductions is to count up to $p(n)$ for some polynomial p, and this can be done in log space as we have amply demonstrated. A number of researchers have identified natural logspace-complete problems for P. The first natural problem we mention is due to Cook [Coo74] and the second is due to Jones and Laaser [JL76]. In both cases the proofs involve generic logspace transformations that result from encoding deterministic polynomial-time-bounded Turing machines into the appropriate structures.

PATH SYSTEM ACCESSIBILITY

   instance A finite set X of "nodes," a relation $R \subseteq X \times X \times X$, and two sets $S, T \subseteq X$ of "source" and "terminal" nodes

   question Is there an "accessible" terminal node, where a node $x \in X$ is accessible if $x \in S$ or if there exist accessible nodes y and z such that $\langle x, y, z \rangle \in R$?

UNIT RESOLUTION

   instance A set C of clauses on a set $X = \{x_1, \ldots, x_n\}$ of Boolean variables

   question Can the empty clause (indicating a contradiction) be derived from C by unit resolution, that is, does there exist a sequence $c_1, c_2, \ldots, c_m$ of clauses, with c_m being the empty clause, such that each c_i is either a clause from C or there exist two previously derived clauses c_k and c_l, $k, l < i$, of the forms $c_k = \{x_j\}, c_l = \{\overline{x_j}\} \cup c_i$, or $c_k = \{\overline{x_j}\}, c_l = \{x_j\} \cup c_i$, for some $x_j \in X$?

The Graph Accessibility problem that we studied in Section 6.2 was shown to be logspace-complete for NL by Jones [Jon75]. Recall that we know that GAP belongs to P (Homework 6.2). (Briefly, A nondeterministic $\log n$ space-bounded Turing machine M accepts GAP by guessing a path vertex by vertex. M does not store the path, it only stores the vertex currently reached.)

Theorem 7.25   GAP *is logspace-complete for* NL.

Proof. Given a language L in NL, we sketch a logspace reduction from L to GAP. First, note that a directed graph with n vertices can be represented by its adjacency matrix of size n^2 and that this matrix can be represented as a string $w = row_1\ row_2\ \ldots\ row_n$ of length n^2 over the binary alphabet. Assume L is accepted by a nondeterministic $\log n$ space-bounded Turing machine M. Let x be an input string to M. Our reduction produces a directed graph G_x, as represented by the string encoding of its adjacency matrix. The vertices of G_x are the configurations of M on x, except that in each configuration I, the input head position is given while the input word itself is not. Thus, the length of each configuration is $\log |x|$ if we assume that our logspace transducer T has a sufficient number of tape symbols. The first vertex of G_x is the initial configuration of M on x. We assume that M has a unique accepting configuration and that it is the last vertex of G_x. T uses its work space to cycle through each configuration of M. For each configuration I, T puts its input head at the position given by I, then T generates an arc for each configuration J such that $I \vdash_M J$. (In this manner T outputs the row of the adjacency matrix that corresponds to configuration I.) Such a configuration J is easily constructed from I and requires no more than $\log n$ space.

There is a path in G_x from the initial configuration on x to the unique accepting configuration if and only if M accepts x. Thus, each language in NL is logspace-reducible to GAP, so GAP is logspace-complete for NL. $\square$

7.5.4   A Note on Provably Intractable Problems

A few interesting problems have been proved to be intractable. The general approach has been to prove that a problem is complete for a complexity class that is known to contain intractable problems. Using the results of section 5.5, we know several complexity classes that contain intractable sets. If a set L is complete (using any of the reducibilities we have studied) for a complexity class C that contains intractable sets, then it is easy to see that L is intractable.

Using this approach, Meyer and Stockmeyer [MS72] proved that the problem of inequivalence for regular expressions with "squaring" is intractable. That is, they proved that this problem is $\leq_m^P$-complete for $\bigcup_{c>0} \text{DSPACE}(2^{n^c})$. Because $\bigcup_{c>0} \text{DSPACE}(2^{n^c})$ includes EXP, and because, by the time hierarchy theorem, Theorem 5.16, EXP contains sets that are intractable, their result follows.

Fischer and Rabin [FR74] proved that the theory of Presberger arithmetic is $\leq_m^P$-hard for NEXP. Thus, the theory of Presberger arithmetic is intractable. Proofs of both of these results can be found in the text by Hopcroft and Ullman [HU79].

7.6   Additional Homework Problems

Homework 7.18   *An* approximation algorithm *for the* VERTEX COVER *problem is an algorithm that runs in polynomial time and that, given a graph G as input, finds a vertex cover of G. For any graph G, let $Opt\text{-}VC(G)$ be the size of a smallest vertex cover of G. We would like an approximation algorithm that finds a vertex cover whose size is as close to $Opt\text{-}VC(G)$ as possible.*

1. *Prove that if there is an approximation algorithm for the* VERTEX COVER *problem that always finds a vertex cover of size $Opt\text{-}VC(G)$, then $P = NP$.*

2. *Find an approximation algorithm for the* VERTEX COVER *problem with the property that, for any graph G, the algorithm finds a vertex cover of G whose size is no more than $2(Opt\text{-}VC(G))$. (Hint: A straightforward "greedy" algorithm for* VERTEX COVER *has this property.)*

Homework 7.19   *Consider the following generalization of decision problems. A promise problem [ESY84] (P, Q) has the form*

instance x.
promise $P(x)$.
question $Q(x)$?

We assume that P and Q are recursive predicates. A deterministic Turing machine M that halts on every input solves (P, Q) *if*

$$\forall x [P(x) \Rightarrow [Q(x) \Leftrightarrow M(x) = \text{"yes"}]].$$

We do not care how M behaves on input x if P(x) is false. If M solves (P, Q), then we call L(M) a solution *of (P, Q). In general, a promise problem will have many solutions, and we are usually interested in finding a solution with low complexity.*

1. *Show that $P \cap Q$ is a solution.*
2. *Show that Q is a solution.*

Homework 7.20   *Let $\oplus$ denote "exclusive or." Consider the following promise problem* PP-SAT:

instance $\langle \phi, \psi \rangle$, *where ϕ and ψ and formulas of propositional logic.*
promise $(\phi \in \text{SAT}) \oplus (\psi \in \text{SAT})$.
question $\phi \in$ SAT?

1. *Show that* PP-SAT *has a solution in* NP.
2. *Show that* PP-SAT *has a solution in* co-NP.
3. *Show that every solution of* PP-SAT *is* NP-*hard.*

Homework 7.21   *Show that if an $\leq^P_m$-complete set for* PSPACE *belongs to* NP, *then* PSPACE = NP.

Homework 7.22   *Define a set A to be* P-immune *if A is infinite and no infinite subset of A belongs to* P.

1. *Show that neither* SAT *nor its complement is* P-immune.
2. *Prove that there exists a* P-*immune set and explain whether the set you construct is decidable. (Hint: Construct one by a diagonalization argument.)*

Homework 7.23   *Define a set A to be* P-bi-immune *if L is infinite, no infinite subset of L belongs to* P, *and no infinite subset of $\overline{L}$ belongs to* P. *Define a language A to be* almost-everywhere complex *if for every Turing machine M that accepts A and every polynomial p, M runs in time greater than p(|x|) for all but finitely many words x [Ber76, Rab60].*

1. *Prove that a set is* P-*bi-immune if and only if it is almost-everywhere complex [BS85].*
2. *Prove that almost-everywhere complex sets exist.*

Homework 7.24   *A function f is computable in* linear time *if, for all x, f(x) is computable in O(|x|) steps. Prove that no set exists that is complete for* P *under linear-time reductions.*

Homework 7.25   *Define a set L to be* sparse *if there is a polynomial p such that for all n, $\|L \cap \Sigma^n\| \leq p(n)$. Prove that* NE = E *if and only if every sparse set in* NP *belongs to* P *[HIS85]. Observe that this result subsumes Theorem 5.18.*

References

[AS89]   K. Ambos-Spies. On the relative complexity of hard problems for complexity classes without complete problems. *Theoretical Computer Science*, 63:43–61, 1989.

[Ber76]   L. Berman. On the structure of complete sets: Almost everywhere complexity and infinitely often speedup. *Proceedings of the 17th Annual Symposium on Foundations of Computer Science*, pages 76–80, 1976.

[Ber78]   P. Berman. Relationships between density and deterministic complexity of NP-complete languages. In *Proceedings of the Fifth Colloqium on Automata, Languages, and Programming, Lecture Notes in Computer Science*, volume 62, pages 63–71. Springer-Verlag, Berlin, 1978.

[BG70]   R. Book and S. Greibach. Quasi-realtime languages. *Mathematical Systems Theory*, 4:97–111, 1970.

[BGS75]   T. Baker, J. Gill, and R. Solovay. Relativizations of the P =? NP question. *SIAM Journal on Computing*, 4(4):431–441, 1975.

[BGW70]   R. Book, S. Greibach, and B. Wegbreit. Time- and tape-bounded Turing acceptors and AFL's. *Journal of Computer and System Sciences*, 4:606–621, 1970.

[Boo72]   R. Book. On languages accepted in polynomial time. *SIAM Journal on Computing*, 1(4):281–287, 1972.

[Boo74]   R. Book. Tally languages and complexity classes. *Information and Control*, 26:186–193, 1974.

[Boo76]   R. Book. Translational lemmas, polynomial time, and $(logn)^j$-space. *Theoretical Computer Science*, 1:215–226, 1976.

[BS85]   J. Balcázar and U. Schöning. Bi-immune sets for complexity classes. *Mathematical Systems Theory*, 18(1):1–10, June 1985.

[Chu36]   A. Church. An unsolvable problem of elementary number theory. *American Journal of Mathematics*, 58:345–363, 1936.

[Coo71a] S. Cook. Characterizations of pushdown machines in terms of time-bounded computers. *Journal of the ACM*, 19:175–183, 1971.

[Coo71b] S. Cook. The complexity of theorem-proving procedures. In *Proceedings of the Third ACM Symposium on Theory of Computing*, pages 151–158, 1971.

[Coo73] S. Cook. A hierarchy for nondeterministic time complexity. *Journal of Computer and System Sciences*, 7(4):343–353, 1973.

[Coo74] S. Cook. An observation on time-storage tradeoff. *Journal of Computer and System Sciences*, 9:308–316, 1974.

[CR73] S. Cook and R. Reckhow. Time bounded random access machines. *Journal of Computer and System Sciences*, 7:353–375, 1973.

[Dav65] M. Davis. *The Undecidable*. Raven Press, Hewlett, NY, 1965.

[ESY84] S. Even, A. Selman, and Y. Yacobi. The complexity of promise problems with applications to public-key cryptography. *Information and Control*, 61(2):159–173, May 1984.

[ET76] S. Even and R. Tarjan. A combinatorial problem which is complete in polynomial space. *Journal of the ACM*, 23:710–719, 1976.

[FR74] M. Fischer and M. Rabin. Super-exponential complexity of Presberger arithmetic. In R. Karp, editor, *Complexity of Computation*, pages 43–73. American Mathematical Society, Providence, RI, 1974.

[Gil77] J. Gill. Computational complexity of probabilistic Turing machines. *SIAM J. Comput.*, 6(4):675–695, Dec. 1977.

[GJ79] M. Garey and D. Johnson. *Computers and Intractability: A Guide to the Theory of NP-Completeness*. W. H. Freeman, San Francisco, 1979.

[Hås89] J. Håstad. Almost optimal lower bounds for small depth circuits. In S. Micali, editor, *Randomness and Computation*, volume 5 of *Advances in Computing Research*, pages 143–170. JAI Press, Greenwich, 1989.

[Hel81] H. Heller. *Relativized Polynomial Hierarchies Extending Two Levels*. Ph.D. thesis, Universität München, 1981.

[Her94] R. Herken, editor. *The Universal Turing Machine: A Half-Century Survey*. Springer, Wien, 1994.

[HIS85] J. Hartmanis, N. Immerman, and V. Sewelson. Sparse sets in $NP-P$: EXPTIME versus NEXPTIME. *Information and Control*, 65(2/3):159–181, 1985.

[HLS65] J. Hartmanis, P. Lewis, and R. Stearns. Hierarchies of memory limited computations. In *Proceedings of the Sixth Annual IEEE Symposium on Switching Circuit Theory and Logical Design*, pages 179–190, 1965.

[Hoc96] D. Hochbaum, editor. *Approximation Algorithms for NP-Hard Problems*. PWS Publishing Company, Boston, 1996.

[Hod83] A. Hodges. *Alan Turing: The Enigma*. Simon and Schuster, New York, 1983.

[HS65] J. Hartmanis and R. Stearns. On the computational complexity of algorithms. *Transactions of the American Mathematical Society*, 117:285–306, 1965.

[HS66] F. Hennie and R. Stearns. Two-tape simulation of multitape Turing machines. *Journal of the ACM*, 13:533–546, 1966.

[HU69] J. Hopcroft and J. Ullman. Some results on tape bounded Turing machines. *Journal of the ACM*, 16:168–188, 1969.

[HU79] J. Hopcroft and J. Ullman. *Introduction to Automata Theory, Languages, and Computation*. Addison-Wesley, Reading, MA, 1979.

[Iba72] O. Ibarra. A note concerning nondeterministic tape complexities. *Journal of Computer and System Sciences*, 19(4):609–612, 1972.

[Imm88] N. Immerman. Nondeterministic space is closed under complementation. *SIAM Journal on Computing*, 17(5):935–938, 1988.

[JK76] D. Johnson and S. Kashdan. Lower bounds for selection in $x + y$ and other multisets. Technical Report 183, Pennsylvania State Univ., University Park, PA, 1976.

[JL76] N. Jones and W. Laaser. Complete problems for deterministic polynomial time. *Theoretical Computer Science*, 3:105–117, 1976.

[Jon73] N. Jones. Reducibility among combinatorial problems in log n space. In *Proceedings of the Seventh Annual Princeton Conference on Information Sciences and Systems*, pages 547–551, Princeton, NJ, 1973.

[Jon75] N. Jones. Space-bounded reducibility among combinatorial problems. *Journal of Computer and System Sciences*, 11:68–85, 1975.

[JS74] N. Jones and A. Selman. Turing machines and the spectra of first-order formulas. *Journal of Symbolic Logic*, 29:139–150, 1974.

[Kar72] R. Karp. Reducibility among combinatorial problems. In *Complexity of Computer Computations*, pages 85–104. Plenum Press, New York, 1972.

[Ko83] K. Ko. On self-reducibility and weak P-selectivity. *Journal of Computer and System Sciences*, 26:209–211, 1983.

[Kre88] M. Krentel. The complexity of optimization problems. *Journal of Computer and System Sciences*, 36:490–509, 1988.

[Kur64] S. Kuroda. Classes of languages and linear bounded automata. *Information and Control*, 7(2):207–223, 1964.

[Lad75] R. Ladner. On the structure of polynomial time reducibility. *Journal of the ACM*, 22:155–171, 1975.

[Lev73] L. Levin. Universal sorting problems. *Problems of Information Transmission*, 9:265–266, 1973. English translation of original in *Problemy Peredaci Informacii*.

[LLS75] R. Ladner, N. Lynch, and A. Selman. A comparison of polynomial time reducibilities. *Theoretical Computer Science*, 1:103–123, 1975.

[Mag69] G. Mager. Writing pushdown acceptors. *Journal of Computer and System Sciences*, 3(3):276–319, 1969.

[Mil76] G. Miller. Reimann's hypothesis and tests for primality. *Journal of Computer and System Sciences*, 13:300–317, 1976.

[MP79] A. Meyer and M. Paterson. *With What Frequency Are Apparently Intractable Problems Difficult?* Technical Report MIT/LCS/TM-126, M.I.T., 1979.

[MS72]   A. Meyer and L. Stockmeyer. The equivalence problem for regular expressions with squaring requires exponential space. In *Proceedings of the Thirteenth IEEE Symposium on Switching and Automata Theory*, pages 125–129, 1972.

[MY78]   M. Machtey and P. Young. *An Introduction to the General Theory of Algorithms*. The Computer Science Library, Theory of Computation Series. Elsevier North-Holland, Inc., New York, 1978.

[Myh60]   J. Myhill. Linear bounded automata. WADD 60-165, Wright Patterson AFB, Ohio, 1960.

[Pap84]   C. Papadimitriou. On the complexity of unique solutions. *Journal of the ACM*, 31:392–400, 1984.

[PF79]   N. Pippenger and M. Fischer. Relations among complexity measures. *Journal of the ACM*, 26:361–381, 1979.

[Pos44]   E. Post. Recursively enumerable sets of integers and their decision problems. *Bulletin of the American Mathematical Society*, 50:284–316, 1944.

[Pos65]   E. Post. Absolutely unsolvable problems and relatively undecidable propositions: Account of an anticipation. In M. Davis, editor, *The Undecidable: Basic Papers on Undecidable Propositions, Unsolvable Problems and Computable Functions*, pages 340–433. Raven Press, New York, 1965. Submitted for publication in 1941.

[PPST83] W. Paul, N. Pippenger, E. Szemerédi, and W. Trotter. On determinism and nondeterminism and related problems. In *Proceedings of the Twenty-fourth ACM Symposium on Theory of Computing*, pages 429–438, 1983.

[Pra75]   V. Pratt. Every prime has a succinct certificate. *SIAM Journal on Computing*, 4:214–220, 1975.

[Rab60]   M. Rabin. *Degree of Difficulty of Computing a Function and a Partial Ordering of Recursive Sets*. Technical Report 2, The Hebrew University, Jerusalem, 1960.

[Reg]   K. Regan. Personal communication.

[Ric53]   H. Rice. Classes of recursively enumerable sets and their decision problems. *Transactions of the American Mathematical Society*, 74:358–366, 1953.

[Rog67]   H. Rogers, Jr. *Theory of Recursive Functions and Effective Computability*. McGraw-Hill, New York, 1967.

[Ros67]   A. Rosenberg. Real-time definable languages. *Journal of the ACM*, 14:645–662, 1967.

[Sav70]   W. Savitch. Relationships between nondeterministic and deterministic time complexities. *Journal of Computer and System Sciences*, 4(2):177–192, 1970.

[Sch82]   U. Schöning. A uniform approach to obtain diagonal sets in complexity classes. *Theoretical Computer Science*, 18:95–103, 1982.

[Sch88]   U. Schöning. Graph isomorphism is in the low hierarchy. *Journal of Computer and System Sciences*, 37(3):312–323, 1988.

[Sch90]   U. Schöning. The power of counting. In A. Selman, editor, *Complexity Theory Retrospective*, pages 204–223. Springer-Verlag, New York, 1990.

[Sel79] A. Selman. P-selective sets, tally languages, and the behavior of polynomial time reducibilities on NP. *Mathematical Systems Theory*, 13:55–65, 1979.

[Sel88] A. Selman. Natural self-reducible sets. *SIAM Journal on Computing*, 17:989–996, 1988.

[Sel89] A. Selman. Complexity issues in cryptography. In J. Hartmanis, editor, *Computational Complexity Theory*, volume 38 of *Proceedings of Symposia in Applied Mathematics*, pages 92–107. American Mathematical Society, Providence, RI, 1989.

[SFM78] J. Seiferas, M. Fischer, and A. Meyer. Separating nondeterministic time complexity classes. *Journal of the ACM*, 25(1):146–147, 1978.

[SG77] I. Simon and J. Gill. Polynomial reducibilities and upward diagonalizations. In *Proceedings of the Ninth Annual ACM Symposium on Theory of Computing*, pages 186–194, 1977.

[Sip78] M. Sipser. Halting space-bounded computations. In *Proceedings of the 19th Annual IEEE Symposium on Foundations of Computer Science*, pages 73–74, 1978.

[SM73] L. Stockmeyer and A. Meyer. Word problems requiring exponential time. In *Proceedings of the Fifth Annual ACM Symposium on Theory of Computing*, pages 1–9, New York, 1973.

[Soa80] R. Soare. *Recursively Enumerable Sets and Degrees*. Springer-Verlag, New York, 1980.

[SS63] J. Shepherdson and H. Sturgis. Computability of recursive functions. *Journal of the ACM*, 10(2):217–255, 1963.

[Sto76] L. Stockmeyer. The polynomial-time hierarchy. *Theoretical Computer Science*, 3:1–22, 1976.

[Sze88] R. Szelepcsényi. The method of forced enumeration for nondeterministic automata. *Acta Informatica*, 26:279–284, 1988.

[Tur36] A. Turing. On computable numbers with an application to the entscheidungsproblem. *Proceedings of the London Mathematical Society*, 42:230–365, 1936.

[Ž83] S. Žák. A Turing machine time hierarchy. *Theoretical Computer Science*, 26:327–333, 1983.

[War62] S. Warshall. A theorem on Boolean matrices. *Journal of the ACM*, 9:11–12, 1962.

[Wra76] C. Wrathall. Complete sets and the polynomial hierarchy. *Theoretical Computer Science*, 3:23–33, 1976.

[Yao85] A. Yao. Separating the polynomial-time hierarchy by oracles. In *Proceedings of the 26th IEEE Symposium on Foundations of Computer Science*, pages 1–10, 1985.

Author Index

A

Ambos-Spies, K., 171, 181

B

Baker, T., 173, 181
Balcázar, J., 180, 181
Berman, L., 180, 181
Berman, P., 144, 181
Book, R., 84, 96, 114, 115, 181

C

Cantor, George, 9
Church, Alonzo, 22, 34, 181
Cook, S., 36, 101, 113, 131, 146, 177, 178, 182

D

Davis, M., 69, 182

E

Eratosthenes, 159
Euler, 18
Even, S., 76, 173, 179, 182

F

Fermat, 17
Fischer, M., 91, 96, 113, 179, 182, 184, 185
Friedberg, 52

G

Garey, M., 77, 131, 133, 142, 148, 182
Gill, J., 143, 149, 173, 181, 182, 185
Greibach, S., 84, 96, 181

H

Hartmanis, J., 75, 80, 82, 90, 108, 110, 180, 182
Håstad, J., 174, 182
Heller, H., 170, 182
Hennie, F., 91, 182
Herken, R., 35, 182
Hochbaum, D., 162, 182
Hodges, A., 36, 182
Homer, Steven, ix
Hopcroft, J., 90, 98, 102, 121, 179, 183

I

Ibarra, O., 112, 183
Immerman, N., ix, 116, 180, 183

J

Johnson, D., 77, 131, 133, 142, 148, 182, 183
Jones, N., 76, 177, 178, 183

K

Karp, R., 170, 177, 183
Kashdan, S., 148, 183

Kleene, 56
Ko, K., 153, 183
Krentel, M., 170, 183
Kuroda, S., 76, 116, 183

L
Laaser, W., 178, 183
Ladner, R., 147, 154, 183
Lagrange, 16
Levin, L., 131, 183
Lewis, P., 75, 80, 108, 182

M
Machtey, M., 36, 38, 147, 184
Mager, G., 76, 183
Meyer, A., 96, 113, 153, 162, 177, 179,
        183, 184, 185
Miller, G., 159, 183
Muchnik, 52
Myhill, J., 76, 184

P
Papadimitriou, C., 170, 184
Paterson, M., 153, 183
Paul, W., 90, 184
Pippenger, N., 90, 91, 184
Post, Emil, 34, 52, 69, 184
Pratt, V., 159, 184

R
Rabin, M., 179, 180, 182, 184
Reckhow, R., 36, 182
Regan, K., 88, 184
Rice, H., 58, 184
Rogers, H., Jr., 69, 184
Rosenberg, A., 184

S
Savitch, W., 102, 184
Schöning, U., 120, 154, 159, 180, 184

Seiferas, J., 96, 113, 185
Selman, Alan L., ix, 76, 153, 179, 182,
        183, 185
Sewelson, V., 180, 182
Shepherdson, J., 36, 185
Simon, I., 149, 185
Sipser, M, 107, 185
Soare, R., 69, 185
Solovay, R., 173, 181
Stearns, R., 75, 80, 82, 90, 91, 108, 110,
        182
Stockmeyer, L., 162, 170, 177, 179, 184,
        185
Sturgis, H., 36, 185
Szelepcsényi, R., ix, 116, 185
Szemerédi, E., 90, 184

T
Tarjan, R., 76, 173, 182
Trotter, W., 90, 184
Turing, Alan, 22, 23, 34, 35-36, 44,
        185

U
Ullman, J., 90, 98, 102, 112, 179, 183

V
Von Neumann, 22, 44

W
Warshall, S., 101, 185
Wrathall, C., 162, 170, 185

Y
Yacobi, Y., 179, 182
Yao, A., 174, 185
Young, P., 36, 38, 184

Z
Žák, S., 113, 185

Subject Index

$\langle , \rangle$, 46
$\subset$ denoting proper inclusion, 109
symbol, 92
$\oplus$, 157
δ, 24
Δ_k^P, 162–163
λ, 1
$\leq_m$, 60
$\leq_T$, 60
$\leq_m^{\log}$, 175–177
$\leq_T^{NP}$, 162
$\leq_r^P$-complete set, 149
$\leq_r^P$-hard set, 149
$\leq_m^P$, 128–129
$\not\leq_m^P$, 147
$\leq_T^P$, 146–147
$\equiv_T^P$, 152
ϕ, 27, 67
$\phi(d)$, 19
$\phi(m)$, 18
ϕ_e, 44
Π_k, 63
Π_k^P, 162–163
Π_0, 62
ψ^A, 60
ψ_{univ}, 54
Σ, 1, 3
Σ_2, 63
Σ_k^P, 162–163

Σ^*, 2
Σ_0, 62
τ_k, 46
$|w|$, 1

A

A_k, 167
A_ω, 171
$\mathcal{A}_k$, 165
$ACCEPT_M$, 172
Acceptable programming system, 54
Accepting configuration, 25
Adaptive reduction procedure, 60
Additive group of integers, 15
Adjacent vertices, 4
Algebra, 11–21
Alphabet, finite, 1
Ancestor, 5
Antisymmetric binary relation, 10
Approximation algorithm for vertex cover, 179
Arcs, 4
Arithmetical hierarchy, 62
Assignment, 6

B

B, 24
B_k, 168
"Big-oh" notation, 80
Binary tree, 5
Boolean circuits, 91

Boolean connectives, 6
Boolean functions, 8

C

Cantor-Bernstein Theorem, 9
Cardinality, 8–10
    same, 8
c.e. (computably enumerable), 47
c.e set
    creative, 71
    simple, 71
Child, 5
Chinese Remainder Theorem, 17–18
Church's thesis, 22, 28, 34–36, 54n
    expanded version of, 35
Clause, 7
Clean segment, 92
CLIQUE, 141
    NP-completeness of, 141
Clique, 33–34
Cnf formulas, 131, 133–134
CNF-SAT, 131, 132
co-$\mathcal{C}$, 62
co-Σ_k, 63
Cobham's thesis, 35, 72
Communications component, 140
Commutative group, 15
Complement, 2
Complete graphs, 4
Complete problems, 52
Complexity, concrete, 75–76
Complexity classes, 74–75
    complements of, 116–120
    complete problems for, 170–179
    space-bounded, 75
    standard, 75
        relations between, 105, 115–120
    time-bounded, 74
Complexity measures, 74
Complexity theory, 72–74
    basic results of, 78–121
    introduction to, 72–77
COMPOSITE NUMBER, 158–161
Computability
    introduction to, 22–40
    relative, 145–180
Computable function, 128
Computably enumerable sets, 47–50

Computation tree, 32
Computing, theory of, vii
Concatenation, 2
Concrete complexity, 75–76
Configuration of Turing machine, 25
Congruence modulo, 12
Conjunction, 7
Conjunctive normal form, 7
Connected graph, 4
Constructible functions, 86–90
Converge, 3
Cook-Levin theorem, 130–136, 168
Cook reducibility, 146
Cosets, 16–17
Countable sets, 8
Countably infinite sets, 8
Creative set, 71
Cycle, 4
Cyclic group, 16

D

Decidable decision problem, 42
Decidable in, 60
Decision problems, 41–43
    instance of, 41
    language versus, 136n
    solution to, 42
Degree of vertex, 4
Degrees, 146
DeMorgan's laws, 7
Depth of vertex, 5
Descendant, 5
Determinacy, 35
Diagonal set, 53, 137
Diagonalization, 9
3-DIMENSIONAL MATCHING, 142
Directed graph (digraph), 4
Disjunction, 7
Disjunctive normal form, 7
Disjunctively self-reducible set, 152
Diverge, 3
Division algorithm, 19–20
DLBA, 75
DSPACE, 75, 80
DTIME, 74, 80

E

E, 75

$\mathcal{E}_k$, 165
Edges, 4
Effective enumeration, 45
Effectively enumerable, 47
Effectively presentable class of sets,
        126–128
Efficiently computable problems, 73
Empty block, 92
Empty set, 1
Empty word, 1
Encodings, 42
Enumerable sets, 8
Equivalence class modulo, 12
Equivalence of Turing machines, 29
Equivalent formulas, 7
ESPACE, 121
EUCLIDEAN ALGORITHM, 14–15, 126
Euler phi function, 18
EXP, 75
Exponential time, 174–175

F
Fermat's corollary, 17
Fields, 11
    multiplicative group of, 15
Finite alphabet, 1
Finite control, 23
Floyd-Warshall algorithm, 101
Full block, 92
Fully space-constructible functions, 86
Fully time-constructible functions, 86
Functional, 66

G
Generator of a group, 16
Gödel number, 44
GRAPH ACCESSIBILITY PROBLEM
        (GAP), 125
GRAPH ISOMORPHISM, 158–161
Graphs, 4–6
Greatest common divisor, 13
Groups, 15–17
    order of, 15

H
HALTING PROBLEM, 51–52
HAMILTONIAN CIRCUIT, 41–42, 73
Hamiltonian circuit, 4, 142

Height of tree, 5
HEX, 76, 173
HITTING SET, 143

I
Immerman-Szelepcsényi theorem,
        116–120
Inclusion relationships, 97–106
Index set, 57–58
Induced subgraphs, 4
$INITIAL_M$, 172
Instantaneous description, 25
Integers, additive group of, 15
Integral domain, 13
Invertible function, 143

K
K, 51, 137
$K^{(\omega)}$, 71
K-adic representation, 2–3
k constant, 140
K^A, 61
k tracks, 30–31, 90
Karp reducibility, 128
Kleene closure, 2
Kleene-Mostowski arithmetical hierarchy,
        62
K^{th} LARGEST SUBSET, 148

L
L, 75
L^+, 2
L^*, 2
Lagrange's theorem, 16–17, 20
Lambda calculus, 34
Language(s), 2
    powers of, 2
    problem versus, 136n
LBA, 75, 76
Leaf, 32
Least fixed point, 67
Length of word, 1
Lexicographic ordering, 2
"Limit" function, 67
Line names, 36
Linear compression and speedup, 80–86
Linear order, 10
Linear speedup, 82–84

Linearly ordered set, 10
Literals, 6
"Little-oh" notation, 79
Logarithmic space, 175–179
Logic, propositional, 6–8
Logspace-computable function, 175
Logspace reducibility, 175, 179
Logspace transducer, 175

M
$M^{()}$, 166
Machine-dependent property, 59
Majorize, 123
Many-one complete language, 52
Many-one reducibility, 51
Many-one reducible in polynomial time,
        128
MAX subsets, 149
maxclique, 142
MIN subsets, 149
Multiplicative group of field, 15
Multitape Turing machines, 29–31

N
N (set of natural numbers), 2
N-SPACE-TIME, 105
NE, 75
NESPACE, 121
NEXP, 75
Next move relation, 25
NL, 75
Nondeterminism, 73, 122
    NP-completeness and, 122–144
Nondeterministic Turing machines, 31–34
Nondeterministic Turing reducible in
        polynomial time, 162
NP, 75, 76, 122–123
    characterizing, 123–124
    structure of, 153–162
NP^A, 167
NP-complete problems, 136–142
    natural, 138–142
NP-complete set, 129
NP-completeness, 128–130
    of CLIQUE, 141
    of CNF-SAT, 132
    of diagonal set, 137
    nondeterminism and, 122–144

of SAT, 136
of 3SAT, 138
of universal set, 130
of VERTEX COVER, 139
NP-hard set, 147–148
NP-hardness, 147–151
    of Kth LARGEST SUBSET, 148–149
NSPACE, 75, 80
NTIME, 74, 80
Number theory, 17–21

O
$o(G)$, 15
Oblivious Turing machines, 91
Off-line Turing machines, 74
On-line Turing machines, 74
$Opt\text{-}VC(G)$, 179
Oracle, 59, 155–156
Oracle calls, 59
Oracle Turing machine, 60, 145–146
Order of group, 15
Ordered set, 10
Ordered tree, 5

P
P, 75, 124–126
$\mathcal{P}(A)$, 10
P-bi-immune set, 180
P-immune set, 180
P_C, 47
P^A, 173
Padding argument, 115
Pairing functions, 46
Parent, 5
Parity counter, 24
Partial computable functional, 66
Partial computable partial function, 28
Partial functions, 3–4
Partial order, 10
Partially ordered set, 10
PARTITION, 142
Path, 4
PATH SYSTEM ACCESSIBILITY, 178
Phi function, 18
POLYLOGSPACE, 75
Polynomial hierarchy, 162–170
Polynomial ring, 19
Polynomial time, 175–179

many-one reducible in, 128
nondeterministic Turing reducibility in, 162
Turing reducible in, 60, 146
Polynomial-time verifier, 124
Polynomials, 19–20
Post's problem, 52
Powers of language, 2
Prefix of word, 2
Presberger arithmetic, 179
PRIMALITY, 159
   algorithm for, 161
Probabilistic polynomial-time Turing machines, 143
PROGRAM TERMINATION, 43–44
Programming system, 54
   acceptable, 54
   universal, 54
Promise problem, 179
Proof, 124
Proper inclusion symbol, 109
Propositional formulas, 6
Propositional logic, 6–8
PSPACE, 75, 170–174

Q
Q, 11
Quasi-real time, 84
Query configuration, 64

R
r-degrees, 146
RAMs, *see* Random access machines
Random access machines (RAMs), 36–40
   equivalence with Turing machines, 39–40
$range(f)$, 47
REACH, 117
Real time, 84
Reasonable encodings, 42
Recursion theorem, 55–57, 66–69
Recursive definition, 67
Reducibility, 146
   Cook, 146
   Karp, 128
   logspace, 175
   many-one, 51
      in polynomial time, 128

self-, 152
Turing, 60, 146
   in polynomial time, 60, 146
   nondeterministic, 162
Reduction method, 52
Reduction procedure, 59, 152
   adaptive, 60
References, 181–185
Reflexive binary relation, 10
Rejecting configuration, 25
Relative computability, 62–66, 145–180
Relatively prime, 14
Relatively prime integers, 14
RELPRIME, 125
Rice's theorem, 57–59
Riemann hypothesis, extended, 159
Rings, 11
Root
   of polynomial, 19
   of tree, 32

S
$S(n)$, 74, 86
S-m-n theorem, 53–55
Satisfaction-testing component, 140
SATISFIABILITY (SAT), 131
Satisfiable formulas, 7
Savitch's theorem, 102
Search problems, 151–153
Segments, 92
Self-reducibility, 152
Self-reducible set, 153
Separation results, 107–111
sim procedure, 93–94
Simple path, 4
Simple set, 71
Simultaneous simulation, 87–90
Sipser's theorem, 116
Solution to decision problem, 42
Space-bounded complexity classes, 75
Space-bounded Turing machines, 74
Space complexity, 74
Space compression, with tape reduction, 80–81
Space compression theorem, 80
Space-constructible functions, 86
Space hierarchy theorem, 108–110
Sparse set, 180

Standard complexity classes, 75
   relations between, 105, 115–120
Strongly connected digraph, 4
Subgraphs, 4
Subtree, 5
Suffix of word, 2
Symbols, 1

T
3SAT, 138
$T(n)$, 86
Tally languages, 113–114
Tally string, 113
Tape reduction, 90–97
   space compression with, 80–81
TARGET, 117
Tautology, 7
TEST algorithm, 45
Time-bounded complexity classes, 74
Time-bounded Turing machines, 74
Time complexity, 74
Time-constructible functions, 86
Time hierarchy theorem, 108, 110–111
Total computable partial function, 28
TQBF, 173
Transducers, 76
Transition function, 24
Transitive binary relation, 10
Translation techniques and padding,
   111–113
Tree, height of, 5
True Quantified Boolean Formulas, 173
Truth-assignment, 6
Truth-setting component, 139
Truth-table, 6
Turing, Alan, 35–36
Turing-machine-acceptable, 26
Turing-machine concepts, 26–28
Turing-machine-decidable, 26
Turing-machine transducer, 76
Turing machines, 22–25
   diagram, 23
   equivalence of, 29
   multitape, 29–31
   nondeterministic, 31–34
   oblivious, 91
   off-line, 74
   on-line, 74

oracle, 60, 145–146
probabilistic polynomial-time, 143
random access machines equivalence
   with, 39–40
space-bounded, 74
time-bounded, 74
universal, 44
variations of, 28–34
Turing reducibility, 60, 146
Turing reducible in polynomial time, 60,
   146
   nondeterministic, 162
Turnstile, 25

U
U, 44
U_{EXP}, 174
U_{NEXP}, 175
$\mathcal{U}$, 130, 137
$\mathcal{U}_P$, 177
Unary connective, 6
Undecidability, 41–72
Undecidable decision problem, 42
Undecidable problems, 43–46
UNIT RESOLUTION, 178
Universal programming system, 54
Universal set for NP, 130
Universal Turing machine, 44

V
Valid formula, 7
$VAR(F)$, 6
Verifier, 124
VERTEX COVER, 139–142
   approximation algorithm for, 179
Vertices, 4

W
W_e, 50
Witness, 124
Word, 1
   empty, 1
   length of, 1

Z
Z, 11
Z_m, 12
Z_p, 13

TEXTS IN COMPUTER SCIENCE

(continued from page ii)

Merritt and Stix, Migrating from Pascal to C++

Munakata, Fundamentals of the New Artificial Intelligence

Nerode and Shore, Logic for Applications, Second Edition

Pearce, Programming and Meta-Programming in Scheme

Peled, Software Reliability Methods

Schneider, On Concurrent Programming

Smith, A Recursive Introduction to the Theory of Computation

Socher-Ambrosius and Johann, Deduction Systems

Stirling, Modal and Temporal Properties of Processes

Zeigler, Objects and Systems